Advance praise for *Faithful Giving*

"*Faithful Giving* is a must-read for practitioners, Imams, clergy, faithful philanthropists, and scholars of philanthropy. This book provides thoughtful insights and practical guidance from experts who daily navigate the challenges of planned giving and legal planning. This book not only is a 'how-to' guide but also provides important thought leadership on the importance of faithful planned giving. The interfaith approach provides much-needed diverse perspectives to our field. This book opens up the opportunity to learn from other faiths while deepening one's understanding of our own faith tradition."

—Shariq Siddiqui, JD PhD, Director, Muslim Philanthropy Initiative, Lilly Family School of Philanthropy, Indiana University

"Rare is the book that offers something for everyone; rarer still one on the topic of giving. But Jim Murphy manages to do just that with *Faithful Giving*. Jim's coterie of contributors has created an incredibly useful resource that will greatly benefit faith communities and organizations across the entire religious and cultural spectrum. What makes it work is that it goes beyond interfaith considerations in planned giving to the 'movement of the heart'—why we give, what motivates us to be generous, and how we can express our generosity. The rich and colorful case studies along with Jim's insightful reflections and exercises will inspire and motivate everyone from committee volunteer and pastor to development committees and fundraising professionals to feel good about their own giving journey and invite others to do the same."

—Charles Buck, CEO of United Church Funds (UCF)

"Jim Murphy has taken on the challenge of outlining the planned giving opportunity for faith-based organizations and has masterfully provided a roadmap that anyone from any faith can follow. The discussions and case studies from the variety of faith perspectives further ingrained in me that faith can be a driving force behind one's philanthropic legacy, and it is up to each of us in our roles to harness and implement those aspirations in our own way. You will take away many practical approaches and reflections to build a successful program no matter how large or small."

—Kevin McGowan, Chief Financial Officer—Catholic Extension

"I found *Faithful Giving* to be incredibly well researched and thoughtfully structured. . . . It is very clear to me that Murphy and all of the contributors see planned giving as a way to help to elevate both humanity and the human. I love this way to thinking about our work in raising these types of funds."

—Dirk Bird, Vice President of Planned Giving and Endowment
for Jewish Federations of North America

"The relationship between faith and philanthropy is profound. Murphy and his guest authors thoughtfully explore this close relationship by examining planned giving traditions of many faiths. Case studies effectively illustrate key observations. This book will be valuable for all who wish to deepen their understanding of the important bonds of faith, philanthropy, and planned giving."

—Philip M. Purcell, CFRE, MPA/JD, Director of Planned Giving—
The Salvation Army, Central Territory, and President-elect,
American Council for Gift Annuities

"Having an active planned giving program is more important than ever for faith communities to thrive, grow, and plan for the future, especially during this critical time of change and transition in organized religion. In *Faithful Giving: The Heart of Planned Gifts*, Jim Murphy features a distinguished group of experts in the field from a wide variety of religious traditions who share their knowledge and passion for this important ministry. Incorporating his own personal and professional insights, Murphy focuses on both the how and why of planned giving in a practical, understandable, yet compelling way. I commend this valuable resource to all lay and clergy religious leaders who are looking for guidance and inspiration in launching a program in their own local contexts."

—Donald V. Romanik, President, Episcopal Church Foundation

"*Faithful Giving: The Heart of Planned Gifts* is a wonderful book for the philanthropic community. Whether you are first starting to incorporate planned giving into your organization's fundraising toolbox or your program has existed for years, this book provides excellent insights and guidance to jump-start your organization's future."

—William D. Samers, Vice President of Planned Giving
and Endowments, UJA-Federation of New York

"James W. Murphy's book *Faithful Giving: The Heart of Planned Gifts* is a thoughtful and eminently practical handbook for anyone working in the field of planned giving with religious institutions. With respect given to each faith tradition, Jim sets forth practical and beautiful examples of institutions and donors working together for the better good. Any professional in the field of stewardship and faith traditions will be happy to have this book to call on for good stories and great resources.

—Meighan W. Corbett, Director of Stewardship and Development,
The Riverside Church in the City of New York

"A must-have book for diverse faith-inspired charities and donors, guiding them methodically and pragmatically to reach their philanthropic goals."

—Sonia Dhami, Trustee, The Sikh Foundation International,
and President, ArtandTolerance.com

"Jim Murphy has written a practical, readable manual for successful planned giving donations that elucidates the best practices in several faith traditions. This is a book I wish I had read ten years ago. I cannot give it a higher recommendation. It is now required reading for all my priests and lay leaders."

—Presiding Bishop Kristina Rake, American Apostolic
Old Catholic Church (AAOCC)

"*Faithful Giving: The Heart of Planned Gifts* is a delightful look at the field of planned giving as seen through the lens of multiple faith traditions. The book, with real examples of planned giving efforts across religious traditions, will benefit both those new to the field and those who are more experienced and looking for new perspectives on their profession and vocation. Jim's deep experience and commitment to building financial support for faith-based organizations shines through in this work.

—Jill Heller, Executive Director and Treasurer, Trustees of Funds
& Endowments, Inc., Episcopal Diocese of Milwaukee

"There are so many great insights in this book! I love the simple yet profound reminder that when an organization receives a planned gift they have become a family member of sorts; that framing is so helpful, as is the interfaith exploration of this crucial topic."

—Mark Elsdon, Author of *We Aren't Broke:
Uncovering Hidden Resources for Mission & Ministry*

FAITHFUL GIVING

THE HEART OF PLANNED GIFTS

JAMES W. MURPHY

CHURCH
PUBLISHING
INCORPORATED

Church Publishing
19 East 34th Street
New York, NY 10016

Cover design by Jennifer Kopec, 2Pug Design
Typeset by Rose Design

Library of Congress Cataloging-in-Publication Data

Names: Murphy, James W., author.
Title: Faithful giving : the heart of planned gifts / James W. Murphy.
Description: New York, NY : Church Publishing, [2022]
Identifiers: LCCN 2022010740 (print) | LCCN 2022010741 (ebook) | ISBN
   9781640654761 (paperback) | ISBN 9781640654778 (ebook)
Subjects: LCSH: Generosity. | Generosity--Religious aspects. | Charity.
Classification: LCC BJ1533.G4 M87 2022 (print) | LCC BJ1533.G4 (ebook) |
   DDC 177/.7--dc23/eng/20220601
LC record available at https://lccn.loc.gov/2022010740
LC ebook record available at https://lccn.loc.gov/2022010741

In memory of my father, the Hon. Charles Nicholas Murphy,
on the 50th anniversary of his death, for his legacy of love and service.
Fortis et hospitalis in aeternum.

General Disclaimer

This material is provided for informational purposes only and should not be viewed as donor, investment, tax, or other professional advice. The writers of this book do not endorse or recommend any of the resources, websites, or entities noted throughout that are referenced for your further research, and we recommend that you always seek your own legal, tax, and financial/investment advice and what is best for you, your family, and your particular situation before finalizing any financial decision or gift.

CONTENTS

FOREWORD

I have had the privilege to follow the work of James W. Murphy for over a dozen years in his tireless efforts to provide state of the art philanthropic planning resources for the Episcopal Church and its faith communities. His work has become a model for others charged with providing gift-planning services for many other faith-based organizations and institutions.

Over the course of more than three decades of helping nonprofits maximize their philanthropic funding, I have come to the realization that there are five components to every charitable gift, regardless of its size or the mission it is intended to support.

Every gift is comprised of a "who," a "why," a "what," "when," and "how." While this may seem obvious upon reflection, there are many fundraising efforts that fall short of their full potential due to overemphasis on one or more of these components and the failure to effectively integrate them.

There are many ways to make charitable gifts that combine these elements in various ways. Some are completed right away. Other gifts are realized over a period of time, or only at the end of a lifetime. Gifts can be funded using any number of types of property.

There are also many planning tools that have been developed over centuries that are designed to facilitate the transfer of property from a donor to a charitable recipient, whether immediately or over time. The process of determining the best property to give, the timing of the gift, tax considerations, and the best way to transfer donated assets and income has come to be known as "planned giving," "gift planning," or similar terms intended to describe the process of determining the "what, when, and how" of a gift, whether large or small.

Jim has mastered the art of combining the myriad of tools that have been developed over the centuries to help charitably minded individuals achieve what might at first seem to be conflicting goals with other underlying motivations for gifts that are as complex as human nature itself.

Jim shared with me once a description of an early form of a life income gift described in the Rule of St. Benedict (530 CE). One of the rules (chapter 59) suggested that parents who were afraid they may be tempted to interfere with their child's vow of poverty might wish to make a donation to the monastery and reserve only the income from the property for themselves, and in doing so, insure they were not tempted to give property to their child "so that the boy may have no expectations whereby (which God forbid) he might be deceived and ruined, as we have learned by experience."[1] Motivations such as these for gifts predate the US Internal Revenue Code by centuries.

In *Faithful Giving: The Heart of Planned Gifts*, Jim ostensibly focuses on helping those who are engaged in fundraising for various faith-based ministries begin, or revitalize, efforts to encourage planned gifts. But on another level, he makes a tremendous contribution to fundraising for all types of organizations by exploring the most often and least understood motivation for making charitable gifts, namely the spiritual dimension of a donor's life.

Only about 11 percent of Americans describe themselves as atheists or agnostics. The remainder profess adherence to a broad range of religious beliefs. Roughly 65 percent of Americans self-identify as Christians or Jews. This percentage has been shifting with the rise of immigration in recent decades.[2]

In this book Jim gives voice, through a fascinatingly diverse roster of contributors, to insights into the nature of philanthropy in a broad array of religious traditions.

In recent years, there has been a growing effort to work to further diversity, equity, and inclusion in all aspects of our society, including the non-profit sectors and the work of those who raise the funds to meet the needs of a myriad of religious, social, educational, healthcare, environmental, and other charities.

While this book can serve as a resource for those who are working to implement more effective gift-planning efforts among various faiths by drawing on principals developed in other settings, I believe it also serves another equally and perhaps more important purpose.

This book can serve as a starting point for those fundraisers who are not necessarily involved in faith-based fundraising to understand how the religious beliefs of those who may be giving to secular charitable endeavors may influence their approach to the philanthropic dimension of their lives.

---

1. Rule of St. Benedict, accessed January 14, 2022, *http://www.archive.osb.org/rb/text/rbeaad2.html*.

2. "Measuring Religion in Pew Research Center's American Trends Panel," *Pew Research Center*, January 14, 2021, *https://www.pewforum.org/2021/01/14/measuring-religion-in-pew-research-centers-american-trends-panel/*.

I have long taught that it is as important to understand a prospective donor's religious beliefs as to know their tax bracket, the property they own, and how they might like their gift to be used. In this work I believe Jim has taken an important step in opening the door to a more inclusive approach to fundraising that will help a new generation of fundraisers be more effective in an increasingly diverse society that will continue to unfold.

It is my hope that this book will be an important part of a movement to ensure that the spirit of voluntary action first described and marveled at by Alexis de Tocqueville in the nineteenth century continues to thrive as a new generation of immigrants finds a nonprofit sector that respects the spiritual dimension of their lives and how it informs a universally inspired desire to build a better world for themselves and future generations.

—Robert F. Sharpe Jr. (1953–2022)

PREFACE

My hope for this book is to inspire and empower. For nearly fourteen years I have worked with congregations and institutions to raise and manage the unique donations known as planned gifts, those contributions which individuals make out of their estate at death or from their retirement, and other, assets. Although my experience has been primarily in Christian churches and their ecumenical connections, and professionally in the world of the Episcopal Church, I have always sought to be a listener and have enjoyed the many stories and experiences of my colleagues and friends in other denominations and faith traditions in the United States, Canada, and Europe.

Something has become clear to me over the past thirty years in my volunteering and my professional work at the Episcopal Church Foundation, the General Theological Seminary, and in so many nonprofit settings. That is, though contexts may be very different and traditions varying, the essentials for moving individuals to make a commitment for a planned gift are basically the same. Primarily it is a movement of the heart; a desire to ensure that the work and ministry of a church, mosque, temple, synagogue, or religious institution continues on and illuminates the lives of others, just as one's own life has been brightened. It is because of all of these central emotional motivations undergirding the work of planned giving that I set this book's subtitle as "The Heart of Planned Gifts." It is our hearts, our deep emotional commitment to the future of our congregations and religious organizations, regardless of our tradition, which draw us to make these special commitments.

Whatever your religion, I encourage you to reflect on what supports the generosity of the members in your faith, whether that be the promotion of tithing in many Christian churches, the tremendous generosity encouraged from Jewish and Sikh traditions, the clarity of Muslim giving guidelines, or the challenging recommendations from Hindu scriptures. Even though not everyone will comply exactly with the stated guidelines of their faith, considering your own traditions in giving is a good starting place. Building on those traditions and your personal insights will enable successful planned giving efforts in your context.

Why an Interfaith Book?

For many years I have been committed to supporting cooperation and collaboration among various denominations and faiths. Why there have not been more substantial attempts to share practical knowledge and resources remains a mystery to me. From my perspective, ecumenical or interfaith collaborations are best achieved not by attempts to adapt and conform/transform worship services. Our earth and its people are best served by the sharing of functional information on issues like fundraising or administrative best practices, and of course by working together to serve, protect, and empower those less fortunate. Those "in the background" efforts taking place in our differing, and sometimes conflicting, faiths can come together under these uncontroversial endeavors. I hope that this volume may continue to help in these ongoing efforts and spread peace and understanding. Though each tradition is unique, we certainly find "common ground" in planned giving.

All of the contributors to this book write from their own experiences and out of their own personal religious tradition and conviction. Some may use terminology or concepts from a faith tradition that is very different from your own and this can spark discomfort in some and, sadly, anger in others. If that happens for you, please read on, and contemplate privately on your reaction. All of us have so much to learn from each other, both in the growing diversity within our own communities of faith and the wider society. There is tremendous wisdom in each religious tradition, even if ultimate conclusions are different from our own. There are many opportunities for each of us to learn from other faiths and to serve God better by working together to make our world more kind, just, and equitable. As is elaborated in Dr. M. Yaqub Mirza's case study, the good work and generosity that each of our faiths call us toward should not only benefit our coreligionists, but also all of God's creation and people. Inclusivity should not be only in our words, but in our actions, charity, and measures of impact.

All the beautiful tapestries of different faith traditions are gifts to God's creation. I believe God's love is all-inclusive and offered to all. Regardless of our culture or faith tradition, either chosen or assumed, I think that God is much more interested that each of us treat one another kindly and well, than if we do everything perfectly. I hope it is obvious that I am convinced that God loves all created beings equally, though also individually. Growing up as a Roman Catholic in a liberal, and traditionally large, Irish family, opinions and perspectives were numerous and I remain grateful that my education and work experiences afforded many occasions for befriending persons from Jewish, Muslim, Hindu, Buddhist, and various Christian backgrounds. Becoming Anglican/Episcopal in my twenties continued my openness and appreciation for the wisdom of those with different perspectives. I hope that my admiration and love of other faith traditions are apparent, as well as my own convictions.

As Dr. Lucinda Mosher will elaborate next, for the many faith traditions now growing in North America through their "congregationalizing" processes, even more useful and practical resources for support should be available in time. I regret that I do not have more denominations and faith traditions represented in this book. (I did try!) If your tradition or denomination has a story or experience you would like to share, please contact me through my website www.murphyjw.com.

A Rose by Any Other Name

I hope that our use of terms is sufficiently inclusive for you. Leadership terms such as board, vestry, parish council, leadership committee may be appropriate for certain traditions or contexts but all perform similar functions. If the words used and roles referenced do not to fit your tradition exactly, please alter them in your own mind to fit your context as you read. (If you own this book, write in the term or role you prefer from your tradition if you wish!) I hope that the numerous ways that different faith traditions name the modes they organize and gather will not be an undue distraction for you. I will use the phrase "congregation/organization" or "charity" as a catch-all for the religious entities, parishes, orders, or other religious organizations for which you volunteer or work professionally.

Constituents is the broadest term used for those who may give financially or volunteer and will be used interchangeable with the term "supporters." These are purposely expansive terms as there are so many levels of connection one can have with their congregation or favorite organization. Members or membership can have a negative connotation in some communities of faith or traditions; that is not my intention, only the use of diverse terms is.

Please apply your own best terminology interpretation for CEO, CFO, boards of directors, etc. (many congregations will have those too of course). Also, many religious orders of men and women in the Roman Catholic,

Episcopal, and other traditions such as in Buddhism, are very much both a congregation when you gather with your associates, visitors, or supporters, and a public service when providing benefits to others, often to those in great need. Please reinterpret terminology as befitting your contexts, especially when considering future efforts with legacy societies and other suggested tools.

Among all the many options for term usage, the clarification of who are clergy or laypeople can be quite complex given the statuses of various roles and the wide disparities among organization and structures. Please read into this work your particular circumstances and context. I will be considering clergy as priests, ministers, rabbis, imams, and other clerics as people doing their work in a more *professional* capacity (whether compensated or not). The numerous leadership and lay volunteer roles I will consider as those whose primary profession or calling is *not* within that "clerical structure." Hierarchies are also quite varied and particular; I will seek to stay as generalized as possible, but please forgive anywhere this does not adequately capture your tradition.

When I refer to donor, I am referring to both the individual making the gift as well as their significant other, normally their spouse. Leaders should never exclude one relationship partner in a discussion. Although one person may be the "speaker" in the relationship, it is rare that there is not a shared decision, even expanding to children in some cases. Be inclusive and be careful not to make the mistake that it is only one person who makes the charitable decisions. Even if the man speaks more, it is often women, who tend to be the more silent partners, who are the ultimate decision-makers for planned gifts. Since wives typically outlive husbands, they may often make the final decisions on planned gifts. (Please note the left-leaning shifts made by McDonald's restaurant heir Joan Kroc from her husband's more conservative preferences for their fortune.)[1]

I ask for your tolerance and a spirit of understanding, as I seek to share the principles of planned giving so that as many different traditions as possible can encourage both awareness raising and those opportunities for gift making. No matter how different our religious traditions are, the basics of encouraging these crucial gifts will be nearly identical, as our case studies will demonstrate. Given the extremely wide audience of different denominations and faith traditions reading this book, I will still attempt to focus on the similar contexts within the United States and Canada. Those reading beyond

1. Lisa Napoli, "Meet the Woman Who Gave Away the McDonald's Founder's Fortune," *Time Magazine*, December 22, 2016, *https://time.com/4616956/mcdonalds-founder-ray-kroc-joan-kroc/*.

these countries, please do not feel excluded but as the potential becomes increasingly diffuse, this was the focus I felt necessary.

Why a Book on Planned Giving?

I chose to focus the writing of this book primarily for the numerous volunteer leaders at congregations and other religious organizations across the faith spectrum. Few religious organizations and even fewer congregations can afford to hire a professional development officer, not to mention a planned giving officer, whose sole duty would be to raise and cultivate legacy gifts. Additionally, over the many years I have done this work, I noticed a consistency among many of the development professionals I have met: many of them do not have a great amount of knowledge or expertise in planned giving. I hope that this book will also help them.

I will mention again later that though many denominations and faith traditions are growing in the United States and Canada, many denominations, especially mainline Christian congregations, are shrinking rapidly. (Please see the studies from the Pew Research Center and others.) Many fear that their denomination or church will cease to exist in a generation or two; this is a legitimate concern for many. No one can predict what the future will bring, but what is likely is that many congregations that cannot support themselves with their annual income will merge with others or shut down. If congregations merge, gifts and funds will continue on in the new context. And, if a particular congregation may close, endowment funds will continue to serve and support ministry long into the future, even if they will be administered differently. Perhaps a focus on planned giving and endowment building will demonstrate an enhanced resilience and new opportunities for confidence and growth in various congregations. Though mainline congregations will continue to evolve in the decades to come, there will still be a future for their communities of faith and their impact: it may just look different from its current incarnation.

As Horizons Stewardship notes, "Despite the negative trends, [during this time of Covid] 30 percent of churches are experiencing growth in giving and 21 percent have seen their attendance rise. Much of the good news is in larger churches, but there are many small congregations who are thriving."[2]

---

2. "Giving and Worship Report," *Horizons Stewardship*, accessed September 25, 2021, *https://www. horizons.net/blog/2021-giving-and-worship-survey-results*.

What is also likely, and has accelerated throughout the pandemic, several congregations and religious organizations will continue to attract supporters if they maintain missional focus and remain good stewards of their resources. Over time, congregations will thrive when they focus on impact, control their expenses, avoid deficits, and diversify their income through building endowments/dedicated funds, and become entrepreneurial with creating additional sources of revenue from rentals and other creative opportunities. Practical challenges have been a part of religious life for centuries; adaptation while still being true to one's faith, will eventually succeed.

Format for Reflection and Action

This book focuses on empowering leaders to raise planned gifts among constituents by reflecting first on themselves and then on the people who compose their supporters and/or members. As you read this book's various case studies elaborating on constituent motivations and the processes described, many will be nearly identical among very different faith traditions and denominations. And though most of our readers will be leaders of a particular community of faith, most of these same steps could be taken by a variety of nonprofits for motivating these gifts among their own varied constituencies.

The main chapters will be structured as follows to enable self-teaching through on-going reflection and sharing of guidance and knowledge:

- Know thyself
- Know your constituents
- Know the basics
- Take the next steps forward
- Evaluate your efforts from time to time
- Summary points

I hope that the study guide for groups or individuals on this book's website will also help you and your fellow leaders to reflect on what you know and what you don't by sharing our various insights learned over the years. Although the case studies may contain gift options or other principles not yet reviewed when you read them, please be assured that those details will be covered in subsequent chapters. The case studies are placed between chapters that are their best contexts.

Final Pointers for Using This Book

I also regret that we will not have the opportunity to drill into the various other cultural factors of ethnicity which greatly influence giving to a congregation or religious organization. I have encountered many of those in my work. This may be the topic of another book in the future, but I hope that my guidance to leaders to trust themselves throughout this book will help.

Finally, I often refer back to other chapters and case studies as I realize that some people will not read this book in page order. That is fine, and I hope my referencing helps. No other book I know is focused on religious planned giving from a multifaith perspective. And my hope is that this book will help level out knowledge and provide a sense of confidence that everyone from congregations to small nonprofits can learn from the many different perspectives shared here.

Blessings to all.

INTRODUCTION

On Sustaining Religion-Community in America: A Glimpse through a Multireligious Lens

Lucinda Allen Mosher

"The Hindu temples we now find all over the United States are part of an amazing American experiment," declares Dr. Asha Shipman, Yale University's director of Hindu Life and a member of the Board of Trustees of Sri Satyanarayana Swamy Temple in Middletown, Connecticut. In India, she explains, many temples are ancient.[1] They were built by kings in fulfillment of their dharmic duty. Most laypersons give but little thought to matters of sustaining those sites. In the United States context, she says, the situation is entirely different: the establishment of a temple is almost always a community effort. Shipman's description from an American Hindu perspective has many other faith parallels. In what follows, I offer some reflections from a multifaith perspective on this phenomenon in multifaith America and its implications for planned giving.

In my teaching, I define "religion" as a constellation of things (beliefs, rituals, doctrines, institutions, practices, stories) that enables people to establish, maintain, and celebrate a meaningful world—and connects them to predecessors who embraced, established, maintained, and celebrated a meaningful world in that way.[2] In the United States, such constellations are plentiful! Religiously, our environment is complex—and has been so for centuries. However, the Immigration and Nationality Act of 1965 triggered an exponential expansion of that complexity in the United States. Diana L. Eck, director of The Pluralism Project at Harvard University, made this point in her 2001 publication, *A New Religious America: How a "Christian Country"*

---

1. I am grateful to Dr. Asha Shipman, Chaplain Aida Mansoor, and Abbot Shim Bo Sunim for conversations in July 2021 that informs this chapter. Any errors are mine.

2. In defining religion in this way, I am following H. Byron Earhart. See his introduction to H. Byron Earhart, ed., *Religious Traditions of the World* (San Francisco: HarperSanFrancisco, 1993), 7.

Has Become the World's Most Religiously Diverse Nation.[3] By the turn of the twenty-first century, a plethora of the world's religions (and multiple expressions of each, in fact) had established themselves in the United States to a degree far greater than ever before. Those who feel called to make certain that, in their present context, the religion—the constellation of beliefs, rituals, doctrines, institutions, practices, stories—they embrace and value deeply are available to the next generation and beyond take on responsibility for that with great determination and love.

During the second half of the twentieth century, the intensification of America's religious manyness made visible differences in the architectural landscape of the United States as dozens of religion communities established places for worship, practice, or study—sometimes in found and repurposed spaces; sometimes in spaces that were purpose-built. Indeed, sheer manyness is now an important dimension of the American religious landscape; so is Christian hegemony. The United States is a "Christian-normative country," asserts Khyati Joshi, a social science researcher and educator on the intersecting issues of race, religion, and immigration.[4] Indeed, in her books, she makes clear that "Christian hegemony" is a powerful force in shaping its "laws, customs, and habits of thought."[5] So thoroughly is Protestant Christian privilege "ingrained in [American] societal dynamics," Joshi observes, that it is persistently "taken as 'normal.'"[6] It should surprise no one, then, that Christians who have a strong sense of denominational affiliation and congregational belonging, make an annual pledge of financial support to it, and elect a governing board responsible for building maintenance and various other congregational concerns may presume that other religion groups take an approach parallel to theirs. In addition, planned giving and the patterns of giving substantial resources to support the institutions and communities of faith that supported and enhanced their lives would naturally flow to them in time. Are they correct? They are—to an extent, at least.

In a region where their religion predominates, average Buddhists, Hindus, or Muslims can simply drop in at their local house of worship or

---

3. Diana L. Eck, *A New Religious America: How a "Christian Country" Has Become the World's Most Religiously Diverse Nation* (New York: HarperOne, 2001).

4. Khyati Y. Joshi, *New Roots in America's Sacred Ground: Religion, Race, and Ethnicity in Indian America* (New Brunswick, NJ: Rutgers University Press, 2006), 4.

5. Khyati Y. Joshi, *White Christian Privilege: The Illusion of Religious Equality in America* (New York: New York University Press, 2020), 23.

6. Joshi, *White Christian Privilege*, 2.

practice on almost any day. The rhythm of its activities is attuned to that religion's unique calendar, paying little heed to the Euro-American work-week. Whether it be an ancient or a comparatively recent structure, it may be maintained by the national or local government. Its operation and upkeep would not, therefore, be the concern of the typical adherent. In the US, the situation is quite different. Multiple expressions of Buddhism, Hinduism, Islam, plus many other religions have established themselves here. When-ever adherents of any of these religions have wanted a specialized and appro-priately furnished worship/practice space, or the services of trained religious professionals, or a center for religious education, they have had to find a way to do so themselves. In many situations, responsibility for an American religion-community's flourishing rests entirely with local laypersons. Some scholars have called this phenomenon "congregationalizing."

By "congregationalizing," commentators mean the putting in place of ele-ments typical of Protestant Christianity. Hence, while a religion-community's unique calendar is maintained, a regular community gathering on the week-end is added or prioritized—and may be as much for fellowship as for wor-ship or practice. A "Sunday school" is established through which the children are nurtured in the religion. (Note Dr. Singh Brar's use of the term in his case study on Sikh giving.) There are regular opportunities for continuing reli-gious education for adults and establishment of a physical space in which all of this can happen. Spending time at the mandir, vihara, mosque, temple, or gurdwara thus becomes a weekend activity for the whole family.

Congregationalizing takes time, patience, and resources. It begins when Buddhists, Muslims, Jains, Hindus, Sikhs, and others in religiously diverse America acknowledge that their religion's practices and unique calendar are better maintained in community. Therefore, they seek out coreligionists who will agree to meet regularly for fellowship and practice—often in someone's home. When the group grows too large to meet in a home, it now seeks a larger gathering place: one that the group can rent, or buy and adapt, or build from scratch.

At this point, the circle of coreligionists must seek answers to questions like "What permits do we need in order to set up a place of worship that will meet our needs?" Going forward, it will need an administrative structure for handling building maintenance, legal matters, fundraising, bill-paying, short-term decision-making, and planning for long-term sustainability and growth through the creation of endowments and other donated funds. In short, in order to thrive, the majority of America's diverse religion-communities have embraced approaches to institutionalizing that are quite unnecessary in their religion's original setting. A collateral benefit of such congregationalizing is this: the closer a religion-community's structure and practices resemble US Protestant Christianity, the more "normal" it seems to those with hegemony. Sensing this to be the case, Shin Buddhists missionaries who came to the United States from Japan in 1893 decided in 1944 to use a Christian term in the name of their network of practice centers. Now the Buddhist Churches of America, the movement also appropriated some aspects of Protestant congregational worship.

Hence, adherents of America's many religions—Hindus, Jains, Buddhists, Muslims, Sikhs, Taoists, Zoroastrians, and others—have established autonomous houses of worship, practice, or study. They have applied for, and have been granted, 501(c)3 not-for-profit status. When incorporated as a "temple society" or a "cultural center," a house of worship then has a constitution and bylaws and a board of directors or officers. Its administrative team is essential for interfacing with governmental matters: tax codes, parking regulations, building codes, and more. It must hire and oversee the staff: ritual experts and other religious professionals, instructors, and youth leaders. It will take (or designate) responsibility for scheduling events, setting rates for services, paying the regular expenses, and investing the assets given through the estates of faithful.

These projects can take a while, Asha Shipman points out. Her father, Dr. Amrutur V. Srinivasan, was instrumental in founding the Connecticut Valley Hindu Temple Society, which built and maintains the Sri Satyanarayana Swamy Temple in Middletown. The temple's groundbreaking ceremony took place in 1979. A full twenty years would pass before the *murtis* (images) of Ganesh and the main deities could be installed and the rites of dedication could be performed. That was May 1999. A recent capital campaign made possible a major expansion of the facility that doubled its size, brought it up to code, and made it fully accessible. Rites of rededication were held in May 2021. This is a familiar pattern for many "church plants" and other new congregations.

For some house-of-worship/practice societies, board membership is the only level of membership. There is no roster of members as would be typical of a church or synagogue. How is support provided? Some house-of-worship societies do have a category of membership subscription and thus maintain a roll of "annual dues-paying members." Synagogues often use this model as do some American mosques and a Shinto shrine located in northwestern Washington. The Tsubaki Grand Shrine of America is open to all. However,

regular attendees and supporters may become members of the shrine association by completing an application form and paying dues. Association members underwrite the maintenance of the shrine's physical property and sacred
objects, which is an outward demonstration of their commitment to work
for the welfare of everyone.

Sri Satyanarayana Swamy Temple in Connecticut invites devotees to reg-
ister as "regular" or "life" members.[7] In fact, Shipman notes, most of this
temple's attendees are people in transit. This should not be surprising, she
says, since the vast majority of Indians in the United States are foreign-born
transnationals. "Since the 1990s," she explains, "when US companies could
invest in India and then train Indians here, and those who were invited
here to help solve the Y2K technical issues, we have had a high number of
transnational visitors. These are folks here for anywhere between a couple of
months and several years."

Yet, the board hopes that devotees will continue to support the temples
they frequent—or hope to visit. After all, Shipman says, one does not have
to live nearby to have a sense of duty toward a temple or monastery. "My
attitude is that we think about what gives us meaning or joy, what traditions
we want to maintain. If a temple helps to make these things possible for you,
then it merits your support." And she stresses, devotees have indeed been
incredibly generous in their support. "We would never have been able to
continue to fundraise during the pandemic for the temple expansion project
without the support of so many devotees. It is so humbling because, in the
beginning, Indian families were not used to the concept of having to fundraise for a temple themselves, so they really did not feel comfortable with the
idea. But that was the only way a Hindu temple could ever have been built in
the United States—at that time, and now!"

More commonly used are the pathways of freewill donation, fees, and
sponsorship. For example, inside an American Muslim, Jain, Hindu, Buddhist, and Sikh house of worship/practice, one almost always finds a freewill
donation box. Hindus call this box a *hundi*. The act of *dana* (giving) is a
dharmic duty; it is also an act of internal purification of body and mind.

Indeed, no matter the religion, websites for American houses of worship/
practice typically provide an easy means for making donations online. Hindu
temples often place a sign near the entrance, detailing the expected donation

7. "Membership Information," *Sri Satyanarayana Swamy Temple*, accessed August 6, 2021, *http://
www.cvhts.org/membership_info.php.*

for the simplest of prayer rites to the most elaborate of weddings—and everything in between. Signage onsite and announcements online solicit sponsors for events—both occasional and frequently occurring. Hence, a Sikh might sign up to provide *prasad* (the sweet distributed during worship at the gurdwara) or *langar* (the meal provided after worship—and often available at other times). A Hindu might also provide *prasad* (and when Hindus use the word, they mean food that will be blessed during their rituals, then distributed to devotees), or she might cover the cost of the many substances needed for an *abishekam* (ritual bathing of a deity-image). Indeed, Asha Shipman explains, "A devotee can sponsor—in part or in entirety—any of the forms of temple worship—a *puja* or a *homa* or an *arthi*. We recommend donations of $501, $101, $51, $21—as these amounts are considered auspicious. This approach keeps things going in the short run."

What about the long run? What provisions are being made for keeping America's Hindu, Jain, Buddhist, Muslim, Sikh, and other houses of worship/practice functioning well into the future and are proper steps being taken to build the trust and relationships necessary for encouraging planned gifts? It is a complex question. One answer is that during the past half-century, an infrastructure for intrafaith collaboration has taken shape in the form of national federations of local worship/practice societies. Examples include JAINA (Jain Associations in North America), ISNA (Islamic Society of North America), and FEZANA (Federation of Zoroastrian Associations of North America). Alongside them are networks of local worship/practice communities and spaces aligned with (and sometimes endowed by) a particular movement or order, such as BCA (Buddhist Churches in America), ISKCON (International Society of Krishna Consciousness), BAPS (Bochasanwasi Akshar Purushottam Swaminarayan Sanstha), the Jogye Order of Korean Buddhism, or Won Buddhism. Relatedly, advocacy organizations look after religion-specific concerns. The Sikh Coalition and HAF (Hindu American Foundation) are good examples. Regional or local organizations, such as the Buddhist Council of New York, also play an important role. Will new foundations, like the various denominational foundations listed in this book, be created to also guide and encourage congregational and other religious leaders to raise planned gifts and/or to manage those funds and endowments to secure the future of these religious bodies? Only time will tell, but all of the roots are forming!

A second answer is that numerous adherents of America's various religions consider financial support of their house of worship/practice an act of faithfulness. For example, Hindus may talk in terms of dharmic giving and dharmic investing. Advocacy for those concepts has been on the rise among America's Hindus in recent years. Some Hindu temple associations have begun to discuss, or may now encourage, making donations of securities in memory of people who have died. The board of Sri Satyanarayana Swamy Temple in Connecticut is doing this. "We see it as an investment in the future of the faith," notes one board member.[8] (See chapter 8 on memorials and Pandit Sharma's case study in chapter 2.)

The Venerable Shim Bo, founding abbot of White Lotus Haven Zen, a center in Connecticut, offers a Buddhist perspective: *dana* (almsgiving) "is a way of voluntarily offering materials, energy, or wisdom (*dharma*) to another, with clarity and intention." For the giver, *dana* is an exercise in renunciation and generosity; for the recipient, it is an opportunity to practice gratitude and dharma stewardship. The Dana Sutra, found in the *Angutara Nikaya* (one of many sacred collections of the Buddha's teachings), makes this clear.

Anyone who wishes to support White Lotus Haven Zen, which is an incorporated not-for-profit organization, may do so by means of a portal on its website. Its abbot and the two affiliated monastics receive no salary, so all financial donations are directed toward basic upkeep, teaching sessions, liturgical ceremonies, and various programs and events. Equally important are the generous donations by community members of their time, energy, and presence. Overhead is kept to a minimum. Currently, the temple is located in rented space. If the lease for this space is not renewed, the community will simply move to another suitable space, the abbot explains. He has no plans to purchase or build a permanent physical temple. "We travel light," he says. It is all about the practice, after all, he stresses. His concern is focused not on bricks and mortar, but on the transmission of the practice well into the future.

Islam eschews usury. Therefore, Muslims who observe the principles of Islamic finance will make use of approaches to mortgages that have been deemed *halal* (compliant with Islamic jurisprudence). Having followed such principles to purchase an existing building for repurposing as a mosque or to erect a new mosque from the ground up, an American Muslim community needs a *halal* means of maintaining this property. Observant Muslims practice *zakat*, the Islamic obligation to return a certain percentage of one's wealth for the benefit of the community. *Zakat* can be a channel toward support of

---

8. See also what Hindu monks in Kauai, Hawaii, are doing in this regard. "How Can I Help?" *Kauai's Hindu Monastery*, accessed August 6, 2021, *https://www.himalayanacademy.com/donations/how-can-i-help*.

a mosque, but there are many other causes toward which it is acceptable to direct one's *zakat*. There is, however, another Islamic category of charitable giving. Called *sadaqah*, it is not obligatory, but it is strongly encouraged. *Sadaqah jariyah* (which means, loosely, "the gift that keeps on giving") is charitable giving directed toward education and worship. "Ramadan puts people in the mood for *sadaqah jariyah*," notes Aida Mansoor. Donations of *sadaqah jariyah* are said to continue to benefit the donor, even after death. To have steady replenishment of its mosque maintenance account, a community might raise funds to purchase a house that can be rented. The rental income generated by the house can then be directed toward mosque upkeep. (See M. Yaqub Mirza's and Anwar Khan's case studies on Muslim giving and the opportunities for planned giving.)

Mosque upkeep can also be funded through *halal* investing—of which the *waqf* is an example. The Qur'an does not mention it directly, but Islamic tradition has much to say about it. A *waqf* can benefit schools, universities, medical schools, land, hospitals, offices, and mosques. The administrative board of the Berlin Mosque in Connecticut established its own *waqf* about five years ago. How does a *waqf* work? To begin, an individual donates. This donation is channeled into a *shariah*-compliant investment. As the fund grows, most of the money is withdrawn and directed toward the projects for which the *waqf* was established. The waqf can be seen as both a major gift to fund capital projects and as a correlating "endowment" for perpetual care of that asset, or—in a more common understanding—simply as a True Endowment, which is diversely invested and spent prudently.

The situation is similar for members of the Sikh faith. For them, ethical financial planning begins with the principle of *dharamsai*: the twin duties of upholding the Sikh legal code and duty to the community. According to the three pillars of the religion, Sikhs are to focus on God; earn a living via hard work through an honest means; and share what is created with others. Related to the third pillar is the principle of *seva* (selfless service) and *daswandh* (tithing): directing ten percent of one's income toward faith-based or charitable purposes. One expression of this is the *langar*—the community meal that is available routinely at *gurdwaras* (houses of prayer) and may be set up at other sites as well. For example, in the aftermath of Superstorm Sandy (2012), Sikhs from New Jersey arrived at St Mark's-in-the-Bowery (an Episcopal parish in the East Village neighborhood of Manhattan, NYC) with everything necessary to distribute a hot meal to the neighborhood in the church's front yard.

These principles have enabled Sikhs in many parts of the United States to gather the funds to acquire and repurpose buildings—or to fund new construction—in order to have a beautiful *gurdwara* for communal worship. These principles inform Sikh preference for stewardship that is environmentally and socially responsible, for distribution of wealth with an eye toward future sustainability (which includes transmission of the faith to the next generation), and for financial management tools and philanthropic projects that promote equality, justice, and responsible management of resources into the future.

Indeed, throughout the United States are individual Jews, Muslims, Hindus, Sikhs, Buddhists, Zoroastrians, and others whose generosity helps to maintain the houses of worship/practice and religion-specific multipurpose centers their religion-community has established. This is an obvious way of ensuring the continued presence of their religion in the US context. But there is another approach: endowment of university professorships, so that one's religion—its history, beliefs, and practices—will be studied deeply; and, crucially, so that new generations of scholars have command of the language(s) of its sacred texts. (As to be referenced in this book, such designated endowments can be created during one's lifetime and be more substantially funded through a planned gift at death.)

An endowed chair for the study of almost any particular religion has been present in North America for decades, with endowed professorships in Islamic Studies and Jewish Studies being most numerous. However, the twenty-first century has seen an uptick in this sort of philanthropy in support of the study of Hinduism, Jainism, Sikhism, and Buddhism. To mention but a few, we now have endowed chairs in Sikh Studies and Sikh musicology at the University of California at Riverside and Hofstra University, respectively—both established in 2008.[9] In 2015, the University of Michigan became the home to the world's first endowed chair in Thai Buddhist Studies.[10] In 2019, the University of California at Irvine filled its own newly endowed chair in Sikh Studies.[11] In the first half of 2021 alone was this flurry of activity:

9. "The Dr. Jasbir Singh Endowed Chair in Sikh and Punjabi Studies," *UC Riverside*, accessed August 6, 2021, *https://spstudies.ucr.edu/*; "Sikh Musicology," *Hofstra University*, accessed August 6, 2021, *https://www.hofstra.edu/music/sikh-musicology/*.

10. "U-M Gift Establishes World's First Endowed Chair of Thai Buddhism," *University of Michigan News*, March 5, 2015, *https://news.umich.edu/u-m-gift-establishes-world-s-first-endowed-chair-of-thai-buddhism/*.

11. "Anneeth Kaur Hundle Named Dhan Kaur Sahota Presidential Chair in Sikh Studies at University of California," *UCI*, February 19, 2019, *https://www.socsci.uci.edu/newsevents/news/2019/2019-02-19-hundle.php*.

the University of Florida received a gift from a coalition of donors for the purpose of creating a Jain Studies program;[12] University of California at Santa Barbara celebrated the endowment of its Dalai Lama chair in Tibetan Buddhism and Cultural Studies;[13] California State University at Fresno appointed a professor to its newly endowed chair in Jain and Hindu Studies, made possible by gifts from two dozen families;[14] and the University of Illinois launched an endowed professorship in Jain Studies.[15]

About stewardship and philanthropy in multireligious America, much more could be said and many other religion communities could be profiled. A thorough investigation of financial planning by America's many religious communities and their efforts to provide and maintain dedicated spaces for worship and practice would reveal stories of headaches and failures alongside the successes. A recurring issue in communities such as the one that founded Sri Satyanarayana Swamy Temple in Middletown, Connecticut, is that providing for the future of a religious community and its facilities takes more than financial planning and philanthropy; it takes new leadership. The process of transition often reveals differences of vision. Yet, the elderly generation must let go—and that is hard.[16] However, as communities of faith and religious organizations continue to grow planned giving efforts by building trust, confidence, and systems of thankful recognition, those substantial legacy gifts, often from the outwardly modest and unexpected donor, will eventually provide the financial resources to support these institutions for generations to come.

12. Andrew Doerfler, "New Endowment to Establish Jain Studies Program at UF," *UF News*, May 13, 2021, *https://news.clas.ufl.edu/new-endowment-to-establish-jain-studies-program-at-ufl*.

13. Shelly Leachman, "An Enduring Connection," *The Current*, May 17, 2021, *https://www.news.ucsb.edu/2021/020289/enduring-connection*.

14. Benjamin Kirk, "Dr. Veena Rani Howard Named Endowed Chair in Jain and Hindu Dharma," *Fresno State News*, May 4, 2021, *http://www.fresnostatenews.com/2021/05/04/dr-veena-rani-howard-named-endowed-chair-in-jain-and-hindu-dharma/*.

15. Staff Writer, "University of Illinois Launches Endowed Chair on Jainism," *News India*, July 6, 2021, *https://www.newsindiatimes.com/university-of-illinois-launches-endowed-chair-on-jainism/*.

16. Asha Shipman notes: "Interestingly we are in the midst of managerial changes at Sri Satyanarayana Swamy Temple; and it is the fundraising leaders, retired gentlemen, who have been fabulous at guiding us through the fundraising and managing the construction for the expansion project through the pandemic. I am not sure how we will replace them—but they want to retire from their Temple positions. I honestly worry that the younger generations will not donate as much because our resources are thinner with decades of economic squeezing of the middle class. Our task is to keep the Temple relevant in the eyes and hearts of the US Hindu communities. I think we can do that creatively and authentically in partnership with the devotees."

CHAPTER 1

Raising to the Level of Family and Legacy Giving

Know Thyself

What motivates you to want to lead a planned giving ministry at your congregation or religious charity, or inspires you to learn more to support others in this effort? How much do you already know about planned giving, or about your various constituencies? What are your own leadership habits and default behavioral actions? Are you a doer or an overseer? Introvert or extrovert, planner or not? (This can be a challenging role if you are not a planner.) As with so many things in life, before we move forward and commit ourselves to an effort, it can be very beneficial to first reflect on "why" we are doing it. Hopefully our "why" self-reflection will demonstrate the reasons we personally believe so deeply in our community of faith or religious organization that we can commit to a planned gift ourselves. However, if the "why" for taking this leadership role is that there seems to be no one else who could do this work at this time or it has simply fallen in your lap with little of your input, you will certainly want to seek out the help of others as soon as possible. You may discover that you enjoy these efforts, but if it is truly a burden, sharing these tasks with others, sooner than later, will enable your charity to keep the effort going well into the future.

Secondly, do you have the tools and ability to complete the tasks? The good news is that for the most part, you already do. You will now have the insights and resources of this book and there are many more tools and resources available to help you online, within your denomination or tradition (and beyond) as well. The key to sustaining a planned giving effort will be a commitment by leaders to continually raise awareness and to thank others who have made this important commitment. However, you should also be seeking colleagues and other advocates to help in your efforts. Not only to keep this effort going after you might stop your work, but additional leaders bring alternative and bright ideas, as well as more hands to support the efforts.

Third, can you be honest with yourself about your abilities and natural inclinations so that you willingly seek the help of others who possess the abilities and personality traits you do not? Do not try to do this effort on your own. Seek the help of at least one other volunteer or staff member to support you, question your ideas, and be a sounding board for how to make your efforts sustainable. No one excels at everything and having others who have skills one does not will complement and enhance your efforts. For example, if event planning is not your forte, or if your preferred spot is organizing in the background, finding an outgoing highly verbal partner who can speak and inspire others can be a benefit. Do you understand the most basic aspects of fundraising? Or the different aspects of giving and types of planned gifts? Are there already denominational resources to help? Can you attend additional education online or otherwise?

Know Your Constituents

Who are the other institutional leaders and participants who can support your efforts? What is the history of doing this type of work at your congregation/ organization? Did your organization fail at this before? What are your faith traditions in this area?

Regardless of your faith tradition, there will always be a variety of levels of affiliation to your church, mosque, or temple by your members and other supporters. Some are dedicated volunteers; many may have other commitments; a few individuals or families may contribute a significant portion of the annual budget; and others will consistently give only tokens of financial support, regardless of their actual financial means. If you work for a religious organization, there are many different types of supporters, from those who may participate in the work you do, and especially for those who give gifts. It is important to know data about your constituents and to make sure that this information is recorded and accessible for reporting, tracking, and planning.

Know the Basics

There are many ways that individuals can support their local community of faith or religious organizations that promote their values. On the whole many people do this through "just showing up" and being present for worship services. Other people will feed their spiritual needs through meditation, prayer, or community focused efforts or social causes. Others connect to the things they value through action and serving others. That service to others can be a wide variety of actions, from serving on boards or congregational councils to directly working with the needy.

Becoming a Part of Something Greater

For centuries people have been drawn to becoming a part of something greater than themselves and our various religious traditions have sought to attract people to that opportunity. This book cannot enumerate all those ways, but what nearly all have led to is the need for communities of faith and institutions to raise funds and resources to support those efforts. For the majority of North American readers of this book, this will mean that you as a leader of your congregation or institution wish to encourage constituents to make financial gifts to support your efforts in the present with gifts supporting your ongoing budget and inviting some supporters who have the means to make major gifts to support a capital campaign or other special efforts. If you are reading this book, your additional goal will be to encourage your constituents to consider making one or more special gifts out of their future estate or retirement assets. Therefore, let's review these basics concepts in the context of religious giving.

Making a Financial Commitment

Personal faith stories are numerous, and each may explain the motivation for us to be committed to supporting our congregation or religious charity with our time and enthusiasm. A natural progression from initial simple involvement for most people is to be moved to support their congregation or other religious organization with their financial resources as well. There are many faith traditions that prescribe specific ways and percentages to give. Although that seems shocking to some, such clarity can be comforting for many. There are traditions where members of a community will know what others have given as an instigation to their own philanthropy. However, for most people, giving will remain a very private matter and something not to be shared publicly. For most contexts in our modern North American society, privacy should always be respected, and amounts of contributions should remain out of public knowledge for nearly every type of gift. In most contexts, if privacy is not respected, that will work against the trust needed to secure planned gifts, which will be elaborated in the next chapter.

In addition to respecting donor privacy, leaders in congregations and religious organizations, regardless of tradition and circumstances, need to demonstrate the impact that giving to your congregation/organization is making. Whether that difference is exhibited in the enhanced spiritual lives of members, or the positive effect that you are having in the local community or beyond, supporters want to know that they are making a difference, through their participation and especially through their giving. Even if traditions required loyal donating to religious institutions, unquestioning financial support can no longer be relied on. There are numerous charities asking for support within every faith tradition, not just yours. Every congregation and organization must demonstrate how they are achieving their intended impact.

A note of caution, although the level of financial commitment will vary among members of congregations, motivating people to give more substantially will rarely be influenced by guilt or emergency requests nowadays. People committed to a cause or to a community of faith will respond to urgent appeals when there is clear need. However, if there is only desperation annually communicated, eventually even those most devoted will reconsider their support. Religious organizations must be perceived as both sustainable and impactful. Interwoven with impact and sustainability, trust and confidence in leadership are also key factors, even if leadership changes. This will be reviewed more in chapter two.

Understanding Types of Giving

There are three main types of financial giving: regular/annual, major/capital, and estate/legacy or planned gifts. Although these types can cross over into each other's territory there are some particular aspects to keep in mind.

Regular/annual giving supports current needs of a charity that are normally a part of an annual budget based on normal activities for worship, salaries, fuel, rent, etc. Generally, these donations come from supporter's current income and the level of giving will rise and fall as individual lives are affected by employment or a lack thereof, as well as many different aspects of the local economy. For the vast number of charities, annual gifts constitute the largest number of gifts.

Capital/major gifts are special commitments given above and beyond normal contributions. These various special gifts can come from several sources: savings, inherited or accumulated assets, windfalls, even from excess income. This type of giving can be coordinated into focused efforts known as capital campaigns or other major gift efforts where professional fundraisers often become involved. Some major gifts may be made to celebrate special occasions, like retirement, the birth of a child, or in memory of loved one. These gifts are consequential to the donor and an outward sign of their commitment to the mission of the charity. In general, seek the help of professional advisors for larger goals and complex plans.

From being involved in various campaigns over my volunteer and professional life, the following are a few helpful notes to keep in mind. Remember to celebrate and thank all donors, as is culturally appropriate for your context, regardless of the size of their individual gift. Everyone who participates in a capital campaign needs to be kept aware of its progress and results. Not every constituent will be willing to make these special gifts, but a significant number of constituents will need to commit to a campaign for it to be successful. Additionally, on the whole, most modern campaigns require a few wealthier constituents to make enough large lead gifts so that campaign goals can be met. Although every donation is important, those large dollar gifts remain crucial for completing a successful campaign in our modern world.

Estate/Legacy/Planned gifts are normally those made from a person's estate assets at death or out of assets held for retirement. They will be made by your most committed donors and since most will be made after someone passes away, will require greater confidence and trust from the donor than other gifts. Not everyone will choose to make these donations, but for those who do, these will often be the largest gifts those individuals will ever make.[1] For some, this will finally enable them to deliver a gift capable of making the significant impact they had always dreamed of having.

There are donors who will consider some major gifts made during lifetime to be a planned gift. I don't wish to split hairs, but if a donor makes it clear that they have consulted with advisors and are choosing to make their "planned" gift during their lifetime, I encourage you to gladly accept them as such. (And potentially include them in your thanking opportunities to be discussed in later chapters.) These "lifetime-planned gifts" are often unique circumstances, as they may be given out of accumulated retirement assets, or from other assets by wealthier individuals. There may also be some faith

---

1. Amy Eisenstein, "Planned Giving and Major Gifts: A Winning Combination," *Amy Eisenstein*, accessed September 18, 2021, *https://www.amyeisenstein.com/planned-giving-major-gifts-winning-combination/*.

traditions such as Muslim and Sikh which encourage more generous "giving while living." You can adapt your thanking efforts to accommodate your contexts. Given the complexity of various retirement and estate plans, leaders should always recommend careful evaluation and planning with the help of personal professional advisors to ensure that everyone's wishes will be properly fulfilled.

Remember, charities generally receive the largest number of gifts from annual efforts and will receive a smaller number of gifts when they conduct a capital campaign or major gifts efforts. Charities raise the smallest number of gifts from the planned gift category. Fear not, though fewer in number, planned gifts are typically the largest gift that someone will contribute to your congregation or organization.[2]

Let me also dismiss a common misperception about raising awareness of planned gifts, which I continue to encounter when I am training leaders. Focusing on planned giving does not reduce annual giving! This has been proven multiple times, including in Dr. Russell James's research over the course of many decades.[3] Additionally, as the source of funds for planned gifts are normally estate assets accumulated over time, most people will not correlate a change to their annual giving since those donations are primarily given out of current income. In fact, both Russell James and my esteemed retired colleague Amy Rome have spoken of how planned giving commitments enhance the current commitments of donors, often prompting them to increase their annual financial support, since they feel more of a part of a charity's future.

What Is Special about Planned Giving?

At every workshop or webinar I do, when explaining the main differences about planned giving from other types, I note the most important aspect to remember for all of your current and future planned giving efforts: **when an individual chooses to make a planned gift to a congregation or religious institution, they are raising that charity to the level of family in their estate**

---

2. "Planned Gifts," *DonorSearch*, accessed September 18, 2021, *https://www.donorsearch.net/planned-gifts-complete-guide/*.

3. Steve Ozinga, "Planned Gifts Increase Annual Gifts, Study Finds," *Kennari Consulting*, June 18, 2015, *https://kennariconsulting.com/planned-gifts-increase-annual-gifts-study-finds/#:~:text=James%20found%20that%20after%20arranging%20the%20planned%20gift%2C before%20and%20immediately%20after%20adding%20the%20charitable%20beneficiary.*

plans. When choosing to enact a planned gift, that person is deciding to place a congregation/organization at the same level as their children or grand-children and others they treasure. (Christian readers, see Matthew 6:21.) For the person making this commitment, they are motivated in a deep emotional way, a commitment to the future mission and ministry of that charity. They believe that a congregation or organization should exist and thrive long into the future and continue to do the good and transformational work which that person and their family have experienced or supported. This deep emotional commitment is just that, impassioned and dedicated.

Because planned gifts primarily come out of estate planning and assets held for retirement, these gifts can be quite large, as many people feel at death or late in life that they can finally make a much more significant allocation since they no longer need those assets. However, each person must be encouraged to do what is fitting for them, their family, and context, as well as their passions. For most Christian traditions, little specific guidance is given for people to consider, and flexibility for context is built in for other faiths such as Islam. As noted in Stacy Sulman's case study, "The Legacy of Peoplehood," to follow and so eloquently reiterated by my new friends Drew Barkley and Leslie Fleisher at Temple Sinai in Pittsburgh, Pennsylvania, "Planned giving for Jews extends beyond just one synagogue. . . . It is a direct engagement to sustain and promote our faith, but also perpetuating Jewish culture and tradition into the future." As you will see in this book's case studies, these central principles prove relevant across different traditions, and whether directly promoted or not, in future years will prove to be a tremendous opportunity for funding future ministry for decades and possibly centuries to come.

Take the Next Steps Forward

Normally most individuals wish to give their assets away at death to family and other loved ones. It is their testimony to those they leave behind and often is intended to express additional meaning beyond simply the bequest itself. Many of us have experienced this through the specific bequests people have made when passing on something like "grandma's ring" or "dad's watch." The tremendous emotion invested in those gifts is demonstrated by the interfamily fights that ensue. (If you have not had this experience, consider yourself very fortunate; it is not pleasant.) When individuals leave gifts to charity at death, those gifts are often invested with just as much emotion.

Leaders must keep this in mind and plan to sustain relationships and thanking programs in the future. Becoming part of an individual's estate plans is much harder than being removed from it—which is why building trust is so crucial and is the focus of the next chapter.

Leaders should remember that these gifts cannot be rushed, as individuals and families have numerous issues to consider and, to ensure that particular wishes are fulfilled, lawyers and other professional advisors should be involved. Planned giving is a congregation/organization's true long-term ministry. Also, planned giving leaders should encourage individuals to notify family members of significant planned gifts to avoid future conflicts or claims of unfairness. It is important that planned giving leaders are not perceived as providing legal, tax, or financial advice, but recognized as simply raising awareness of options that constituents may consider. Therefore, leaders should never appear overly pushy or aggressive regarding planned gifts and especially not actively promoting specific types. Different individuals will need different things from their estate and retirement planning, not simply due to different levels of economic wealth, but also for context and various family commitments. Chapters 4 and 5 should help leaders with the necessary tasks of raising awareness for the many options that exist.

A caution from my experience: if too much attention is paid to the money aspects of planned giving and not to the development of a relationship with the individual, a psychological switch will be flipped in many people's minds. That switch will make people of more moderate means think that their ultimate gift would be incidental and so they may not choose to make any planned gift at all. A secret to share with you is that the publicly or obviously wealthy do not usually make the largest planned gifts to congregations and religious organizations. Those who make larger and more significant planned gifts are the "unexpected" people of more average means. They may not be able to make significant gifts during life but may make very significant donations at death. Please note this in your minds now; it will be a principle we will return to many times in this book. I have witnessed this multiple times and most recently confirmed it again in a conversation with a Roman Catholic diocese; they received an unexpected seven-figure bequest from a person who, though a consistent donor, had never before given more than $300 annually.

Evaluate Your Efforts

I shall state the obvious (a bad habit, or my calling, you decide): many people will resist your best efforts as a leader regarding encouraging a planned gift, even if they are devoted to your charity. Difficulties with issues of ultimacy and superstitions around planning for the end of one's life cut across many different cultures and faith traditions, so please remember to be sensitive, gentle, and as already indicated, patient in all your planned giving efforts. Some people will avoid planning even though it is so tremendously beneficial for them and their family. Your goal as a planned giving leader is to raise awareness gently over time and share resources and information for people to make these decisions at their own unique pace. However, there are many things you can do to motivate and enable people to take the next steps; these will be covered in the chapters that follow.

Summary of Main Points

- When an individual commits to a planned gift, your congregation/organization has been raised to the level of family in their estate plans. This is an immense and very emotional commitment and one which has been made with the deepest trust and confidence in your charity's future.
- Not every person will make a planned gift, only those who are the most committed to the future ministry and mission of the congregation/organization.
- Those who have made initial financial commitments often grow in their commitments over time and in response to several motivations to enhance that relationship.
- It is often the "unexpected" giver who makes the larger planned gifts; wealthier people make more gifts during their lifetime.

CASE STUDY

The Legacy of Peoplehood

Stacy B. Sulman

The American Committee for the Weizmann Institute of Science, where I oversee estate and planned giving, may not appear on its face to be an appropriate charity to discuss in a book focused on religion. Although located in Israel, the Weizmann Institute of Science is not a religiously affiliated scientific research institute. Our sole focus is as secular as they come: science for the benefit of humanity.

That said, the original Weizmann donor base, which still makes up its estate and planned giving core, is united by something found in many religions: a shared cultural identity. This peoplehood, if you will, stems from shared experiences, including the horrors of the Holocaust—whether witnessed or learned about—and the consequential establishment of the State of Israel. More broadly, this peoplehood extends to a shared sense of purpose related to the endurance of the Jewish people in the State of Israel and the world stage. It is aspects of this shared identity that inspire many individual donors to make legacy gifts to support a scientific research institute in the middle of what was once an Israeli desert.

Legacy Society to Create Community

Much of my core estate and planned giving base includes donors who have informed us we are in their estate plans (Legacy Donors), and older donors who make modest annual gifts (Loyalty Donors). Through carefully analyzing our data, we have found that about 40 percent of our estate gifts come from Loyalty Donors who never inform us of their estate plans. While our donor base shares a common understanding of peoplehood, our donors represent a large group of individuals from around the United States. They do not know one another except for pockets in different communities.

It therefore falls on us—the Planned Giving Department—to create a community from a wide range of supporters through our legacy society.

Named after the founder of the Weizmann Institute and his wife, The Vera and Chaim Weizmann Honor Society strives to create a community of visionary supporters like its namesakes. Except for a focus on donors over age seventy, our society is open to anyone who indicates that Weizmann is somehow in their estate plans. We also include donors who make planned gifts, whether by transferring retirement or other significant assets to us during their lifetimes or entering into a life-income relationship through a charitable remainder trust or charitable gift annuity.

Donors do not need to sign anything to join our Honor Society because we simply want to create, as easily and as openly as possible, opportunities to thank, connect, and steward such donors through their lifetimes. Through this strategy we hope to achieve our goal: to maximize planned and realized estate gifts, whether received currently or after the donor's passing.

We make a deliberate effort to steward both Legacy and Loyalty donors with a variety of communications, token gifts, and engagement opportunities. Our principal effort before the Covid-19 pandemic (and hopefully post-Covid) has been to invite Legacy and Loyalty donors each year to luncheons in communities around the country. At these luncheons, I would interview a scientist or our CEO, who would highlight recent scientific achievements and the role of the Weizmann Institute in Israeli society. In short, we aimed to connect donors and prospects to our mission and to one another.

An ancillary benefit for me of these luncheons, relevant here, has been the opportunity to meet our planned giving donor base—men and women around the country who share an interest in the Weizmann Institute and, in most cases, the State of Israel. While each donor is unique, with their own interesting personal stories, I witnessed the shared values and commitments firsthand. I also refined my understanding of some common concerns and motivations for giving. And, in discussing legacy gifts with so many donors around the country, I have come to realize that I am able to offer donors a means to connect to their peoplehood: by finding a family; making a meaningful impact; helping others; and in their way, being part of the course of Jewish history.

Legacy to Find a Family

Sonya, a single woman who lived in an Upper East Side New York City apartment, was in her eighties and not well. Aside from an older brother, she had no living relatives. She needed an executor for her estate and someone to hold her healthcare power of attorney. Her primary asset was her apartment. Her connections to the Jewish community were not strong, but she had been making modest donations over many years to local and national Jewish organizations.

What could we offer Sonya? Our gift acceptance policy prohibited any staff person from serving in a fiduciary or similar role, as she wanted, but we could suggest attorneys to fill that role. More significantly, we could offer her a way to connect. We suggested she establish a retained life estate, which means she would make an immediate gift to Weizmann of her apartment—her primary asset—but retain the right to live there for the rest of her life. She agreed to this arrangement, which gave her a simple way to secure her estate gift while she was alive and fairly well; it would not have to go through the lugubrious and expensive process of probate.

Beyond that, by making a legacy gift, Sonya became part of a large, extended family. She would have the chance to become close to the staff and scientists working within the Weizmann Institute. She would be stewarded along with our legacy society members, and therefore receive invitations to luncheons, updates, and other outreach. More existentially, and perhaps most importantly, by making the Weizmann Institute the heir to her estate, she fixed her place in the continuum of Jewish peoplehood.

Legacy to Create a Lasting Impact

Fred was an eighty-plus-year-old single man who lived in Florida. Like Sonya, he had no children. Over the years, many of his friends had passed away, and his closest contacts were an attorney and financial planner. While he lived a modest life, he had significant funds in an IRA from his years working in the public school system from which he did not need to draw for living expenses. One day, I sat next to him at one of my legacy luncheons and he shared his desire that his estate should have impact and meaning. His connection to Weizmann was closely linked to his passion for the State of Israel as a homeland for the Jewish people, no matter where they came from.

Initially, we discussed the possibility of his making annual Qualified Charitable Distributions (QCDs or often called "IRA Rollovers"). While normally any distributions from an IRA are taxable, under current laws at the time of this writing, donors can distribute up to $100,000 from their

IRA each year directly to a charity without income tax consequences. This distribution could be used to satisfy the required minimum distribution (RMD) he would have to take from his IRA by law.

Then we discussed how his gifts could have a lasting impact, an important goal for Fred. He suggested the idea of starting an endowment fund, where the income supports a program in perpetuity. I agreed that such a fund was a great way to create perpetual support. But then I posed a perhaps idiosyncratic idea: what if his gifts were left simply to the discretion of the president of the Institute instead?

Flexibility, I suggested, means the funds would be available to support the Institute's most current work in scientific research. I explained how recent estate gifts were used to fund two of our newest initiatives: a cell-sorting facility that was part of an integrated cancer center and a building that will house research in space exploration. Neither gift instrument (charitable remainder trusts) specified a restricted purpose, which was a good thing, given that the trusts were set up so many years ago. Who could know where science would take us in the intervening years? Because the gifts had wide-open possibilities, the president of the Institute was able to satisfy pressing needs and use the gifts to ensure the Weizmann Institute's primacy in the scientific world.

The suggestion of making an unrestricted gift resonated with Fred and, from our conversation, he now understood that flexibility enabled him to have the greatest impact on the Institute, on science, and on the State of Israel. To satisfy his desire to have his gift recognized with something permanent, we discussed the idea of inscribing his name now on the International Donor Wall, located centrally on campus in Rehovot, Israel. For further permanence, I recommended he consider entering into a binding gift agreement where he would pledge a specific amount in exchange for a predetermined naming opportunity. He promised to discuss that with his advisor and follow up with me shortly. Ironically, the most flexible gift has the most impact and longevity.

Legacy to Help Others

In Southern California, I met a couple, Harry and Anna, who had been together over sixty years. In their late eighties, they had been to the Weizmann Institute many years ago when Harry was a visiting scientist. Their wealth was in retirement vehicles and the proceeds from several of Harry's successful patents. They were most impressed with research that addressed hunger and medicine, especially as it affected developing countries. As we spoke, it became very clear to me that, while they would love to support the Institute, their *competing* concern was for their daughter, Susan, a fifty-five-year-old single mom who taught public school.

We spoke about a charitable gift annuity, which is a contractual arrangement in which the donor agrees to make a gift in exchange for a fixed annuity for life. (See chapter 4.) I explained how charitable annuities can indeed be set up for another party, like Susan, though typically payments would be deferred until she was at least at an age to ensure a charitable gift at the end. We discussed how the arrangement would guarantee a payment to Susan for life no matter what, and whatever remained after she passed away— usually about 30 to 50 percent of the gift—would go to Weizmann. They were happy to hear that we could recommend that such remaining funds support research affecting the developing world, their philanthropic passion. Broadly written, such a preference was sufficiently flexible even though the gift would only be available to Weizmann upon Susan's death, hopefully far into the future.

Anna asked how we guarantee the funding stream, especially if the gift runs out. I assured her that not only are we are required to hold sufficient reserves to ensure the payment stream, but we are also overseen by relevant state agencies. Moreover, the payments are backed by any unrestricted funds in our endowment. This gift addressed at once seemingly competing goals of providing some security for their daughter, helping Israel, and helping the world.

Legacy to Make Your Mark on History

Finally, while most of my donor stories come from my interactions with donors at legacy luncheons, phone calls, and other exchanges, sometimes I learn the donor's story through estate documents and underlying assets. This is always fascinating and provides inspiring stories that I can then share with future donors.

I learned about Felix, a Holocaust survivor who ended up in Chicago, in just this way. Felix left us the remainder of his estate, which was initially a meaningful six-figure gift received in the late 1980s. Unbeknownst to him, his estate would come into possession of significant real property in Germany.

Several years after he died, the Berlin Wall fell and we were contacted by an asset recovery firm because Felix's father had owned substantial land in Berlin prior to World War II, which now belonged to us as Felix's beneficiary. The land had been confiscated twice, first by the Nazis, then by the East Germans. The East Germans had used it for factories, and the land had significant environmental damage. The land had also served as a training camp for the Stasi, the East German secret service. Some of it was immediately marketable, and we have a seven-figure endowment for scientific research as a result. Twenty years later, a big chunk of the land remains unmarketable, although now, finally, we are in the rather long process of converting it into residential housing.

I visited the site on a cold, gray February day in the waxing days of the Covid-19 pandemic. As I wandered abandoned factories on unkempt land upon which both Nazis and East German Stasi officials walked, I felt the weight of history more tangibly than I had ever felt before. The Holocaust sought to destroy the Jewish people. But through the legacy gift of Felix, I was standing on formerly confiscated land representing an Institute established by the first president of the State of Israel, Chaim Weizmann, as part of his goal to provide a home for the next generation in Israel. Felix's dream of supporting scientific research in Israel was realized (and is still being realized) to a degree he could never have imagined. And those officials who confiscated the land are long dead, their plans undone.

I have spoken to another survivor, Charlotte, over the years. She had a sad and tragic Holocaust story, which fortunately led her to the United States. Her family's farm had been confiscated by the Nazis and was returned to her family at some point in the last thirty years. Felix's story inspired my conversations with Charlotte. The ability to turn an asset that had been confiscated by Nazis into a gift to secure the future motivated her too. Sadly, Charlotte recently passed away in her late nineties. She named us as a beneficiary of the proceeds of the sale of her family's farmland in Northern Germany. Like Felix, she used her legacy to rebuke the Nazi's plan of destroying her family and the Jewish people.

Founders of the Future

These last illustrations highlight most starkly the common theme in many of my donor conversations and stories: the desire to make a mark in history by providing funds, through estate and other planned gifts, to secure the future.

Each donor in his or her own way is fulfilling some kind of commitment—personal or moral, if not religious—to their culture and people. A legacy gift, therefore, offers donors a way to fulfill this commitment, while also providing security to the charitable organization.

But, in truth, nothing is assured. Since the pandemic, we have moved to webinars and conference calls, and it is not clear when—and to what extent—we will be able to have face-to-face visits with this donor base. The effect of this shift in communications, whether significant or not, will take years to evaluate. More existentially, the next generation of planned giving donors, made up of baby boomers, seems to have a different and more diffuse commitment to peoplehood and the role of the State of Israel.

Motivations will change no doubt. But, thanks to the generosity of past and current estate and planned giving donors, we have come this far, and we can look to the future.

CASE STUDY

Legacy Planning in Islam

M. Yaqub Mirza

Legacy planning is a central topic in Islam. Muslims tend to understand the concept of legacy in broad terms that include both "giving while living" as well as longer term ways of bequeathing wealth. This chapter describes Islamic lessons for legacy planning as I have understood them in my work as an investment manager and in my life as a practicing Muslim. I do not profess to be a theologian or cleric, but I am a lifelong student of Islam, as well as the founder of a mutual fund specializing in investing following Islamic principles. My book, *Five Pillars of Prosperity: Essentials of Faith-Based Wealth Building* (White Cloud, 2014), outlines some of the key Islamic principles related to wealth management. As *Five Pillars* explains, Islam teaches that one's legacy involves both what one leaves behind, as well as the model and lifelong example set for one's family and community.

As compared to other Abrahamic religions, Islam is perhaps the most structured in its approach to charitable giving and bequeathing one's wealth. It might come as a surprise to followers of other faiths that Islam is quite specific about how much to give and who should benefit from the giving. The Qur'an defines righteous behavior in the following terms: to "spend of your substance, out of love for Him, for your kin, for orphans, for the needy, for the wayfarer, for those who ask, and for the ransom of slaves; to be steadfast in prayer, and practice regular charity" (Qur'an 2:177).[1] This verse provides the foundation of several categories of charitable giving in Islam:

- *Zakat* is a pillar of Islam and refers to obligatory giving, like a tithe.
- *Sadaqah* refers to voluntary giving beyond and above *zakat*.
- The rules of **inheritance** in Islam are specified by the Qur'an and the normative practices of the Prophet Muhammad, known as *sunnah*.

  o Muslims must follow these rules unless their heirs agree to a different arrangement or forego their rights to the inheritance.

---

1. All Qur'an references are from Abdullah Yusuf Ali, *The Meaning of the Holy Qur'an*, 10th ed. (Beltsville, MD: Amana Publications, April 2001).

○ Muslims are permitted to allocate any portion—but not to exceed a third of their wealth—to discretionary bequests.

○ The rest is distributed to inheritors as defined in Islam.

Islam encourages inheritors to share wealth with the needy. "If other near of kin, orphans and needy are present at the time of division of inheritance give them something of it and speak to them kindly" (Qur'an 4:8–9). This verse allows for people who do not have any legal claim to the inheritance to be considered, especially if they are in need. In this way, Islamic law ensures that inherited wealth is widely distributed throughout society. Islamic tradition also specifies eight categories of people who are entitled to receive charitable gifts. Those groups include: the poor, the needy (destitute), *zakat* administrators, those whose hearts are to be reconciled, captives, debtors, wayfarers (those who are stranded), and those receiving it in the cause of Allah.

To a non-Muslim, this specificity might sound surprising. However, Muslims interpret the guidelines as clear instructions about how to live a spiritual life, manage one's wealth, and distribute one's giving. To Muslims, the clarity reduces confusion when we find ourselves in unexpected situations. What if we discover gold in our backyards? Alternatively, what if our wealth is destroyed due to a natural disaster or other calamity? In each of these cases, Islam is clear about how we provide for ourselves, our families, and our communities in terms of *zakat* and discretionary giving. The instructions reduce confusion when our circumstances change unexpectedly, and they minimize cheating and disagreement. For example, Muslims pay a 2.5 percent *zakat* for many categories of wealth. The rate is 10 percent for riskier types of wealth, such as total returns on risk investments.[2] These differences depend on the ways which Islam categorizes different types of wealth and investments.

Zakat—or mandatory tithing—is considered so important that it constitutes the third of the five pillars of Islamic faith. "The prescription of *Zakat* is a clear and unambiguous signal of the Divine desire to assure that no one suffers because of lack of means to acquire the essential need-fulfilling goods and services," notes M. Umer Chapra.[3] In Islam, *zakat* helps organize and realize a world in which neighbors take care of each other and extra wealth

---

2. For a lengthy discussion of different categories of *zakat*, see M. Yaqub Mirza, *Five Pillars of Prosperity: Essentials of Faith-Based Wealth Building* (Ashland, OR: White Cloud Press, 2014).

3. Mirza, *Five Pillars of Prosperity*, 83, *https://www.contemporaryislam.org/uploads/1/2/2/1/122197478/yaqub_mirza_five_pillars_of_prosperity.pdf*.

is channeled to those in need. It disciplines believers and reminds us to align our worldly, material goals with a larger spiritual vision.

Giving beyond *zakat* receives a special designation in Islam, called *sadaqah*, or voluntary giving. Muslims are encouraged to give during their lifetimes, rather than keeping wealth to bequeath upon death. "It is better for a man to give a *dirham* as *sadaqah* (charity) during his lifetime, than to give a hundred at the time of his death," Abu Sa'id al-Khudri, God's Messenger, is reported to have said.[4] In *sadaqah*, we have a great deal of discretion regarding how to direct giving according to the legacy we seek to realize. But how do we determine how to allocate that giving? What priorities should guide our legacy planning?

The Hadith (a narrative record of the sayings or customs of Muhammad and his companions) directs us to focus our legacy planning in three broad categories. These categories are often understood as: (1) giving to institutional charities, (2) giving ideas and knowledge, and (3) enriching human capital. The categories come from the companion of the Prophet who reported the Prophet to have said that three kinds of giving define our legacy after we die: "a perpetual charity, knowledge that others will benefit from, and offspring who do good and remember them with their good prayers."[5] Several Hadith and other sections of the Qur'an help us understand how to interpret these types of giving.

"Perpetual charity," or institutional charity, is often understood as focusing on the creation of endowments. "Endow it for the sake of God, so that it cannot be inherited or sold forever,"[6] said the Prophet, directing a leader to dedicate a piece of land to be given as charity. In endowing the land, "it cannot be inherited or sold forever, and its produce would perpetually go to the poor, your relatives, freeing slaves, sheltering wayfarers and the homeless, and in the way of God in general. And those who manage the land and work in it could also benefit from it with moderation."[7]

---

4. Narrated by Abu Sa'id al-Khudri *2860*, Abu Dawud, Sulaiman. Al-Sunan. Ed. Shu`aib Al-Arna'ut. Beirut: Al-Risalah, 2009.

5. Narrated by Muslim 163 (Muslim, Abu al-Hussain. *Sahih Muslim*. Ed. Mohammad Foad Abdul-Baqi. Beirut: Dar Ihya al-Turath al-Arabi, w.d.), Abu Dawud 2880 (Abu Dawud, Sulaiman. Al-Sunan. Ed. Shu`aib Al-Arna'ut. Beirut: Al-Risalah, 2009 ), Tirmidhi 1376 (Al-Tirmidhi, Mohammad. *Al-Jami, Al-Sahih Sunan a-Tirmidhi*. Ed. Ahmad M. Shakir. Beirut: Dar Ihya al-Turath al-`arabi, w.d.), Nasa'i 3651 (Al-Nasa'i, Ahmad. Al-Sunan Al-Kubra. Ed. Shu`aib Al-Arna'ut. Beirut: Al-Risalah, 2001).

6. Narrated by Bukhari 1392. Al-Bukhari, Mohammad. Al-Sahih. Ed. Mustafa al-Bagha. 3rd ed. Beirut: Dar Ibn Kathir, 1986.

7. Narrated by Nasa'i 3651. Al-Nasa'i, Ahmad. Al-Sunan Al-Kubra. Ed. Shu`aib Al-Arna'ut. Beirut: Al-Risalah, 2001.

Endowments can provide a range of services and fulfill diverse functions, according to another Hadith. The Hadith outlines the activities as: "knowledge that he/she taught, a pious offspring that he/she left behind, a book that he/she bequeathed, a mosque that he/she built, a shelter for the refugees that he/she constructed, a water channel that he/she unblocked, or a charity that he/she decided in their life while healthy, which will continue after their death"[8] As this passage notes, endowments can support a wide range of projects designed to help one's community, such as:

- Establishing health clinics
- Improving access to preventive medicine
- Delivering meals to patients at a local hospital
- Reading to residents at a nursing home
- Cleaning a local park
- Developing local recreation facilities
- Improving lighting and safety on poorly lit streets
- Petitioning town leaders for better recreation facilities
- Volunteering for trash cleanup in parks or public areas
- Cleaning up after natural disasters

Endowments develop a community's support system to make such services available, and they help align our legacies with realizing spiritual goals.

Pooling resources is another way to strengthen one's commitment to perpetual charities. Let's say that in our legacy planning we want to support the development of science by funding a university laboratory. Such an act might exceed our financial ability to give, but by pooling resources with friends and likeminded donors, we can help realize the vision. Pooled giving allows the university to receive the desired funds over time, invest the funds until the necessary amount is obtained, and proceed with building the laboratory. Pooled giving for an agreed upon purpose is an excellent way to realize collective goals and expand the impact of our legacy planning. (See Chapter 8.)

"Knowledge that others will benefit from" constitutes the second major area of legacy planning in Islam. Giving the gift of knowledge is a service that

---

8. Narrated by Ibn Majah 200, Tirmidhi (Al-Tirmidhi, Mohammad. *Al-Jami, Al-Sahih Sunan a-Tirmidhi*. Ed. Ahmad M. Shakir. Beirut: Dar Ihya al-Turath al-`arabi, w.d.) and Nasa'I (Al-Nasa'i, Ahmad. Al-Sunan Al-Kubra. Ed. Shu`aib Al-Arna'ut. Beirut: Al-Risalah, 2001).

can pay dividends long beyond the lifetime of one individual. The Qur'an and Hadith define education not only as religious instruction but as providing all kinds of useful knowledge. In Islam, Muslims are rewarded for the knowledge they share with others in their lives, as well as the education they leave behind in terms of books or increasing educational capacity of institutions. Modern examples of supporting education could be as grand as endowing a chair at a university or donating a building. But the scale of investment need not be so large and visible. Other activities for legacy planners at all income levels include: donating books to a local library, teaching computer skills to the elderly, and supporting literacy training for incarcerated people.

Finally, the third category of legacy involves supporting "offspring who do good and remember them with their good prayers." Like many Muslims, I understand this category more broadly than simply referring to one's children, and we often interpret the Prophet's words to apply to our communities. Legacy planning that supports this category could include both direct action and support for institutions that enable services such as tutoring children, mentoring students, and investing in human capital to develop character and ethics.

As this discussion has suggested, in Islam, one's legacy is not simply a matter of the material possessions and charitable gifts we leave behind. Instead, it is a more holistic matter of the way in which we live our lives, the example we set for our families and neighbors, and the impact of the institutions that we support through our financial giving and service. According to Islamic teachings, if I move a stone out of the road, my actions are considered a form of charity. Such actions become part of our legacy when we exemplify the spiritual life, perform charitable acts regularly, and demonstrate public service without insisting on rewards in return.

Our motives matter in thinking about our legacies as well. The allure of fame or vanity draws many into charitable giving. After all, doesn't it sound appealing to be known for having one's name emblazoned on a university building or donating a wing of a children's hospital? Motivations such as vanity or celebrity-seeking do not completely invalidate charitable actions. After all, a donated building still benefits student education, and a new hospital wing will help children get medical treatment. However, in Islam, it is recommended that giving comes from the heart rather than from a desire for recognition. "Deeds of charity are of value when they emanate from love, and no other motive," said Yousuf Ali, who translated the Qur'an and included commentary, about verse 2:177.

The final consideration in understanding Islamic legacy planning is the importance of family and one's community. In Islam, the duty to provide for one's family is one of life's most significant commitments. It is the responsibility of parents to care for their children, and this care extends beyond providing for their material needs. In our family, my wife and I consider education to be one of the most important investments we can make in our children's lives and ensuring that our children have access to knowledge and development is one of the cornerstones of my own thinking about legacy. My wife and I believe that education is more than simply access to schooling. We want to help our children and grandchildren understand how to be good members of their communities and responsible custodians of their own wealth and legacies.

One strategy that worked for our family was to establish a family foundation. (Note, many people now create donor-advised funds in place of family foundations and as an important part of their legacy.) The foundation is an official legal entity, created in accordance with Internal Revenue Service guidelines, that provides charitable grants from its funds and investment earnings. In 2008, we came together as a family and decided to create the foundation to give back to the community and formalize our family's legacy in terms of philanthropic giving. The Foundation allows us to support projects that align with our spiritual vision and goals. My wife and I have designed a number of ways for our children to participate as board members, donors, and cocreators of the foundation's mission. For example, as parents, we have committed to helping our children purchase their homes with the understanding that when they are financially able, they will give the same amount to our family foundation. One of our daughters was quick to see the financial upsides: "This is a great deal," said Asma. "There is no due date, no interest, and no rent sharing, and when you pay it back, you get a tax deduction!" Such a financial vehicle helps ensure that our children and their spouses have a long-term structure for continuing our family's tradition of giving, and it creates a common purpose that deepens connections among family members.

The most important reason to establish a foundation is to do good. Foundations create a stream of money for charitable purposes that may continue into perpetuity, otherwise known as a *sadaqah jariyah*, or a perpetual charity. In Islam, perpetual charities give God's rewards to the donor even after death. Second to doing good, there are financial, practical, and family-oriented reasons to form a foundation. Foundations often have tax advantages and serve estate-planning goals. Moreover, our family foundation has helped ensure that we are all involved in charitable work. After deliberation, we decided as a family to focus our foundation on several funding priorities, such as community building, disaster relief, education, poverty alleviation, and social justice. The Foundation pools our resources and allows us to have a larger and more long-term impact than we could have individually or without such a structure.

Whether you have thought extensively about legacy planning, or the topic is a new area of consideration, Islam shares a great deal of common ground with other Abrahamic religions. Even though Islamic categories of giving are structured and explicit, the overall goal is to help followers live compassionately, spiritually, and with a long-term view of the betterment of the world.[9]

---

9. All Qur'an references are from Abdullah Yusuf Ali, *The Meaning of the Holy Qur'an*, 10th ed. (Beltsville, MD: Amana Publications, April 2001).

CHAPTER 2

Building Trust with Donors and Leaders

Know Thyself

In the earliest stages of my career in development, a comment was made to me that I have never forgotten. (Margaret Holman, I think you were the one who said it!) "You are your organization's most likely donor." I had already known the maxim that "your previous donors are your organization's best new donors," demonstrating that you can cultivate current supporters to make new types of gifts. However, I had not taken to heart yet that my own perspectives for giving and trusting in institutions could help guide me in my own work. If you have chosen to read this book, you should also "trust your gut" on many things as you move forward in cultivating planned gifts. What would motivate you to raise your congregation or favorite religious organization to the level of family in your estate plans? If you are working for a nonprofit or giving of your time and talent as a volunteer to your community of faith, you are likely already making a financial commitment and may be planning to make an ultimate gift to them one day. In all likelihood, you already finalized it. Why? Because you believe in its future mission and ministry, and you want that to continue to flourish and benefit others!

However, your belief in the mission of your organization or congregation should be bolstered by a belief that you can also trust its current and future leaders. If you did not trust them, why else would you chose to give so generously? This is the main focus of that multifaceted aspect which motivates one to make any gift but will be crucial in decisions to make ultimate/planned gifts.

Know Your Constituents

Moving now from your own perspective to those of your constituents, how do leaders enhance and cultivate trust in the current and future leaders of their organizations? There are certainly many ways to enhance trust and demonstrate that a religious organization is well run and taking actions to fulfill its mission (impact). In my experience there are three main ways to enhance this for planned giving: First, ensure you have gift acceptance and endowment/designated fund policies in place and easily available to constituents. Second, create open communications between current leaders and constituents which demonstrate the congregation/organization is having an impact in the lives of the people of the congregation and beyond or evidence that the stated mission of the organization is being accomplished. And third, recognize donors in appropriate and ongoing ways. (As you will read later in chapter 7, the building of this level of trust and relationship for thanking or appreciation is best done through creation and maintenance of a legacy society or taking its equivalent actions.)

Existing within One's Means

A caution for all leaders, avoid ongoing budget deficits! Although it would be unthinkable for most nonprofits, and literally not possible for many ventures, ongoing budget deficits for religious organizations are not as uncommon as one would hope. Running regular deficit budgets is one of the most dangerous behaviors of current religious leaders that will likely cause declines in current donations but will certainly dissuade planned gifts in the future if ongoing deficit budgets and spending beyond your congregation/organization's means persists. Supporters will forgive a single, possibly two, year's negative budget with reliance on reserves or a special fundraising appeal, but ongoing deficit budgets destroy trust in leaders and their organizations. Regrettably, some mainline Protestant congregations with reserve assets will choose to spend down all their available funds solely to maintain their current level of program over the course of several years. Arguments to support this behavior can vary, but leaders will often claim that they are trying to "grow the church out of a deficit." Yet, once reserves have been exhausted, living within their means becomes the only option. Please note, the confidence of many donors will likely have also evaporated by that time of forced practicality. Such irresponsible behavior will likely dissuade even the strongest supporters from making a planned gift. Please be aware and exist within your means! As financial challenges accelerate at many congregations and religious organizations, this prohibition could never be more important.

Know the Basics

Leaders, both volunteer and paid staff, hope that all donors and constituents will share the conviction they have about the future mission and ministry of their charities. However, that may not be uniformly true. How leaders build that support among constituents is complex and requires transparency and effective communication to help supporters feel a part of the mission, and so build trust that leaders are fulfilling their charities' goals. Although this book cannot address how to solve all of these issues for each congregation or organization, there are some basic guidelines which should help to solidify your efforts for planned giving.

Building Trust and Confidence

Documentation is one of the primary starting places. This will be mentioned again, but one of the main ways to build trust in the current and future leadership of an organization is to focus on putting gift acceptance and endowment/designated fund policies in writing and to make those clear and publicly available. This is one of the best ways to demonstrate that leaders are being good stewards (caretakers) of current assets and gifts, so as to enhance the trust necessary for receiving more. Additionally, as will be discussed later, in tandem with these policies, being transparent with budgets and straightforward with financial reporting will benefit all giving by increasing trust and clarity. Pandit Sharma's case study elaborates on much of this from a Hindu perspective. Building trust through clear documentation is beneficial in all contexts. As Dr. Manzoor Tariq of the Islamic Foundation of Greater St. Louis (MO) told me, "Giving is the best feeling in life . . . but endowment documentation is crucial for accountability and building confidence that gifts will be properly invested and used as the donor specified."

The concepts of endowment and separately tracked funds in congregations may be very new to many leaders from a variety of traditions. (See Church Publishing's *Faithful Investing* for more information.) Some traditions such as Islam, various Reformed Churches like the Presbyterian, or the Anglican Communion (of which the Episcopal Church is a part) have promoted and cultivated types of endowments for centuries. For some traditions, endowments are prohibited or discouraged, or at least not very prevalent at the congregational level. My hope in concentrating so much on endowments and designated funds throughout this book is not to try and convert you to implementing such funds, but so that you understand their benefits as they apply to planned gifts. (On the whole, most endowments grow incrementally through proper investment management, but exponentially from planned gifts.) I would encourage you to review the additional resources provided on this book's website as well as to consider reading Church Publishing's *Faithful Investing*, which reviews endowments at length (and their investment from a socially responsible perspective). That book also clarifies the important differences between true and quasi-endowments, the importance of fiduciary responsibility and trust building, as well as the beneficial guidance of the Uniform Prudent Management and Institutional Funds Act (UPMIFA), which governs the use and investment of True Endowments in all states, except Pennsylvania, which has its own similar laws, and the District of Columbia.[1]

Second, demonstrating that a congregation or organization is having expected impacts within their stated mission and making a difference for the better are key ways to build trust. If the congregation or organization which you support financially is not making a difference for the better, why bother giving now, and why on earth would you raise them to the level of family with a planned gift? Even if one feels a strong cultural obligation or instruction for giving, one may choose an alternative charity for a planned gift, or they may seek out another charity that is doing a better job of having an impact. For congregations, the impact most members or other supporters are hoping to witness is that the community of faith is guiding people to be strengthened in their religious tradition and to a greater connection to the divine and humankind, as well as to their fellow congregants. However, most people also wish to be inspired by worship, sermons, community service, and good examples from their leaders.

Returning to an earlier principle, reflect on your own motivations and instincts for giving to your own congregation or organization. What motivates you to be a dedicated giver? For example, speaking for myself as an Episcopalian, I give to my parish because I am inspired by my worship experiences which bring me closer to God and encourage me through communal prayer and reflection. I am inspired to be a better person, kinder to those around me, and more willing to be generous. My congregational worship

---

1. Tom Sneeringer, "Top 5 Missteps to Endowment Management Under UPMIFA," *RSM*, October 30, 2020, *https://rsmus.com/what-we-do/industries/not-for-profit/top-5-missteps-to-endowment-management-under-upmifa.html#:~:text=The%20Uniform%20Prudent%20Management%20of%20Institutional%20Funds%20Act,the%20accounting%20standards%20were%20also%20updated%20in%20response.*

and its sacraments inspire me to serve my fellow humans better in my daily behavior and I hope guides me to make good moral choices that foster a healthier, happier, and more just world. Also, I know that any financial gifts to my congregation support various social justice and other activities which improve the world. How do I know this? Because, in addition to inspirational sermons and evocative worship, my parish does a great job of sharing their impact through regular updates on its website and other media. What would your reasons for being financially generous be?

Congregational experiences may be different for others, but through a variety of means, we all want to see evidence that the charity is being true to its mission. Certainly, given the intimate experiences of congregations, even large ones, members are more forgiving if updates on impact are not shared constantly, but leaders need to be proactive on building trust. Communicating impact and transparent financial accountability builds trust. Regular reporting to constituents regarding budgets and demonstrating that funds are being used for their intended purposes are all part of this. Some members of congregations may often *seem* disinterested in finances but skimping on reporting is a dangerous path to travel, especially for endowment or special purpose funds to which people give both during life and in planned gifts at death. A lack of good reporting will sow both distrust and eventually create greater headaches for leadership in the future.

Although needs change, leaders should choose a variety of methods desired by constituents, such as posting on social media, sending printed materials, taking explanatory time during worship opportunities or meetings (especially around the offertory/donation/collection time), or sending regular e-mails etc. for updates. Supporters need to know that their gifts are making a difference now and need to witness the responsible decisions and actions of leaders to indicate that future decisions will be well handled too.

For religious organizations, communication that missions are being fulfilled and impacts achieved, is witnessed through the various methods most appropriate to the type of institution. For a great example of how an organization has effectively engaged their constituents through the sharing of updates on their ministry over many decades, please see Fr. David Uribe's case study for the Missionary Oblates of Mary Immaculate. The Oblates have effectively motivated many to make a planned gift through their efforts. It will be a challenge to encourage planned gifts if your organization does not communicate its mission and impact.

The third important aspect of trust building is recognition and thanking of supporters. Please let me dissuade you from an unfortunate, but common misunderstanding, especially in many congregations: donors need to be thanked! Believing that religious donors do not need to be thanked since people should be satisfied by simply giving because it is "required" or prescribed by specific scripture is a notion that should no longer be relied on. In our modern age, skipping thanking will break down relationships and all leaders should seek more opportunities to thank their loyal constituents. Not only because other nonprofits regularly thank their donors multiple times, making religious charities appear privileged and disinterested, but also because ongoing thanking draws constituents closer into our congregations and organizations and makes them feel a part of the "family." (Remember this from chapter 1?) I regret to share this, but my experiences have demonstrated that avoiding thanking comes more often from laziness than any true theological conviction.

Enhancing Relationships with Thanking

Your goal as a planned giving leader is to develop relationships that mutually enhance well-being. It is crucial as a leader to build trust actively by thanking your donors and demonstrating that you will continue to do that after they have committed to a particular gift. Thanking donors is the key to relationship development and to receiving a gift in the future. As previously mentioned, as leaders you need to build trust by being transparent in reporting and updating donors on how past donations are being used. This helps build confidence that leaders will treat everyone's future gifts with respect. A lack of reporting and thanking will discourage supporters from making a planned gift to a congregation/organization, and donors may choose another charity perceived more worthy of their trust and financial support.

What are the best ways to thank? That will ultimately be up to leaders to decide what is most culturally appropriate and will best build relationships and trust. However, I wish to share a few initial guiding thoughts. As soon as it is known that a planned gift has been put in place, I consistently recommend that a donor should receive a personal note of thanks (preferably handwritten) from the main clergy of the congregation or the organization's CEO. Ultimate gifts are of such great importance to the donor that this simple action will endear the charity to the giver. Leaders do not know at the time the plan is completed which gifts will be the largest, but these are often the largest a committed donor will ever make. Additionally, individuals who commit to one planned gift may well make others such as Life Income Gifts (LIG) in retirement, increasing their allocations or updating their plans from time to time as needs or estate plans change. Establishing that initial demonstration of respect is crucial for further opportunities. Other leaders can also send notes of thanks, but for congregations, I believe it is crucial that the primary clergy person (or a strategically designated leader) send a note, preferably handwritten. (Yes, I wrote that twice in this paragraph.) Donors will be so impressed that they received a handwritten note, they will likely keep it for years and remember the level of respect demonstrated to them as they consider changes to their estate plans in the future. I have personally confirmed this with several donors through the years and Arlene D. Schiff's case study reaffirms this practice.

However, you know your context best. Caryn Feldman, executive director of Temple Shaarei Shalom in Boynton Beach, Florida, which has a very successful planned giving program in place, confirmed that instead of their rabbi sending handwritten notes, those welcoming and thank-you notes are handwritten by peers in the legacy society at the congregation. This practice has worked well for them and affords new opportunities for member engagement.

I also promote that creation of a legacy society is the best way to enhance trust from relationship building and the best way for awareness raising to expand planned giving efforts. A discipline for leaders for maintaining their planned giving efforts, and an essential aspect to legacy societies, is to set annual thanking events into their congregation/organization's calendar so that they are accountable to maintain them year after year. (If a legacy society will simply not fit your cultural context, focus on the regular thanking and relationship development that a society would promote.)

Leaders should always remember that the majority of planned gifts are revocable by the donor during their lifetime. This is a good and beneficial thing, as the donor may need to use those assets during lifetime to support themselves or their loved ones. It is also an important caution for all leaders to remember that given the highly personal nature of these gifts and the deep emotions that are involved, a breakdown of trust or negative experiences at the congregation or with the organization may motivate the donor to change their plans. Not to mention that just as all human relationships change throughout life, a breakdown of affiliation may also prompt someone to feel they should change the ultimate beneficiary of gifts. This is true even very late in life with revisions made to individual wills and estate plans. In certain studies, nearly half of the bequests to charities were finalized or revised within three years of death.[2] It can be difficult to get included in someone's estate plans, but somewhat easy to be removed if trust and relationships break down.

The Importance of Gift Acceptance and Fund Policies

Many mainline Christian and Jewish foundations provide written policies which can be provided for free and adapted for your own context. You can review this book's online resources to find your denomination's or faith tradition's resources which may include these important documents. You may also review the online resources for sample endowment and gift acceptance policies that are connected to our previous book, *Faithful Investing*. It is helpful to show how any gifts made would be invested for the long term and many denominational foundations and other entities provide those services too. In time, resources like these for some under-resourced faith traditions should only increase and become more readily available.

The standard policy documents recommended in Karl Mattison's case study following chapter 5 are: gift acceptance, gift purposes or disposition, investment policy statement, and other guidelines and highlights. Samples are easily found searching the internet, but you may find the samples in the online resources of this book more useful. Once customized for your congregation/organization, they will benefit your charity for years to come.

One of the other guidelines I strongly recommend would be a threshold amount to create any new separate purpose or endowment fund that may also be designated for a specific use, expense, or in memory of someone. Determining that threshold amount will be particular to your context and the general wealth of your constituents. Your goal will be to avoid maintaining too many small funds which must be accounted for separately, while still inspiring creation of these special funds. All leaders should know that once a charity accepts a gift that creates a separate purpose fund, you are legally bound to track it separately (or through subaccounting for each fund if you invest all your assets together to get better pricing and investment or

2. Robert J. Sharpe Jr, "Has a Bequest Boom Begun?" *Sharpe Group*, September 1, 2014, *https://sharpenet.com/give-take/bequest-boom-begun/*.

service options). Of course, unrestricted donations, including planned gifts that do not require creation of a subaccount, can be comingled with other unrestricted invested assets or, if undesignated True Endowment gifts are donated, into the general endowment fund.

True Endowment funds are specified as such by the donor to exist in perpetuity and have various guidelines a charity must follow due to UPMIFA laws in the United States.[3] If encouraging the creation of new funds, be careful to select a threshold amount that will inspire individuals to begin giving during their lifetime, as well as encouraging others potentially to contribute additional donations during life, and, especially planned gifts. However, if a fund is set up for a particular purpose and to be fully spent over a certain amount of time, be sure to put those guidelines in writing to guide leaders on its proper spending and investment for its specific time horizon.

Putting fund and gift acceptance policies in place helps guide and instruct leaders by providing buy-in and enabling them to understand what is possible. It also provides references to guide the actions that future leaders should take. The clarity of fund and gift acceptance policies guide leaders on how the gift must be treated both in how it should be invested for the long term as well as how it should be spent. As referenced above for non-endowment gifts meant to be spent over time on a particular purpose, it may also be beneficial to create gift instrument documentation and share those with potential donors. This can be an important decision and one which may aid both donor and charity. Clear records remain a wonderful benefit and a way to reference goals and preferences if there is ever a need for discussion about how to spend a gift.

If you are in a denomination or tradition where you are not able to hold endowment or separate funds for your congregation, please check with your judicatory or denomination on what is appropriate for your congregation to put in place. If you are able to hold separate designated funds but choose not to encourage endowment funds for some reason, this can be an opportunity for encouraging a variety of giving options for your donors, including memorial funds, which will be discussed in chapter 8. Whatever your leadership ultimately decides, having specific documentation to clarify the use and pattern for investing assets will be beneficial. Other congregations or organizations within your religious tradition may also have insights on available

---

3. Sneeringer, "Top 5 Missteps."

options for investing, documentation, and accounting for those funds. A Community Foundation or designated denominational entity might separately hold certain funds on behalf of your charity, f/b/o (for the benefit of). Although this will work well for a few, if a charity can maintain direct control of assets, that is normally best.

Although not everyone will ask to see copies of endowment, special funds, and gift acceptance policies, having them easily available or posted conveniently online can create a congregational/organizational culture which demonstrates trust and transparency. Such clear and confident guidance will help supporters be more willing to consider making a planned gift. However, there are also other considerations below to keep in mind from the donor perspective.

Take the Next Steps Forward

Donor Desires and Goals

Although most donations are unrestricted, it is important to keep in mind that it is the donor who determines what is to be accomplished with the gift, and legally, if a restriction is made on a gift, once your congregation/organization accepts it you must conform spending to its specified purpose. Also, it is the donor who clarifies if a fund is a True Endowment to be held in perpetuity. (See *Faithful Investing* for a brief overview of endowments and other funds.) Though endowments are normally the best place for unrestricted planned gifts, that destination is not always the donor's wish. There are some individuals who wish that their planned gift be spent on specific ministries or for known capital/building needs and not for perpetual funds. The donor's specifications are what matters most. There may be occasions where a charity cannot accept a gift because of the excessive restrictions placed on it or because it is not something that the congregation or organization does.

In addition, there are some faith traditions, notably Roman Catholic, where endowments normally cannot be created and held directly by a specific parish. This is not a simple situation, as many Roman Catholic dioceses have divergent practices for how parishes may invest and spend planned gifts. Some Roman Catholic dioceses have separate foundations that can assist with investment, or planned giving efforts, and some do not. For leaders, understanding your specific context is important so that donors can be guided well. No one wants to decline a gift (especially from a loyal supporter), and that is why having policies publicly available and openly discussed can help guide donors and leaders on what is appropriate.

It is clearly important for leaders to get to know the structural and legal differences which will impact planned gifts. Those denominations which are more centralized may require that planned gifts received be delivered to a higher judicatory, like a diocese, for safe keeping or there could be the exact opposite where a congregation has full control over what to do with a windfall planned gift. Various traditions may mix a variety of possibilities when a portion of a planned gift would need to be turned over to a judicatory or there may be strict requirements to invest them in a particular way. There are far too many variations to go through all of them here, but it is important for leaders to know how their traditions and denominational restrictions impact gifts.

Sadly, when many congregations receive estate gifts, they often spend them immediately. This has also become a common place activity in many financially challenged communities of faith who may come to rely on a few estate gifts coming in annually to balance their budgets. However, if there are ways to preserve those planned gifts in separate funds held at the judicatory or restrict their use to capital and future-focused expenses, that will help to build that importance sense of trust among donors for raising additional planned gifts. However, it must be apparent to supporters how all these funds will be maintained.

Building Trust and Confidence among Leaders

It is not only among potential donors where trust and confidence need to be put in place, but also among leaders. Not every leader will be supportive of efforts to raise planned gifts, nor will everyone understand why a congregation or religious organization should bother. However, the three main areas of focus suggested for building donor confidence and trust can also assist in building consensus and support so that leaders can trust each other and the effort to raise planned gifts. More on this in the next chapter.

Though a legal obligation, which can be reviewed by your state or governmental authority (in the United States, typically the attorney general), I encourage your leaders to consider any restrictions placed on a fund created by a gift as another opportunity to connect with your donors and their families. You can use the reporting on these funds as a means to build trust and to encourage new donations from other family members. Even if the original gift was from a deceased donor, that person's spouse or family may well be encouraged to make additional gifts in the future, especially if done in memory of that loved one. (See chapter 8.)

Evaluate Your Efforts from Time to Time

Reflection on how much work your congregation/organization may need to do to increase the level of trust both among supporters and leaders is important. In the next chapter, reviewing the clarity in roles and expectations should continue to enhance trust as well as put systems in place to ensure ongoing support from leaders.

If a choice is made to have someone other than the main clergy or CEO to write the official planned giving thank-you notes, I recommend that you monitor feedback from recipients. If feedback is not positive or if people are not feeling significantly engaged, changes to this procedure should be considered.

Summary of Main Points

- Building trust through documentation, reporting, accountability, and recognition is essential for any planned giving effort.
- Many religious leaders feel overburdened nowadays. Unfortunately, this may cause some leaders to shortchange the importance of communicating impact of the mission of the congregation/organization. However, skipping or minimizing communication of a charity's impact will diminish the trust that is necessary for encouraging all giving.
- Unless strategically decided otherwise, handwritten thank-you notes should be sent by the main clergy or CEO to someone who has self-identified as a planned giver.

CASE STUDY

An Invitation to Donors to Be Co-Missionaries in Our Ministries and Missions

David P. Uribe

When it comes to fundraising, especially for planned gifts, for religious ministries and missions in the United States and around the world, there are multiple strategies to adopt and engage in that should reflect an organization's core mission and character. For the purposes of this case study, the core strategy engaged is that of relationship-building. In our own experience, our foundational aim in obtaining and retaining donors who support us spiritually and financially is to invite them into a relationship with the good work being done domestically and abroad with our missionaries. Through a well-established direct mail program and an integrated digital and electronic program (e-mails, social media, and live streaming) as well as a major donor/planned giving program, we continually invite our donors to support our religious efforts in being the body of Christ to the poor and marginalized of our missions through our missionary charism. Our planned giving efforts go hand-in-hand with our direct appeals through mail and electronic media. Many of our planned giving donors have been long-term and major donors, and by sharing our stories we enhance our relationship with them.

The Missionary Oblates of Mary Immaculate is a Catholic male religious community of priests and brothers numbering 3,800 today in 60+ countries around the world. Founded in 1816 in Aix-en-Provence, France, St. Eugene de Mazenod saw the devastating effects on the poor in post–French Revolution France. St. Eugene wanted them to know their rightful place with God and the Church, regardless of their struggles and challenges in life. After ministering tirelessly in the beginning years, the small group was given papal approbation (approval) in 1826 and began to move beyond France. The first missionaries went to remote places in the Canadian Arctic and southern Africa. All along, the founder invited people to be part of the missionary efforts in building up the local Church where they were invited to be. And the people responded with their prayers, charity, and engagement.

At the invitation of Bishop Jean Marie Odin, bishop of Texas, the Oblates landed in Port Isabel/Brownsville, Texas, in 1849. As the initial base for the missionaries, the Oblates invited people to be part of the building of churches and missions along the Rio Grande Valley, the San Antonio area, and north into west Texas in the following decades.[1] Fundraising efforts were coordinated formally and informally through the local churches. The local faithful saw the progress made by the missionaries and wanted to be part of that expansion. In 1885, the bishop of San Antonio asked the Oblates to move further north along the Rio Grande River into west Texas. In return, the Oblates requested from him that an established parish in downtown San Antonio be given to the Oblates as the new Texas headquarters, as well as to help finance the mission expansion. The bishop agreed and this proved to be very successful for the Oblates and the parish.[2] St. Mary's Parish became intimately aware of the Missionary Oblate charism to reach out to the poor in these remote Texas towns and missions. Because parishioners were engaged through constant stories coming from missionaries themselves, this affluent parish aided in the founding of many parishes and centers in this new area of Texas. As a direct result, the parish became mission-centric, thus becoming co-missionaries in the missionary charism.

Expansion in Texas continued for several decades, with Oblates moving into New Mexico, Oklahoma, Colorado, and Louisiana. In the late 1930s, a formal fundraising effort began with a direct mail program. The Oblates made the decision to accept a bishop's invitation to begin a mission in the Philippines, specifically on the island of Mindanao. Seven pioneer Oblates from the United States were chosen to take on this new mission challenge and arrived in Manila in 1939.[3] One particular Oblate volunteered for the mission to fulfill his lifelong desire to go to the foreign missions. Because of his talents, Fr. Cullen Deckert, OMI, was told to remain back in Texas for the sole purpose of fundraising for the new mission in the Philippines. Reluctantly, he agreed and officially began the Missionary League of Mary

1. William L. Watson, OMI, "Oblates of Mary Immaculate," *Handbook of Texas Online*, last updated September 29, 2015, *https://www.tshaonline.org/handbook/entries/oblates-of-mary-immaculate*.

2. "History of St. Mary's," *St. Mary's Catholic Church, A Spiritual Oasis on the Riverwalk*, accessed April 10, 2021, *https://www.stmaryschurchsa.org/history*.

3. "U.S. Oblates in the Philippines," *Missionary Oblates of Mary Immaculate, United States Province*, January 29, 2010, *www.omiusa.org/index/php/2010/01/29/us-oblates-in-the-philippines/*.

Immaculate to write mission stories and publish letters to existing and potential donors.

As time would prove, more mission stories were requested as donors felt part of the Mindanao missions. With the ongoing success of fundraising through the direct mail program, Oblates built churches, mission centers, hospitals, the Notre Dame high school system, Notre Dame College, and various airstrips to fly between the various missions.[4] It was reported that when Fr. Deckert passed in 1973, he fundraised an equivalent of $80 million US (in today's standard) simply by inviting donors as part of the missionary efforts, not only in the Philippines, but also in other parts of the world. Other missions were begun in Haiti, Mexico, Zambia, Guatemala, and Cuba. Oblate Missions, as part of the Missionary Association of Mary Immaculate for the Missionary Oblates, still writes stories about various missions around the United States and the world.

A same effort began in the early 1940s in Belleville, Illinois, from an existing letter writing effort to support St. Henry's Seminary. When Fr. Paul Schulte, OMI, arrived in Belleville in 1941, he inherited the role of thanking donors who donated to the seminary. With permission from the seminary rector, Fr. Schulte began to incorporate stories of his missionary efforts in the Canadian Arctic, focusing on his devotion to Our Lady of the Snows[5] and the founding of several missions along the northern Arctic coast. Because he was a trained pilot in the Great War in Europe prior to his seminary training, he obtained a used plane and flew from mission to mission delivering the Catholic faith, sacraments, and built missions for the indigenous Arctic people. He also aided in the building of hospitals and schools by delivering supplies and materials on his scheduled trips. Many times, while in flight, the weather would change at a moment's notice, making it difficult to land with the inclement weather on the surface. In his letters, he wrote that he

---

4. Jesse Pizarro Boga, "Oblates of Mary Immaculate: 75 Years of Missionary Work," *Minda News*, September 25, 2014, *www.mindanews.com/top-stories/2014/09/oblates-of-mary-immaculate-75-years-of-missionary-work/*.

5. Devotion to Mary, the mother of Jesus, under the title of Our Lady of the Snows is one of the oldest devotions to Mary. It has direct ties to the legend about a marvelous snowfall in Rome in 352 CE. Mary had indicated in a dream to a wealthy, childless Roman couple that she wanted a church built in her honor and the site for this church would be covered with snow. On a hot, sultry morning on August 5, Esquiline Hill was covered with snow. All Rome proclaimed the summer snows a miracle, and a church to honor Mary was built on the hill in 358 CE. Restored and refurbished many times, this church, now the magnificent Basilica of St. Mary Major, still stands today as the seat of devotion to Our Lady of the Snows in the Catholic Church. "About Us," *National Shrine of Our Lady of the Snows, Missionary Oblates of Mary Immaculate*, accessed April 9, 2021, *https://snows.org/about-us/*.

simply looked at the image of Our Lady of the Snows pinned on the cockpit panel and prayed for a safe landing.[6] In every case, the plane landing, whether smooth or rough, was always achieved. The more Fr. Schulte wrote of his devotion to the Blessed Virgin and experiences of the Arctic missions, more mail would arrive with the next delivery. Donors wanted more first-hand stories from Fr. Schulte. And he complied for several more years until his time came after World War II to return to Germany.

Over the decades, the Missionary League of Mary Immaculate (later renamed the Missionary Association of Mary Immaculate) operated as two separate and independent fundraising organizations in the United States: Oblates Missions in San Antonio, Texas, and the Missionary Association of Mary Immaculate in Belleville, Illinois. With a variety of ministries and missions throughout the United States and the world, many stories were written in the direct mail program to keep donors informed and engaged with ongoing projects and needs in the missions. In 2009, these two fundraising entities came together as one organization to support the formal fundraising efforts of the Missionary Oblates in the one US Province. Known today as Missionary Association of Mary Immaculate (MAMI-USA), the organization continues a direct mail program, along with a growing digital and electronic program that incorporates online giving through e-mails, websites, and social media efforts.

Within MAMI-USA, the charitable and planned-giving department is made up of donor advisors and support staff for the sole reason of developing and maintaining relationships with major donors. A high percentage of planned gifts and those who became major donors came from the direct mail program, with many donors giving to the Oblates over a span of decades. Many gave on a consistent basis to appeal letters and campaigns. Over time, they gave more when they felt part of a growing effort with specific Oblate priests and brothers in a particular mission or ministry. Many have felt engaged in efforts to help the poor and less fortunate. Today, when asked why they give generously to the Oblates, many say they want to be part of the support system in missions around the world. When I recently spoke with a donor, I asked for his connection to the Oblates. John S. in California stated, "I received a prayer card from a family member and noticed it

---

6. "SURVIVE-MIVA Carries on an Oblate's Dream—Fr. Paul Schulte, OMI," *Missionary Oblates of Mary Immaculate, United States Province*, January 17, 2017, *www.omiusa.org/index.php/2017/01/17/survive-miva-carries-on-an-oblates-dream/*.

came from the Missionary Oblates. I looked over the website and was very impressed with the ministry and work done, especially in the poorer areas. Now, I really enjoy the stories I receive in the mail and online." Another donor was asked the same question. Harold M. in Maine stated, "I have fond memories and enjoyed my time with the Missionary Oblates in Ottawa in the early 1950s. They do good work in ministry and in the missions. That's why I'm so generous with them." This is a repeated comment among donors; they believe they are co-missionaries along with the Missionary Oblates.

As in the past, the Missionary Oblates continue to go to difficult places to build up communities of faith and to work alongside people. In speaking about established institutions and parishes/missions because of the financial support from donors, it is currently happening today. One particular mission that has drawn much interest from donors is the Oblate mission in Tijuana, Baja California, Mexico. In the mid-1980s, the Oblates moved into an undeveloped section of the metropolitan city. As more immigrants from Central and South America migrate to the United States through California, many are stopped in Tijuana. Unwilling to return to their home countries, many settled in the eastern section of Tijuana. With no running water or electricity and open sewers, many would find a plot of land and build a home using anything they could find. In this district, the Oblates opened a parish and built chapels in various parts of this undeveloped area. This parish and set of chapels brought one aspect of life many are familiar with: their Catholic faith. As the parish grew, the need to help people grew beyond faith—many needed assistance with food and other basic needs. Soon, the Oblates opened a health and dental clinic to meet the people's physical needs. With support from local and regional donors, a small school was founded and soon a youth group. A few of the fifteen chapels became centers of faith and assistance and began to operate like mini parishes. After thirty years ministering and working in that area of town, roads, utilities, formal sewers, commercial development, and public safety agencies began to be part of the neighborhood. All of this was possible after people began working together in forming the neighborhood of their choice. Many of the major donors, through annual giving contributions and planned giving, wills, and other methods, were a key part of this effort alongside the Oblates there.

In recent years, pastor and superior of Mary Immaculate Parish in Tijuana, Fr. Jesse Esqueda, OMI, noticed a perpetual and vicious cycle that many young adults were falling into. He saw many of them being lured into factory jobs that paid low wages and worked them for 70+ hours per week with Sundays being their only day off. Fr. Jesse recognized that many could be trapped in these jobs for a lifetime if they did not pursue higher education while young. Since tuition was at a reasonable cost in the public university system in Mexico and a bit higher at the local private colleges, Fr. Jesse saw the opportunity for a scholarship program for these young adults. With a dedicated parish youth group already in place, he solicited sponsors for a new scholarship program. Starting with just a handful the first semester, he awarded scholarships to cover tuition and for other incidental fees. In return, recipients had to report to a scholarship coordinator every month, participate in youth and parish ministry every week, and call for help when needed, especially with academic help. This empowered that first group to be successful. Many studied for professional degrees, such as teaching, medicine, nursing, psychology, dentistry, business, and marketing. Four years later, that first group graduated and became professionals in the community. Most have remained in leadership roles in the program and offer help to the new youth pursuing their academic dreams. A few are now offering their professional services to members of the parish. They have stated they will always support the parish community, just as they supported them in their academic pursuit.[7] Testimonies from those who were leaders shared their stories with donors and inspired many to complete planned gifts.

In past decades, we have seen high success with our direct mail campaigns, so much so that we had resources to expand our places of ministry and presence in other nations and countries. We built up infrastructures to accommodate the good work being done on many levels. However, as we move into the twenty-first century and into an ever more connected world, we are met with challenges in our traditional fundraising efforts. While our direct mail program is still successful and sustainable for encouraging planned and other gifts, we recognize our donor file is shrinking due to the aging of current donors and that newer generations are moving away from postal mail appeals for cultivating new donors. In response, a digital and electronic program has been developed to meet the trends of younger generations that prefer to give online through digital-pay options. Our efforts now include social media (i.e., Facebook, Twitter, Instagram, and YouTube)

---

7. Fr. Jesse Esqueda, OMI, "The Power of Faith and Education," *Missionary Oblates of Mary Immaculate, United States Province*, April 2, 2021, https://www.omiusa.org/index.php/2021/04/02/jesse-letter.

to send out stories occurring in our ministries and missions. Through social media campaigns that include prayer, devotions, stories, news updates and appeals, our online participation is growing every day. However, we continue to build our relationships with all donors by drawing them close through telling our stories of impact, only now through new channels.

All the while, donors inform us they feel part of our mission and want to contribute to worthy causes they can relate to on many levels. For Oblates, we have done this for decades through our missionary charism and through our wonderful relationships with supporters and co-missionaries. Let His will be done!

CASE STUDY

Endowment Program for the Hindu Community

Pandit Roopnauth Sharma

It is stated in the Hindu Scripture the Bhagwat Geeta 18:5 as I have translated it to English, that the lord said, "Personal sacrifice for the betterment of all, Charity, Austerity and Good actions are the key pillars of living a spiritual life, leading to purity of body and mind."[1] The Hindu way of life very clearly stipulates the value of charity as a key element in the fulfillment of our divine duty. The Hindu Scriptures strongly encourage giving, from 10 percent and much more as appropriate to circumstances.[2] Given the long-standing tradition of generous giving in the Hindu tradition, planned and major giving should be a wonderful opportunity to promote both benefit to society and the sustainability of Hindu culture long into the future.[3]

In my experience, most donations to Hindu temples come from about 70 percent of the congregation and will vary from $50 to $1,000 annually. There are several efforts throughout Canada to support the building of new temples and various capital drives to support those endeavors to create new faith communities. Unfortunately, on the whole, there are few coordinated efforts yet in temples to encourage estate giving from their members. I hope that as greater clarity and awareness raising efforts continue, this will also improve. I believe that by focusing on the ways that individual can give, and putting in place various procedures and documentation, planned and other major gifts could be expanded in many Hindu communities of faith.

---

1. Online translation: "The practice of sacrifice, charity and austerity is not to be abandoned; it is surely to be undertaken. Sacrifice, charity and austerity are verily the purifiers of the wise." Bhagavad Gita, accessed September 16, 2021, *https://bhagavadgita.io/chapter/18/verse/5/*.

2. "How Much Percent of One's Income Should Be Given to Charity?," Stack Exchange, accessed September 17, 2021, *https://hinduism.stackexchange.com/questions/12258/how-much-percent-of-ones-income-should-be-given-to-charity*.

3. Amar Erry, "Charitable Giving in Hinduism," *Canada Helps*, accessed September 16, 2021, *https://www.canadahelps.org/en/giving-life/featured-series/hinduism-and-charitable-giving/*.

Donations of a larger scale are given by wealthy families and individuals in major gifts to fund endowments or to support needy causes such as new hospitals, educational institutions, temple building, and research foundations. Additionally, there are areas where there is a great need for the Hindu community to consider directing their efforts that will benefit both society in general and contribute to the propagation of the Hindu way of life.

One of these opportunities is the need for the Hindu community to work with academic institutions to establish faculties for Hindu studies and is one where endowment programs will be most needed. As the Hindu community continues to grow in the United States and Canada, the need for a better understanding of customs and traditions will increase as well as the need for certification of Hindu clergy. It is most important that the Hindu community give serious attention to establishing funding programs that will sustain the different faculties in the academic world. (Please see Dr. Lucinda Mosher's introduction to this book.)

There will also be new opportunities to encourage giving to designated and memorial funds to celebrate the lives of loved ones, which will be reviewed in the final chapter of this book. Encouraging Hindus to make commitments, both during life and through planned giving, will enable both for creating funds to support our expanding communities of faith and offer more opportunities to commemorate loved ones. Prompting those of greater and lesser means to create focused funds during life and in death will enhance our community's impact on society.

The intention of this document is to provide guidance to the Hindu public and related charitable institutions as to the value of planned contributions and the best approach to manage the process.

Similar to other appeals in a variety of faith traditions, I believe that the methodology should be guided by the tax regulations of the country where the gift is made, the bylaws of the institutions receiving the gift, and the desire of the donors.

The key factor is how to match the desire of donors with the mission of the temple or institution. As has been written throughout this book, helping donors to have greater confidence and trust in a religious charity is often centered on clarifying how gifts will be used and building relationships with donors so that they feel thanked, appreciated, and especially confident that their temple or favorite Hindu institution or program is having the impact they would expect.

As with so many charities, the starting point is building trust and confidence with clear documentation. All institutions receiving donations for annual support and endowment creation must have defined policies and procedures to guide the process of giving and build up donor confidence. I recommend the following for all Hindu temples and institutions who wish to encourage more planned and major gifts (please see this book's online sample resources for several of the following suggestions): solicit donations through a major marketing plan, including encouraging various methods for making gifts to support the annual budget, such as cash, credit card, and the easy set-up of regular electronic contributions. Clearly explain how individuals could make gifts of securities directly to the organization and how donations should be valued for tax deductibility purposes, such as objects of art, real estate properties, and other items of financial value, especially various types of securities. Clarify methods of disposition of all such items. In general, all gifts would be sold with proceeds invested into existing endowments or, if intended for annual support, tracked for its intended purpose. Demonstrate through clear and public documentation the methods for investing and managing long-term endowments, scholarships, and other funds so that all donors are aware of this before they make their gift.

I would also recommend that all organizations are transparent and clear with their reporting and auditing processes, especially if a family or individual has created a specific fund. Providing timely reporting (or subaccounting statements for comingled endowment assets) will demonstrate that a temple or Hindu institution is committed to accountability, which will build trust on how gifts will be managed over the long term and provide confidence to donors considering a planned gift from their estate. This should be a holistic effort to create a financial audit trail for budgeting, financial reporting, audit, investment policies, and spending policies.

The institutions receiving donations must also have clearly defined long-term objectives that will indicate the need and the method of solicitations and disbursement of funds to meet those objectives. As of the date of this document, it was very evident that there is no known documented process within the Hindu community to address endowments or any such initiatives other than the basic tax laws of the country. This document is intended to be an initial guideline for all Hindu institutions that may wish to explore and implement an endowment program.

As of the date of this writing, The Mississauga's Ram Mandir (Hindu Temple) in Ontario, Canada, a registered charity where I have been very involved, has in principle agreed that endowment is a way for all Hindu temples to ensure the financial stability of their organization. The following are some of our efforts to secure the future of our temple and to enable the generosity of our members. Looking to our future, in June of 2020 we established a committee to define and implement a strategy to move the organization in the direction of encouraging endowments. The team was given a mandate to develop a marketing campaign that will be focused on our senior members. The approach will be to host a series of forums to discuss financial retirement planning and to highlight the need for long-term contribution plans to support seniors' programs, such as retirement homes and women shelters, as well as to encourage seniors to review their estate plans and to make a will.

Our mandate also stipulated that we encourage seniors to donate personal items such as artwork, vehicles, a portion of a life insurance policy, portions of Registered Retirement Saving Plans (which are tax deferred investment accounts in Canada commonly known as RRSP, similar to IRAs in the United States), investments, or possibly portions of other pension plans. Such contributions are opportunities that are rarely considered as elements that can be donated to a charitable organization in the Hindu community.

The committee was further tasked to establish scholarship programs to assist students with the cost of education at the university level. These scholarships would be financed by long-term endowments from families who would be credited by having the scholarships being named after the family. Those endowments could be funded throughout life and by several other family members and receive planned estate gifts to bolster their value.

In my capacity as president of the Hindu Federation (Canada)[4] I have initiated discussions with key members to get feedback from their management teams on the subject of endowment. In general, there has been a very positive response. However, my experience has taught me that these matters would need time to be digested by the decision makers of the Hindu community over time. As noted in many places in this book, these are endeavors that will grow and evolve over time.

In conclusion, I believe that all Hindu temples and institutions could greatly expand their impact by focusing their fundraising efforts and clarifying their documentation and processes. These efforts not only improve the greater society and enhance the Hindu contribution to it, but they also enable donors and supporters to fulfill their goals and become generous partners in these exciting undertakings.

---

4. *https://www.hindufederation.ca/.*

CHAPTER 3

Choosing Planned Giving Leaders and Other Leadership Issues

Know Thyself

Are you the leader who will move your planned giving efforts forward at your congregation or religious organization? You might very well be. However, before you make that commitment, please ask yourself if you have the extra time and energy to devote to this effort and if you are willing to guide others into leading this effort as well? If you think immediately, "I cannot do this alone!" as noted in chapter 1, good. You should not want to go this alone and should want to discover at least one other individual to assist. When encouraging Episcopal Church leaders to consider taking this role (at ECF we call them Planned Giving Shepherds), we always encourage at least two people to take this on together. Such a collaboration leads not only to better decisions and broader understanding, but it also allows for compensating where the other may be lacking in one skill or another. In addition, if one of the pair chooses not to, or cannot, continue in these efforts, there will be someone left to seek a new second colleague leader. What is your default style when working with others? Is it collaborative, directive, or somewhere in between? Do you easily share information? Knowing this about yourself will certainly help you to work more effectively with others. With respect to planned giving efforts, it will help leaders to delegate tasks to others which suit them best.

Know Your Constituents

For congregations, you may be challenged to find that second person due to your size or a lack of volunteers who may wish to do this work. For organizations, you may be the volunteer board member or the development staff who also struggles to find someone to assist in these efforts for some of the same reasons. However, even if you are a paid staff member officially responsible

for this endeavor, I will still encourage you to seek an additional leader, preferably a volunteer from among your organization's supporters to assist. You
should seek someone who works well with others, is a good listener, and
actively shares information. If choosing from among your constituents, pick
someone who is well respected and has already made arrangements for a
planned gift. They should also be someone who has enough time to devote
to this effort and is not overburdened with other duties. These two planned
giving leaders should both have sufficient free time to devote to learning
more about planned giving as well as a willingness to work with other leaders
at the congregation and beyond, at the judicatory or denominational level,
and perhaps even outside your denomination or faith tradition. In time your
charity can expand to a larger planned giving committee, but for most small
religious organizations and congregations, starting out with at least two leaders will work well.

Know the Basics

Choosing Planned Giving Leaders

Neither leader must be an expert in planned giving, but both should be willing to expand their current knowledge so that they can share basic information with both donors and other leaders. It is often tempting to assume
that one or both planned giving leaders should have experience in estate or
financial planning. In some contexts, having a practicing attorney or financial planner could appeal to some constituents and that specialized knowledge might prove valuable in some cases. However, professional certification
is not necessary to be an impactful planned giving leader. What is required is
a willingness to work with others and a dedication to raise awareness of various options for planned gifts to constituents while encouraging them to seek
their own legal/tax/financial advice. Yvonne Lembo's and Perkin Simpson's
case studies to follow demonstrate the importance of leadership involvement
and knowledge, as well as a caution for leaders to remain focused on vision as
they promote aspects of planned gifts.

I am reminded of an Irish proverb from my youth (originally from Epic-
tetus, a Greek philosopher in Rome ca. 60 CE), *God gave us two ears and one
mouth, so we ought to listen twice as much as we speak.* An important factor in
choosing a leader will be to pick someone who is willing to listen to people
who express an interest in creating any type of planned gift. Although the

leader does not need to have all the gifts in the next chapter memorized, it is vital that they are willing to learn the basics and be receptive. Many of our case studies highlight the importance of listening and collaboration.

Whom Not to Choose?

Choosing amenable planned giving leaders is important and crucial to your success, but who should not be the main planned giving leaders? I recommend the following do not take on this role: main clergy leader (pastor, rector, rabbi, or executive director), main financial leader (treasurer, endowment chair, or CFO) or main congregational lay leader (pastoral council chair, churchwarden, president of the assembly, or board chair). Although the individuals in these important roles need to be supportive of planned giving efforts and should work together with the designated planned giving leaders by sharing information and interacting with donors, due to extensive existing duties, they should not take on this additional responsibility. While the main clergyperson in a community of faith should be available to speak with donors and could share important pastoral guidance with planned giving leaders, their role should be to remain mainly supportive.

The main congregational leader or board chair of an organization can be a very tempting option to choose as main planned giving leader since that person is often so well-known and well connected. That individual can certainly be consulted and brought in to speak with donors and constituents, or of course, to convene events as, I would hope, the main clergy or executive leader would desire such opportunities. However, the people in those roles hold enough responsibility and adding these duties to their plate may cause efforts to be delayed. There will be exceptions, of course, especially as congregations and organizations may be too small not to mix these roles, but if it can be avoided, that choice will benefit the overall efforts by having a leader with a dedicated focus.

Though financial leaders will be crucial for enabling proper management and oversight of donations, it is best to demonstrate that the planned giving leader is not so deeply involved in finances. Planned gifts are made out of conviction and devotion. The more that "money" is highlighted, such as having the planned giving leader "report to the Finance Committee," the more that regular individuals will think the organization is only looking for large dollar gifts. I have seen this occur many times. In my experience, overfocusing on money will inhibit your most likely (and potentially largest) donors from thinking they should finalize a planned gift. This is because most of them do not think of themselves as wealthy, and they may become convinced that their future gift won't be significant enough. Please avoid that typical psychological switch from being flipped in the mind of constituents, causing them to think that planned giving efforts are primarily about largesse from the wealthy.

Also, there is a danger in appointing a practicing attorney or financial planner to this role. Appointing such professionals who are currently active might be interpreted as an opportunity for them to seek new clients. That also creates a legal and reputational risk for the charity. Perception that any leaders are offering professional advice regarding particular gifts should be consistently avoided for the same reasons. Planned giving should be perceived as a natural extension of your donor cultivation and stewardship efforts.

Among many mainline churches, stewardship is now a common understanding on the proper use of one's time, talent, and "treasure." Our personal resources are from God and intended to be shared to build up God's kingdom on earth. Many of these concepts echo within other faith traditions. Religious organizations can apply this wisdom to their own donor cultivation. When I speak to congregational leaders, I often say that planned giving is a natural extension of your ministry of stewardship and not something new and separate. For an in-depth review of giving from a Christian perspective, please see Henri Nouwen's *A Spirituality of Fundraising*.

Self-Knowledge and Reflection for Planned Giving Leaders

Even with the wide agreement on planned giving shared within this book's case studies, there is still significant cultural diversity between congregations and religious traditions. The bottom line is that you know your own community of faith better than someone from outside of it. You will have insights to guide your planned giving efforts and can usually determine the best steps forward. You as a leader have insights into the mindsets and predispositions of your members, which should provide clues into how you should adapt any suggestions in this book for helping people to consider planned giving. Balancing what you know along with a willingness to attempt new things is important. Remember, leaders who solely know their congregation might maintain "blinders" on witnessing certain truths which keep them from valuing outside perspectives. Those outsider insights may help your congregation to grow and evolve.

Please do not be dissuaded from trying something new or raising aware-ness of planned giving because "our people are just not the type who want to talk about death" or some similar predisposition. Your knowledge of constit-uents should empower you to know what can be tried now versus later and certainly the best ways to get started on raising awareness for considering planned giving. Even if your constituents are predisposed only to leaving assets to family, there are suggestions featured in the book and its case studies that may give you new ideas. Take advantage of them.

As a leader, you will know the particular aspects of your context, in addi-tion to the particular variations to tradition and culture that evolve in spe-cific congregations or organizations. Knowing your religious tradition and its structures is also important. However, one cannot assume that all lead-ers are aware of the many intricacies of their own faith. Do not assume if leaders grew up in your denomination that they know its particular gover-nance or guidelines. Many "converts" may actually know much more detail on its structure better. Bottom line, be confident but also receptive to new possibilities.

The Importance of Senior Leadership Support and Administrative Coordination

The ongoing support of planned giving efforts by the main clergy/CEO and official lay leaders (board chair, treasurer, etc.) is key to ensuring efforts con-tinue for the long term. If the main leaders do not demonstrate support, the effort will eventually fail, just as if they openly opposed it. The support of the treasurer, or similar role, is also very important for ensuring that when gifts are pledged and eventually received that accurate reporting on their use or investment can be provided.

If clergy and other senior leadership are not supportive, eventually planned giving efforts will falter by neglect, and no new or additional leaders and resources will be given toward this effort. Although many clergy and senior leadership are comfortable with fundraising, some are not. Regrettably for congregations, some clergy consider the cultivation of planned gifts as one more way of pandering for money and a distraction from their main pas-toral duties. Even though raising gifts is an essential aspect of ministry, some clergy prefer to focus on the traditional pastoral aspects of their role, misun-derstanding that encouraging planned gifts is not primarily about the money from an eventual gift, but that it is about the opportunity for an individual to feel a part of the future of a congregation or institution. The extra good news for clergy who struggle with fundraising is that since clergy should not be the primary planned giving leader, but a supporter to other leaders, this effort will not consume extensive time but will call upon their pastoral acumen. (See Randall Nyce's case study following chapter 4.)

Coordinating with Other Fundraising Efforts

As affirmed by the staff at Temple Sinai Pittsburgh, Pennsylvania, collaborating closely with others doing development/fundraising at organizations or congregational stewardship work is important for updating giving materials and coordinating various fundraising efforts. As previously mentioned, planned giving will not interfere with annual giving efforts, as planned gifts are provided from accumulated assets and are future focused. However, if a capital campaign or major donation effort is underway, that is a great opportunity to raise awareness of opportunities for supporters also to consider future gifts from their estate. I emphasize "also," as you still want those people with current means to make an actual multiyear pledge to any capital campaign. Although not everyone will choose to give to such a campaign, you want to encourage everyone to consider it. There is a small risk that some people, who may not be desiring to make a current pledge to the capital campaign, may try to use the excuse that they will make a future "planned gift" instead of major donations now. It will be important to clarify with all donors that there are three types of gifts, and the congregation/organization needs to ask for each of them at different times for different reasons.

Other Leadership Challenges

From time to time, there are also challenges when there is a history of bad pastors who misspent funds or CEOs who broke trust in various ways. Though I hope you do not have this history, these memories long outlast the problematic past leader and can cause donors to delay or choose not to make a gift at all. There is no perfect solution to this, but I would recommend being honest about previous problems and being clear on how procedures or policies were put in place to help make things better.

Additionally, planning for leadership changes will be important. No planned giving leader will do their work forever, and although seeking to have two main planned giving leaders and good data base records will alleviate some of the problems, leaders should be mindful of putting their procedures and activities in writing to pass on information to guide future leaders. It will be crucial to understand what had been done and how records were kept in the past. Administrators may be able to help with this by confirming they could maintain written records to pass on to future leaders. It could be as simple as a shelf in parish office or possibly a dedicated folder on a network drive. Don't forget to keep data updated on websites and social media sites! (See chapter 5 on raising awareness.)

Collaborating with Other Roles

Administrator roles can be very broad, especially in a small organization or congregation, and may be consolidated in a single person's job in many cases. The "administrator" role may also be expanded to include the leaders or staff involved in communications if your congregation or organization is large enough to have that role separated. However, many congregations task a single administrator with data collection, record keeping, and communication efforts, including document/letter production and website maintenance. If your charity has a small staff, who is the "administrator" in your context? That dedicated person is very important for your planned giving's future success.

Whether they are the long-term "church secretary" or similar role in other traditions, he or she is not usually given the accolades they deserve for carefully tracking records in addition to all of their other tasks. Consider gestures of appreciation or small gifts from time to time to show them how much you value their mostly unseen but vital work. In addition, it will be a great idea to keep them as a strong supporter of your planned giving efforts. The main record keeper will be crucial to recording when someone has made the commitment of a planned gift, as well as the person who will often facilitate the sending of e-mail, receipt of checks, thank-you notes, birthday greetings, and follow up on materials to estate attorneys, banks/brokerage firms, and ultimately condolences to family and friends of planned giving donors. Build up this important relationship as often as possible. (Trust me.)

Database Issues

Ensuring that future gifts are properly recorded is very important so that there is not a loss of data if leaders change, or for that matter, databases switched. Keep back up records secure so that if system failures or other trag-edies cause a loss of data, you will still know who has raised your charity to the level of family in their estate plans. Planned giving efforts often lag in-between planned giving leaders (if guidelines previously discussed are not followed), but if records are well kept, individual commitments and gifts will not be forgotten. I have personally experienced numerous cases where gaps in planned giving leadership caused annual thank-you events/actions to cease for several years. This is another reason for having at least two leaders work-ing together to ensure records and relationships are maintained.

Good use of databases and record keeping can truly benefit all of your fundraising efforts, but especially planned giving. Keeping gifts private and informing supporters that databases are secure will benefit the ongoing effort of trust building as well. Databases can be used to track important infor-mation about constituents to enhance relationships, such as birthdays, spe-cial commemorative dates of deceased loved ones (especially those related to a memorial fund), and notations about a donor. Be careful not to record embarrassing or truly confidential information in a donor's record. Not only is that inappropriate, but every donor has the right to request a copy/print out of records kept on themselves. Few things would destroy trust and con-fidence more than witnessing that inappropriate details have been kept on a treasured donor. However, basic information can greatly enhance a relation-ship, such as sending thank-you notes on a birthday or, for congregations, to notify a confirmed planned giver that they or their deceased loved one will be remembered in daily prayers on a particular anniversary. This is a long-standing tradition in many Roman Catholic parishes, synagogues, and mosques. Reflect on what is best to record so that leaders at your congregation/organization can enhance relationships with supporters. (Please see data tracking suggestions in online resources.)

Spending and Investing Planned Gifts

The fastest way to dissuade potential planned giving donors is to take actions that would break down trust! As previously mentioned, though the donor may no longer be living, family members, spouses, and friends will keep a watchful (sometimes hawklike) eye that their loved one's gift is being spent properly and is being recognized. One very dangerous activity is the practice of spending planned gifts as a part of the regular annual budget. (Generally planned gifts are best placed in existing endowment funds so that those gifts will be well managed and continue to fund the future of the charity; undesignated gifts can become a part of the assets managed or, if meeting preset criteria, could be subaccounted for purpose or naming.) If the practice is simply to fill budget gaps or fund "pet projects" when unrestricted planned gifts are received, eventually people will stop making planned gifts or will reduce them to insignificant token gifts. Remember leadership actions today inform potential planned giving donors on how leaders will treat their own gift in the future.

I once consulted with a formerly prominent and large parish in the Northeast United States on a variety of issues with their finances and giving. One of the first things I discovered when reviewing their income statements and financial documents was that they listed a line for "planned gifts" under ordinary income, following "rental income" instead of being segregated to show how special the gifts are. I asked the person representing the parish to tell me how long they had listed these types of gifts in this way, and she told me about fifteen years. I then asked how many years ago they had received their last significant planned gift. Her response was, "Sixteen years ago." That conversation literally proved my point of the direct and dangerous correlation to their leadership. It also highlighted the importance of demonstrating proper care and use of these important donations.

To Endow or Not to Endow

I recommend that, if possible, most, if not all, undesignated planned gifts received should be invested along with general endowment funds by default, including small planned gifts. By doing so, leadership demonstrates to their supporters that they will treat every gift with similar care and respect. In fact, by showing that leadership will care for small allocations as well as they care for larger ones, more people will be willing to trust the charity with these donations that are so important to the donor. (For our Christian readers, please see Luke 16:10–13.) Of course, if a donor specifies their planned gift to be spent presently and not placed in the endowment but dedicated to an acceptable purpose, that should also be carefully followed, with its impact communicated effectively to the rest of your constituents, as another demonstration of trustworthiness.

There may be cases when an undesignated planned gift could legitimately build trust even if the board/parish council/vestry chooses to spend it in the present. The most reasonable situation would be when there might be a capital expense, such as replacing a roof or implementing crucial building improvements or some other future-focused project that could be easily justified since the planned gift would be used to enhance the future mission or ministry of the congregation or organization. I am sure you can conceive of a number of appropriate situations to explain to donors. However, the danger will always be if a governing board becomes comfortable with creating "emergencies" or new future-focused opportunities simply so that a planned gift could be spent in the present. This will be an ongoing challenge for your senior leadership on the board to use their authority well over windfall planned gifts. They must use that power of choice carefully so that trust is built among potential planned givers, and not diminished. Clear gift acceptance and endowment/designated fund policies can help guide leaders at those times of great temptation.

For those charities that choose not or cannot hold endowments, be certain to share the impact that the unrestricted gifts or designated funds are having to better people's lives. This should also be done for endowments too. However, since endowments are typically more publicly known, sharing impact will normally be encouraged. Other designated funds should also remain in the minds of supporters through regular reporting and communication of impact by leaders. This demonstrates that such assets are making a difference but also prompts potential donors to consider future gifts from themselves as well.

Take the Next Steps Forward

Choosing appropriate planned giving leaders and their effective collaboration with other roles is clearly a starting point in your planned giving efforts. The next steps of education, raising awareness, and relationship building are in the chapters to follow. Though we hope this book and its many resources will help as you move forward, if you are a part of denomination or faith tradition with a national or regional foundation or other beneficial organizations which can assist to give you additional resources, please take advantage.

Documentation and the Future

Getting procedures and plans formalized in writing is one of the best actions to keep your planned giving efforts moving forward. We have already discussed the importance of putting in writing appropriate endowment and gift acceptance policies. These policies will build trust among donors and constituents by outlining how future planned and other gifts will be prudently invested and spent. They will also guide leaders. Setting out a calendar for upcoming events and when communication to potential donors would go out will also help keep leaders on track for taking action and planning ahead. (See Yvonne Lembo's case study to follow as well as chapter 5 on raising awareness.)

It should not come as a surprise, but religious people will not always agree on what is best. As leaders are confronted with new challenges, there will always be a variety of ways to address an issue related to planed giving too, such as how to spend a windfall gift or whether to accept a particular kind of gift. I would recommend that returning to your official gift acceptance policies will be best, but if a situation is not clarified there, a gift committee could be set up for that review. Whatever decisions are reached, ensure that the results and reasoning are recorded in notes for future leaders.

I also recommend that if separate funds, either endowment or special purpose funds, are created from gifts, a basic record of the donor, date of gift, and copies of any original documentation such as wills or attorney's letters specifying purposes of gift are all kept on record in perpetuity. Taking the time after a donation is accepted to carefully record in a summary document all the basic details of the gift and the donor will be extremely beneficial when issues or questions arise in the future about spending purposes, especially when identifying if a fund is to be added to or used to create a new True Endowment or designated for a specific use. This extra detail can be kept as a part of the official endowment and fund policies and will greatly assist leaders.

Reaching Beyond

I strongly suggest that you reach out to other communities of faith both within your own tradition, and those different from your own. Other traditions, or even others within your denomination, may be more direct or subdued in asking for planned gifts than yours, but you may learn many new ideas regardless. Perhaps others will have a new way to do a legacy society gathering, or a successful way of inspiring knowledge about types of planned gifts you have not raised awareness of yet. Also, I have been amazed how some churches in the same denomination within a few miles of each other have absolutely no relationship or regular communication. Although I hope that is not your experience, I fear this may be a problem for some traditions. So please reach out among and beyond your own faith tradition if possible. It may be beneficial to connect with another community of faith in your denomination that is similar to your own demographically, even if they are much farther away or possibly with one nearby from a completely different tradition. Ask them what has been working well for them and what they are considering trying next in their planned giving efforts. More knowledge is always beneficial.

These outreach efforts may open not only new opportunities to enhance your local community and build new friendships, they may also afford a new opportunity to collaborate on a future educational event. I had been involved in several interfaith events which gathered large numbers of potential planned giving donors together and, for a shared cost among several communities of faith, professional speakers were able to provide their insights on planning for the end of life, basic estate planning, as well as information on some of the more complex planned gifts. The pooling of resources, both financial and professional, may enable more effective education on the common choices of medical care, end of life/funeral preferences, and estate and retirement planning that may be very different among individuals even within the same family.

Evaluate Your Efforts from Time to Time

Planned giving leaders should seek the insights of other leaders to evaluate how efforts are progressing. As previously noted, one of the biggest challenges I have witnessed in sustaining planned giving is not having more leaders involved in those efforts. Though collaboration with senior leaders benefits your endeavors, a central lesson is that the main planned giving leader should always have a partner to complement their strengths and weaknesses and protect continuity. If only one leader has been cultivated to focus on planned giving efforts when that sole person burns out or departs, planned giving efforts often cease. The damage to the charity can be great when activities simply end, as those supporters who previously committed a planned gift may no longer feel connected to the congregation/organization and also feel that their gift and commitment are not being appreciated. The wound leaders cause may be so deep, donors may choose to change an ultimate charitable designation. Consider well what you are doing to build up your relationships in the future.

Summary of Main Points

- Appoint at least two planned giving leaders for mutual support and continuity.
- Form affiliations with other leaders and plan for record keeping.
- Retain records and secure backup copies for the next planned giving leaders.
- Ensure clear documentation is in place and that procedures for recognition and record keeping are followed to ensure that trust and accountability can be maintained.
- Even if actions in the past damaged trust, recognize what went wrong and how it was corrected, then focus on the future and how that trust can be sustained going forward.

CASE STUDY

Helping Faithful Congregations Lift Up Planned Giving

Yvonne Jones Lembo

"Estate planning—isn't that something for the rich and famous? I don't have those kinds of assets."

"Planned giving? Our congregation is doing okay with annual giving, and we have a capital campaign coming up—we'll get to planned giving later."

These are a couple of the most common reservations I encounter in my work as a regional gift planner with the ELCA Foundation.[1] Our mission is two-fold: (1) To help families leave a legacy for the people they love and the ministries they care about by creating a comprehensive gift plan and (2) to help congregations prepare to receive and manage legacy gifts by establishing gift policies and creating or growing mission endowment funds.

Our method centers on building relationships with congregations through a system we call the Ministry Funding Plan. Here's an example of how this process played out in a congregation I've worked with. With a few modifications, you and your congregational leadership can adapt this process to create a Do It Yourself (DIY) Ministry Funding Plan for your congregation.

A City of Hope in the Hills of Coal Country

I first met Pastor Bob[2] by phone. The bishop's assistant in his area referred him to me as a resource person to discuss planned giving with members of City of Hope. In addition, a previous gift planner had been in conversation with the congregation about establishing a mission endowment fund through our foundation.

---

1. *www.elca.org/foundation*.
2. Names and identifying details have been changed to preserve confidentiality.

Congregational Discovery

In our initial conversation, I got to know a little more about Pastor Bob, the congregation, and their ministry funding goals. A DIY Congregational Self-Discovery process among leaders in your congregation can be accomplished by discussing some of the following questions together:

Concerning the Pastor and Congregation Council/Vestry:

What's your vision for the congregation?

Concerning the Congregation:

What kind of ministries is your congregation currently engaged in?

How are these ministries funded?

Concerning Planned Gifts:

If your congregation received a bequest of $100,000 today, how would it be used? Would it be fought over?

How many bequests do you receive a year now?

Concerning Endowed Funds:

Do you have an endowment?

How do you use it? Who manages it?

How much is in the endowment? Are there separately designated funds?

Are bequests consistently deposited in your endowment fund?

Pastor Bob had been serving City of Hope for two years. His goal was to ensure that the congregation was on firm and sustainable spiritual and financial footing for the years ahead.

About one hundred members gather weekly for worship at City of Hope. Music ministry is a focal point for the congregation. A childcare center housed on the church grounds is a daily hub of activity and constant community connection as well as a source of income. City of Hope also generously supports the local food pantry. These ministries are all funded by annual giving.

City of Hope's operating budget is about $330,000 per year raised through weekly offerings, special appeals, and interest income and cash transfers from reserve accounts. The combined total of these reserve accounts was about $500,000. A "Special Memorials" account held about $230,000 in congregation bequests and memorial gifts. Although the congregation called it a "Memorial Endowment," it was a savings account typically earning less than 2 percent annually.

Course of Action: Council, Group Meetings, Family Meetings, Results

Pastor Bob and I agreed that I'd first meet with the congregation council. Next, I'd meet with groups of families to discuss planned giving. After that, I'd schedule follow-up meetings with families who were ready to create a gift plan. Then we'd reconvene to assess results.

During my meeting with the council, I presented "The Three-Legged Stool" to show how planned giving and endowment funds fit into the congregation's overall stewardship plan. This simple illustration responds to the two reservations I mentioned earlier: "Estate planning is out of my reach" and "Planned giving is something our congregation will do later." You can use the three-legged stool to present a picture of balanced stewardship that includes current, major, and planned gifts.

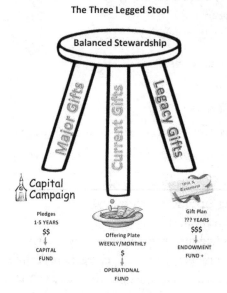

The Three Legged Stool

Balanced Stewardship

Major Gifts | Current Gifts | Legacy Gifts

Capital Campaign
Pledges
1-5 YEARS
$$
↓
CAPITAL
FUND

Offering Plate
WEEKLY/MONTHLY
$
↓
OPERATIONAL
FUND

Gift Plan
??? YEARS
$$$
↓
ENDOWMENT
FUND +

Council gave the go-ahead and Pastor Bob identified six families in the congregation, including the pastor and his wife, who were interested in learning more about planned giving. We scheduled a planned giving presentation.

Together with your congregation leadership, you can identify families in your congregation who may be interested in learning more about planned giving. Think through the following checklist as you identify families for an initial meeting:

1. Lead by example. Start with you and your own family.

2. Invite your pastor and council (or vestry, board, etc.) members to join you.

3. Consider senior families in your congregation who have a history of consistent (*not necessarily extravagant*) giving to your congregation.

4. Consider families who have been actively volunteering and who are enthusiastic about your congregation's ministry.

5. Focus on members aged fifty-five and over who are near or in retirement.

6. Give special attention to single seniors and couples without children, for whom the congregation may be the focus of their legacy.

7. Don't forget about others in your community who have a positive relationship with your congregation: service people and local business owners, those who attend seasonal congregational events, families connected to the neighborhood or congregation school, leaders of social service organizations, etc.

Planned Giving Presentation

My initial planned giving presentation does not focus on specific gift instruments, but rather on the heartfelt motivations that encourage families to create a lasting legacy: "Planned Giving Starts with the Heart." Here are the three heart pillars for a good gift plan:

1. **The people you love:** Parents, children, grandchildren, other relatives, and loved ones.

2. **The ministries you care about:** Religious and charitable organizations that make a difference in people's lives and help build strong communities and a better world. Your congregation may head the list, along with other significant organizations such as your alma mater, social service agencies, or other charities that you regularly support.

3. **The assets you own:** Some typical assets we build during our lifetimes are a) our home, b) our retirement savings, c) life insurance, d) investment accounts. Totaling up the approximate value of these assets helps you see your capacity to make a lasting difference with your legacy gift plan.

You can create a simple list of these three pillars to serve as a personal guide.

You can host a DIY planned giving workshop by showing a short planned giving video from your denomination/denominational foundation or a legacy planning organization or by simply inviting a local professional who is knowledgeable about estate planning to provide a simple introductory presentation about planned giving. However you do it, completing the 3-point "Starts with the Heart" inventory will provide a solid start for you and others in your congregation to begin or renew the legacy planning process.

Cultivating Relationships

Beyond conveying information, one of the chief goals for planned giving group meetings is to establish rapport, build trust, and whet families' appetites for creating their plans. Because of Pastor Bob's influence and example, five of the six families who attended the group meeting scheduled one-on-one gift planning appointments with me.

Having an advocate to work with is the key to cultivating relationships for planned giving in congregations. (See chapter 3 on appointing leaders and the concept of a planned giving shepherd.) It doesn't have to be the pastor. It may be an enthusiastic committee member who opens doors of access to decision makers and builds a bridge to connect with key families. It may be a family of stature who had a great gift planning experience and influences others. (Consider recording such an event for those who will miss it.)

How can you build rapport in your congregation? Instead of setting up a once-and-done legacy presentation by an outside expert, consider inviting a few families to form a planned giving support cohort. Over the course of several months, these families could commit to meeting regularly, learning more about planned giving, holding each other accountable as they schedule confidential meetings with professionals, and celebrating together as they complete their plans.

Creating A Gift Plan

Over a period of about three months, I met with each family at least twice to help them create their gift plan. Here are three planning options to consider:

1. **Adopt ministry as another child in your legacy plan.** For example, if you have two children, adopt ministry as the third child and distribute 33 percent of your assets to each.

2. **Leave a tithe for ministry in your legacy plan.** A tithe or 10 percent represents a significant legacy gift—$10,000 for every $100,000 in assets. In contrast to bequests of a specific dollar amount, a tithe can grow or contract as a family's assets change over time.

3. **Consider a Charitable Remainder Trust** also known as the "Give It Twice" option. Give a percentage of your assets into the trust and the trust (often invested by your denomination's foundation) will invest those assets to continue growing over time. Family members will receive income of at least 5 percent per year from the trust for life or for a term of up to twenty years. After that, your congregation and/or other charitable organizations will receive the charitable remainder of the trust. This option enables families to leave a much larger share of their assets for ministry than if they were to divide their assets between family and ministry immediately upon death. Your denominational foundation, financial planner, or estate attorney can help you set up a Charitable Remainder Trust.

Finally, consider how you will distribute the charitable part of your legacy gift:

1. **Outright gift**, which can be spent immediately and in full by the receiving organization.

2. **Endowed gift**, which will be invested for long-term growth and generate stable distributions in perpetuity in support of your congregation.

A family could endow their annual congregation contribution by multiplying that contribution by twenty-five and gifting that amount to their congregation endowment fund or setting up their own endowment fund with their denomination or community endowment and designating their congregation to receive the distributions. (See chapter 8.)

Documenting and Acknowledging Planned Gifts

Although families will create their plans confidentially in consultation with their own professional advisors, it's still important for your congregation to create a reliable record of planned gifts or *expectancies*—gifts planned now that will be received by the congregation in the future.

In some cases, a gift plan will be the fruit of detailed conversations between your congregation and the donor family as the gift is taking shape.

In this case, your congregation will know more about the gift in advance and help guide how the gift is structured for mutual benefit.

You can use something as simple as a planned gift confirmation card or letter of intention to keep a record of families who have created planned gifts that include your congregation. Here's the essential information you should include:

1. Donor contact information.
2. Contact information for the executor or other planning professionals who will administer the gift on behalf of the donor's estate.
3. Whether there is a restriction on how the gift is used. (If there is, you should meet with the family to discuss this in advance to ensure that the gift can be used as intended.)
4. Whether the donor wishes to remain anonymous.

Here's some optional but *very helpful* details to collect:

- Basic details about the structure of the gift such as: bequest through will or trust, beneficiary designation of selected assets, gift to congregation endowment or distribution from an independent endowment, gift of appreciated securities, gift of real estate, or tangible personal property.
- Estimated value of the gift. (Please note, though we do not recommend directly asking the dollar value of the gift for a number of reasons discussed in this book, some donors may volunteer an estimated value. If you choose to record a general value, according to surveys from 2019, average bequests to charity were $78,630;[3] so perhaps $50,000 for each confirmed gift could be a conservative estimate.)

As an incentive, consider creating a Legacy Society to acknowledge families who establish and document a planned gift for your congregation. (See chapter 7 and Peter Pereira's case study from his work in the Episcopal Diocese of Hawaii.)

It's *essential* to express thanks to each person who includes your congregation in their plans. Once you receive a completed planned gift card or letter of intention, your pastor or designated congregation leader

---

3. Eden Stiffman, "Survey of Wills Created by Everyday Donors Shows an Average Bequest of $78,630," *The Chronicle of Philanthropy*, August 28, 2019, *https://www.philanthropy.com/article/survey-of-wills-created-by-everyday-donors-shows-an-average-bequest-of-78-630?cid=gen_sign_in.*

should promptly prepare a thank-you letter or card and mail or hand deliver it to the donor. If you establish a Legacy Society, you may also include a small but meaningful memento to commemorate their new membership in the society.

Results!

Five families at City of Hope completed gift plans representing $5.5M in combined family assets distributing $740,000 in planned gifts for ministry, including nearly $120,000 designated specifically for City of Hope. On top of that, shortly after our gift planning work was complete, Pastor Bob received a call from a musician who had been a visiting artist for one of City of Hope's organ recitals. Pastor Bob invited him to attend Easter service. He was so moved by his experience in worship that he gave a gift of $30,000 in appreciated securities to City of Hope to establish an endowment fund for their worship and arts ministry. Spurred on by this surprise gift, Pastor Bob quickly convened the congregation council, and we went right to work in setting up their endowment funds—yes, funds with an "s." The seed gift for the worship and arts endowment fund became a springboard for the congregation to transfer the $230,000 in their savings account "Endowment Fund" into an investment account managed through the ELCA Foundation's Pooled Trust Endowment Fund. Today, City of Hope's two endowment accounts provide $10,000 in annual support for City of Hope's worship, music, and outreach ministries.

This example shows how *a single legacy gift* can become a seed that yields an abundant harvest of generosity for your congregation. That gift could start with you!

Follow Up! Follow Up! Follow Up!

Planned giving workshops are not once and done. Scheduling workshops at set times each year ensures that families in the congregation are regularly invited to consider creating a planned gift. Creating a simple planned giving message or tagline that appears on your congregation website and in weekly bulletins serves as a constant, silent reminder to help families build planned giving into their generosity habits.

Regularly "rediscovering" your congregation's plans, hopes, and dreams for the future will keep a fresh vision in front of families as they consider how to contribute to your congregation today, tomorrow, and beyond their lifetime. As families mature into new seasons of stewardship, or new families become part of the congregation, hearing this message with fresh ears can lead to new gift plans.

Closing Blessing

In closing, here's one of my favorite passages from Paul's second letter to the congregation in Corinth:

> He who supplies seed to the Sower and bread for food will supply and multiply your seed for sowing and increase the harvest of your righteousness. You will be enriched in every way for your great generosity, which will produce thanksgiving to God through us; for the rendering of this ministry not only supplies the needs of the saints but also overflows with many thanksgivings to God. Through the testing of this ministry, you glorify God by your obedience to the confession of the gospel of Christ and by the generosity of your sharing with them and with all others, while they long for you and pray for you because of the surpassing grace of God that he has given you. Thanks be to God for his indescribable gift! (2 Cor. 9:10–15)

CASE STUDY

Connecting with the Vision

Perkin F. Simpson

For both faith-based and secular organizations, ensuring that the vision and mission of the organization remains at the forefront while educating members and supporters on planned giving options requires an intentional effort. From an experiential and observational perspective, when planned giving is introduced into the stewardship (the giving of time, talent, and treasure by members in the religious context) conversation, there is a tendency to transition from "why" a person should give (the mission) to then focus on "how" and "what" they should give. Tax-benefits and gift specifics become the focus and the true motivation to give and the donors' connection to the vision and mission of the organization is placed in the background, if not displaced altogether. The overemphasis on the technical side of planned gifts can also diminish the opportunity to expand planned giving opportunities, where the complexity of these gifts can serve as a deterrent to explore or establish them. Technical details of planned gifts are important and there is a time and place to discuss these elements. Recognizing when and how to merge these aspects along with discussion about mission and vision can increase the opportunities for successful planned gift development. Fortunately, there is a recognizable roadmap that most organizations already have in place in their current development efforts. Capital campaigns and fundraising appeals for (current dollars) tend to do a much better job at keeping vison and mission at the forefront of the conversation. A similar prescription can and should be put in place when soliciting and creating awareness about planned giving options. Ensuring that the vision and mission is intentionally included will also simplify and strengthen the message.

The disconnect between planned giving appeals and the vision and mission of the organization is often evident from the awareness stage. As a former executive director of a denominational planned giving organization, several invitations to speak about planned gifts to members and supporters of various ministry partners were personally received. In a large percentage of the cases, these requests centered around conducting a seminar or workshop to speak to the benefits of establishing a will, charitable gift annuity (CGA), charitable trust, or other type of planned gift. These requests would further include the desire to see tax calculations or some analysis of planned giving from a cost-savings perspective. Tax attorneys and other financially focused individuals would sometimes attend or speak at these events, often reinforcing the focus, or in this case, overfocus on the technical side of planned gifts. The treatment of bypassing capital gains, obtaining the biggest tax deduction, or finding creative ways to establish lifetime income for individuals and their families would be discussed as the main drivers to establish planned gifts. What was usually missing was the discussion about the impact of the gift on specific areas of ministry and how the donor's generosity would aid ministry for generations to come. The idea of leaving a legacy, when presented, tended to be from an individual benefit perspective and the coordination of legacy goals with organizational and ministry goals was left wanting.

In fairness to our planned giving development officers, tax and legal professionals, and church and other religious leaders, I have found that the giving environment has conditioned us to think about and introduce planned giving predominantly from the technical benefit side. Establishing a gift illustration detailing numbers seems to be the desired initial goal and communicating the financial benefits of the planned giving is placed on a pedestal. Conversely, fundraising and capital campaign communications rarely lead to an environment where a gift illustration is even considered as a desired objective. Although these current dollar appeals result in donations manifested in the form of cash or a check, it is possible to detail the potential tax incentives of these gifts or to calculate savings based on an individual's income tax bracket and donation level. The practice is not applied. There is often no desire to focus on technical details of campaign and current dollar gifts and gift specifics are usually handled at tax time or acknowledged after the gift is made. The argument can be made that current dollar appeals and planned giving appeals cater to different types of givers and different levels of giving; however, there are no current studies, of which I am aware, that demonstrate any less of a connection to mission evident for the planned giving prospect when compared with the current dollar steward. If anything, the connection to ministry arguably must be stronger for someone willing to give a more substantial planned gift than a much smaller current donation. Yet, there is a minimization of the vision and mission message when there appears to be a greater need to reinforce this message. There is merit to understanding and communicating the financial benefits of various planned gifts. There is validity in preparing gift illustrations for complex gifts. There is appeal in realizing tax benefits. In financial planning, these elements are very important and will aid in securing planned gifts, but not to the exclusion of including the vision and mission message.

It may be beneficial to converse on why keeping vision and mission as part of current dollar appeals is much easier than accomplishing the same when introducing planned giving options. From professional experience and observation, capital campaigns and fundraising goals tend to be more proximate and time sensitive, and a large focus includes tugging on the heartstrings of the potential giver. The call to action is more urgent. This immediacy prescribes that the emotional appeal may be the best course of action. In my experience, there is merit in this approach since better mission-driven, impactful appeals tend to result in more gifts. In successful fundraising campaigns, the goals of the appeal and organizational need are clearly stated. What will be done with the funds, once received, is often at the forefront of the communications. The sense of partnership with the mission is put at the forefront. Motivational aspects for giving are celebrated and drive the appeal.

In my experience, when transitioning to planned giving appeals, these aspects seem to diminish. Why is this intentional connection to ministry in the planned giving discussion minimized? Why does a shift from vision and mission to technical details happen when planned gifts enter the scene? Why does the conversation transition from meeting the needs of the organization and ensuring the continuation of key ministries to placing most of the emphasis on what the prevailing CGA rate is, or trying to determine and explore the benefits associated with various individual tax brackets or income levels? Organizations are not forced to make these communication shifts; however, the tendency to do this is often without inhibition.

Much of the answer as to why there appears to be a need to maximize the technical details and minimize the vision and mission message may lie in the perceived complexity of the planned gift. Closing a planned gift does take more intentional effort than completing a simple online gift or donation from a text message. Establishing a charitable remainder trust does take more coordination with legal and tax advisors than writing a small check for a donation. A gift from a will requires greater consideration since it likely has broad-reaching implications for the giver, the ministry, and their personal financial goals. The perceived complexity of planned gifts appears to contribute to the tendency to want to address complexity with complexity from the start. The initial motivation appears to be to lay out the numbers and show the ultimate tax savings or benefit that will make the reason to create the planned gift more compelling. As humans, donors can only digest so much information, so why not devote as much energy as possible to describing and analyzing the numbers? This desire appears to drive the process for many planned giving appeals. In appealing to these motivations, the connection to ministry, which is the true motivation to give, is often taken for granted where the organization assumes that the potential donor will automatically make this connection. Donors often do not.

In helping to ensure that ministries and organizations do not fall into the technical detail trap when reviewing planned gifts, my professional experience suggests the following practical considerations. At the introduction of planned giving appeals or workshops, begin with the stated goals and accomplishments of the ministry or organization. Affirm the desire to see these objectives continue and expand indefinitely. Express the introduction of planned giving options as simply providing additional pathways to support. Since giving is beneficial to the donor, these additional ways to give provide avenues for additional blessings as a measure of faith. Avoid the initial inclination to introduce legal and tax jargon early into the process. Avoid the emphasis on creating gift illustrations as the initial primary goal. Instead, create an avenue for the donor to affirm what they would like to see happen as a result of their gift. Do this with the confidence of knowing that there will be time for sharing those other technical details in time. Speak to the how that gift will benefit and be appreciated by the ministry and organization. Testify to how others have demonstrated their generosity by establishing similar gifts.

Analogous with how a current dollar gift contributes to present goals, there is merit in investing time and conversing with a donor about how their bequest can benefit a ministry they love in perpetuity. There is value in discussing how the establishment of an individual or family endowment can help ensure the continuation of ministry by providing provisions to replace their current tithe with endowment income after they are gone, without the initial focus on the numbers. Speak to the scholarships that may be awarded and how lives of many will be impacted. Ask the donor where and how they would like their gift to benefit ministry and keep that message alive throughout the conversation. Make the vision and mission element a continued and intentional effort.

The vision and mission conversation will simplify the planned giving message. Instead of meeting complexity with complexity and numbers with more numbers, focus the attention on the organizational impact and goal. Ministry goals are much simpler for the donor to understand, and when they realize how their personal gift can help, their receptiveness increases to exploring planned giving options capable of making their desires a reality. Recognize that donors also have other advisors. They may prefer to hear tax details, gift specifics, and legal implications from their accountants or attorneys, rather than hearing that message from individuals more closely connected to the ministry. For the messenger, this also relieves the tension of needing to become a gift planning expert. Come equipped with understanding of where to direct gift guidance, rather than feeling that you have to be the ultimate guru on all things planned giving. If a gift illustration is desired or if there is the overwhelming urge to conform to meeting the gift illustration creation goal, present it to the donor. After your conversation, encourage them to review that information with their advisors. More importantly, if the message is not already clear, remember to include mission and vision as a significant part of your conversation.

Intentional vision and mission conversations will also better align the planned giver and their gift to the mission of the organization. Demonstrating the ability to save thousands or hundreds of thousands in taxes is remarkable and oftentimes will result in the establishment of a planned gift; however, without the vision and mission discussion, the ministry or organization is left keeping its fingers crossed that the gift will be usable. The consequence of speaking predominantly to gift specifics to the exclusion of mission objectives is often evident in resulting gifts. Without vision and mission awareness, planned gifts tend to be established with too many restrictions or not in line with ministry and organizational priorities. For example, there have been pipe organ funds where the pipe organ at a church no longer exists. There may be cemetery funds established to contribute to the upkeep of a cemetery where another donor has already satisfied that need. There may be provision for gifts to be used for "ministry only" along with no provision established to reduce or relieve the administrative burden of maintaining the objectives of the gift. The vision and mission discussion does not guarantee that all gifts will be usable, but experience has demonstrated that impact on ministry will be more beneficial when that conversation is placed at the forefront.

At times, there will be donors who want to focus on the numbers. Do not ignore their desire to see the numbers and address these needs first but be sure to proactively include the conversation about vision and mission.

As long as credence is shown to what the number-focused donor wants to see, the integration of the mission message is usually met without resistance. When vision and mission is included in the message, the overall conversation becomes more meaningful, providing an avenue for deeper discussion and strengthened relationships. Numbers people like to talk about numbers; however, most ministry connected individuals like to talk about mission as well, even though they may not proactively bring that aspect to the conversation. Remember that in the arena of planned giving, donors have also been conditioned to meet complexity with complexity and numbers with more numbers. Many enter the conversation believing that this is the way it is and always has been done. Provide some relief for them as well.

If it helps, consider the planned giving appeal as an extended current dollar appeal when it comes to speaking about vision and mission. This is not an exact analogy but may help to steer considerations in the right direction. Fundraisers and capital campaigns tend to keep the organizational objectives at the forefront. The mission message is one of inspiration and should be included and celebrated as often as possible. There are obvious differences between current dollar campaigns and planned giving appeals. There are differences in contributing a gift to the offering plate versus establishing one through a beneficiary designation in a retirement plan or life insurance policy. However, the chasm that appears to exist between current dollar stewardship and planned giving with respect to mission message seems to exist because of social conditioning and historic practice. Numbers and illustrations are inherent aspects of the planned giving message. They are important and beneficial to the process, but not to the exclusion of the vision and mission message.

CHAPTER 4

Types of Planned Gifts

Know Thyself

As a leader, it may be useful to reflect on what you have considered for yourself for a planned gift, as was previously suggested in chapter 1. Given your stage of life and context, what gifts would most appeal to you or be best for you and your family? And why am I asking you now? It is for two reasons: if you are making the choice to lead this effort at your congregation or religious organization, by making this decision for yourself, you can be a personal example to others. The second reason is so that you can recognize some of the challenges that people encounter when making these choices. These are very important decisions for all individuals, and it is vital to understand that not everyone will make the same ones as you. Obviously, family commitments will vary from person to person; some will have commitments for the care of disabled children or elderly relatives. There may be concern for protecting heirs from bad spending habits. One person may find that a life income gift is a great solution in one scenario, but not in all. This is also why it is so important to seek professional assistance to ensure that one's wishes and commitments (including those encouraged by your faith tradition) will be properly fulfilled.

The other issue for yourself and eventually those you may speak to about planned giving, is to be cautious and mindful when making any gift, but especially planned gifts made during one's lifetime such life estate gifts of real estate or life income gifts. These are wonderful gifts that may satisfy several personal needs, from providing significant current tax deductions, or an income for the rest of one's life and making a significant gift to a charity at death. (These will be explained in greater detail.) However, remember that once a donation is given, it is truly final and cannot be returned.

This is why so many people of average (or self-perceived average) means will choose to make an allocation out of their estate at death so that they have access to the assets for as long as they need them during life and can maintain the option to revoke gifts that they have set up as well. Many charities would prefer the certainty of a current donation, as there is never a guarantee of receipt when an estate gift is planned. However, it is in the donor's best interest to retain the right to revoke, and honestly, that is also in the interest of the charity ultimately, so that congregations/organizations demonstrate their care for the individual and that they desire donors to make the most appropriate choices.

Know Your Constituents

The fellow members of your congregation or your organization's constituents are much more diverse than they may appear at first. Supporters will be drawn to different options at different times of their lives and for many diverse reasons. If you are a volunteer leader or a staff member, the most important thing to remember when raising awareness is not how to calculate life expectancy tables for charitable gift annuities; it is the fact that different people will consider different types of gifts. Having a basic understanding of the various options will help you as a leader to raise awareness of them and better serve the interests of your supporters.

As will be mentioned again, as planned giving leaders it is not our role to instruct people which type of gift is best for them, but to listen to people's concerns and challenges, as some choices will fit better than others. For a great review of how listening to needs will lead to good outcomes for both donor and charity, please review Stacy Sulman's case study following chapter 1 on her work with a variety of donors.

Know the Basics

Take a deep breath. No one ever remembers all of the details that will be reviewed in this chapter for the many different types of planned gifts. For an insightful case study on the balance between technical details and mission discussions, see Perkin Simpson's article just before this chapter. Everyone, including professionals who have done this work for many years, will go back and refer to "cheat sheets" and other summaries to double check or ensure that they are giving correct information about a particular type of planned gift. (For a brief summary of the most common planned gifts, see our online "cheat sheet.") Most of the options reviewed in this chapter are options in Canada as well as the United States. Other countries may have some similar vehicles, but those cannot be clarified here.

For many mainstream Christian denominations, there are resources to aid in the support of these gifts from denominations or their foundations. Several regional Jewish foundations also provide similar resources and as "congregationalizing" continues, one day various additional resources will be available to Muslim, Sikh, Hindu, and other faiths. In addition to educational materials and tools to reuse for your donors (like descriptive brochures), several denominational entities and foundations offer access by congregations and related religious organizations to programs for more complex vehicles such as LIGs.

Review chapter 6 for ways to help constituents discover how they can ensure that their wishes can be fulfilled through estate planning. Although some people and traditions focus on making significant donations during lifetime, and that is certainly a part of planned giving, these gifts normally are received after a constituent has died. There are numerous ways to make these types of gifts and each individual must reflect on the best ones for them at their particular stage of life. However, circumstances for individuals will change, retirement may come earlier than expected or shift to being farther out, windfall inheritances or career successes may alter one's assets suddenly and can occur at unexpected times, and of course the birth and death of children, spouses, or other family members can all radically change one's plans.

Considerations for Leaders and Donors

The bottom-line lesson for leaders in congregations or religious organizations is to be mindful that because circumstances will change over time, planning/estate documents need to be updated to reflect that. I recommend that you are regularly raising awareness of all the different ways to make a planned gift regardless of a supporter's age or perceived economic circumstances. Seeds planted today may grow into useful new ideas in the future for your constituents. I have had numerous discussions with leaders who felt that raising awareness of the many diverse types of planned gifts would be distracting and confusing, and there is a risk for that. However, due to the importance of keeping people informed while always respecting their privacy, gentle and simple awareness raising will allow for people to self-select what is best for them and their families throughout the changing circumstances of their lives.

Providing information on websites and through written materials of basic information on the different types of gifts will allow supporters not to feel rushed into decisions but will also enable them to be aware that they know where to go when they are considering one or creating/revising estate plans. As Heraclitus said, "Change is the only constant in life,"[1] and as elaborated in several parts of this book it should be a part of your ministry of planned giving to your supporters that you are reminding them to update their estate plans from time to time as circumstances change so that their specific wishes will be fulfilled.

It is good practice to encourage your supporters to review their full estate plans at least once a decade and perhaps more often if they move their state/province of residence, have grandchildren, or have significant life changes such as retirement or the death of a spouse. Tax laws also change, and many people would benefit from a professional review of assets to ensure that allocations to heirs and charities remain in their best interest. Some assets are better suited as a gift to charities and others to individuals, but circumstances and best choices can change over time. Taxes are not the prime motivator for making a donation, and according to Rob Reich, "Religious organizations are minimally influenced by tax incentives."[2] However, a number of factors including tax considerations and timing can impact the choice of assets and sequencing of giving.[3]

I also strongly recommend that all leaders urge their constituents to seek their own independent professional advice as appropriate when they make their end-of-life plans and before finalizing most gift plans. All religious institutions should be cautious about providing too much advice which could be perceived as undue influence or misinformation, but leaders should certainly share basic information so that options are known.

This chapter's basic review of gift types is not intended to turn you, dear reader, into a planned giving expert. Its intent is to ensure that you are aware of the many ways that your loyal constituents can raise your institution to the level of family in their estate plans, as fitting for their circumstances. Planning to ensure that one's wishes are fulfilled is a demonstration of your care for donors, even if in the end they choose to make no gift at all to your charity.

---

1. Staff Writer, "Who Said "the Only Thing Constant Is Change"? Reference.com, March 24, 2020, *https://www.reference.com/world-view/said-only-thing-constant-change-d50c0532e714e12b.*

2. Rob Reich, "Would Americans Make Charitable Donations Without Tax Incentives?," *Stanford Social Innovation Review,* Winter 2005, *https://ssir.org/articles/entry/would_americans_make_charitable_donations_without_tax_incentives.*

3. Michael Barvick, "Do Taxes Motivate Charitable Giving?," *Linked In,* December 7, 2018, *https://www.linkedin.com/pulse/do-taxes-motivate-charitable-giving-michael-barvick/?articleId=6476896228037652481.*

Allocations at Death

Bequests are the most common form of planned gifts, through wills and designated allocations in revocable and living trusts (set up to exclude assets from the probate process and distribute them at death), as well as many other accounts that have designated beneficiaries (like IRAs, 401(k)s, etc.) that normally fall outside of a probated estate. (Fewer assets are becoming part of probated estates governed by a will, due to the popularity of trusts and specific account designations.) For many years the standard guideline has been that around 80 percent of all planned gifts come from these allocations; estimates vary and in certain years measured as high as 90 percent.[4] Though some recent studies point that it may drop closer to 60 percent.[5] Overall, 70 to 80 percent is a good estimate, so that it is clear that this is where leaders should focus most of their efforts. Because these are the most common ways that people make a planned gift, it is important for leaders to focus on encouraging individuals to make end of life plans to ensure that their wishes are properly fulfilled. Bequests are normally revocable by the donor up to the time of death or final estate plan revisions.

Generally, estate gifts of these kinds follow a similar pattern for allocation to individuals and charities: (1) a specific dollar amount, (2) a percentage, (3) the allocation of a specific asset, and (4) the remainder value after other allocations are made in most wills and trusts. A qualified attorney should be able to assist in choosing what is best for individuals based on the types and how one holds assets, as well as the best gift choices. As I have said at now hundreds of workshops, webinars, and donor conversations, each choice has considerations which can be reviewed with professionals to ensure one's wishes are fulfilled in making allocation for family, friends, and those charities raised to the level of family. (Your religious tradition may have very specific guidelines for allocation to family and others, a few of which are noted in our case studies, but should by no means be considered totally inclusive of every perspective.)

There have also been great strides in improving online legal forms for making wills and trusts for estate planning. Some charities have even partnered with various online vendors. I cannot recommend any particular

---

4. Gabrielle Weiss, "Planned Giving 101," *Every Action*, May 9, 2018, *https://www.everyaction.com/blog/planned-giving-101/*.

5. "Planned Giving Programs That Are Limited to Bequests May Be Leaving Money on the Table," *Pentera*, accessed August 10, 2021, *https://pentera.com/blog/planned-giving-programs-are-limited-bequests-may-be-leaving-money-table*.

service, but it would be vital that any online service used demonstrate that they are affirming or recommending appropriate legal review. It is better to pay the necessary expenses to ensure that personal choices get fulfilled.

Specific dollar amount bequests are quite simple. "I bequeath $X to Y." Those allocations must be paid out directly from the estate or trust to the named beneficiaries before other allocations. One challenge with this option is if too many specific dollar bequests are made from an estate that ended up being much smaller than one anticipated, their use may deplete remainders intended for other individuals or purposes. In my workshops, I often share a story of someone I knew of who made twenty-five specific dollar bequest in her will to a number of individuals and Roman Catholic charities, leaving any remainder to her surviving children. Unfortunately, this individual never updated her plans as the decades passed, and long after her children grew up, her health declined. This forced her to liquidate most of her assets, including her home, to pay for extended nursing home care. At her death, her numerous specific dollar allocations severely depleted what was left in the remainder of her estate for her adult children. So much so that I can assure you that those "children" will never give a penny to those charities that "stole" much of their inheritance away.

Percentage allocation often works well for most bequests and may be required for allocating remainder designations for retirement and other accounts. Percentage can work well for charities, as allocations can be made to family and others as appropriate. (See Fr. Charles Cloughen's case study following chapter 8.) As a dear friend of blessed memory, Terry Parsons, former stewardship officer of the Episcopal Church, would often say when speaking of giving and the biblical tradition of tithing (giving 10 percent one's earnings), "If you could never find it in your heart to tithe while you were living, you ain't going to miss it when you're dead."

Bequeathing **specific assets** at death like tangible personal property, artwork, jewelry, etc., can certainly be a benefit for individuals to receive in some cases and certainly if they held great sentimental value. However, most charities would prefer not to receive specific assets unless previously confirmed with the leadership of an organization or congregation. Please note that gifts of tangible personal property not related to the work of a charity may produce a smaller deduction for the donor.[6] Additionally, many

---

6. "Charitable Contributions," *IRS*, accessed May 20, 2021, *https://www.irs.gov/publications/p526#en_US_2020_publink1000229768*.

charities may not be able to accept certain assets, including real estate, unless previously approved.

Remainders or "remainderman" are distributed after all other allocations have been made. These can be the largest gifts that charities receive.[7] However, that large bequest may be intentional or unintentional. Intentionally if someone chooses to leave the majority of their estate to charity or to an individual; sometimes unintentionally if not properly planned.

Contingent Beneficiary

For any of the options above, a charity or individual could be made the designated or a contingent beneficiary. If your congregation or organization is made a contingent beneficiary, it would only receive the bequest on the condition that the originally designated beneficiaries cannot receive the bequest for some specified reason, usually that the initially designated persons are deceased. Regardless, I encourage leaders to promote the contingent option for their congregation/organization. That will allow for a charity to be included in current estate plans even if receiving the gift may be unlikely. This could be a good choice for younger donors who may have children or other people they need to provide for first and opens the supporter to the possibility of including the charity in their ultimate plans "permanently" at a later time. As wills, trusts, and other designated allocations are changed or updated in the future, the contingent allocation may switch to a designated one. In my experience, staying within the estate plans is always preferred to being out of them completely.

Allocations from Designations in Various Accounts

A current growing trend is the ability to designate a specific beneficiary of a personal investment or bank account. Through this direct designation, when a person dies, the account can pass directly to another individual or to a charity without becoming a part of the assets governed by a will and therefore not part of the probated estate. Many people find this a convenient way to make a nearly immediate transfer of assets to children, spouses, or others at death. Charities can also be designated as the ultimate beneficiary on such accounts.

---

7. Robert J. Sharpe Jr., "Has a Bequest Boom Begun?," *Sharpe Group*, September 1, 2014, *https://sharpenet.com/give-take/bequest-boom-begun/*.

For your future planned giving efforts, as more and more people place the majority of their assets for retirement in tax deferred accounts like IRAs, 401(k)s, 403(b)s, etc. (similar accounts exist in Canada), these accounts will be the source of more and more planned gifts. As you may be aware, these special accounts allow people to deposit monies prior to being taxed so that assets may grow tax free, and taxes are only paid as withdrawals are made. (More on this later.) These accounts are great opportunities for people to invest for their retirement nest egg as fewer and fewer companies provide classic pensions. At death, these accounts can be transferred to spouses and other individuals (though recent tax changes in the United States under the SECURE Act have complicated some of the transfers)[8] with those individuals paying taxes as withdrawals are made. However, under current law if these assets are left to your congregation or organization, the charity receives the bequest tax free![9] There have already been many substantial gifts to congregations and other religious charities made in this way, and they are expected only to increase in the future as more and more assets are added to these types of accounts.

Life Income Gifts

One of my favorite Christian saints is St. Benedict of Nursia, the author of the *Regula* or Rule, and founder of the Benedictine Order in Italy in the early sixth century. I had written my seminary thesis on the application of his Rule to the business world and to daily living outside of a monastery. In my research I discovered that he may have been the first person to suggest the use of a life income gift (LIG). St. Benedict suggested in chapter 59 of his Rule[10] that a noble could offer lands that would have gone to the son entering the Order directly to the monastery, but the parent could keep receiving the income from the property for their lifetime. A clever idea indeed, and one that clearly has been recycled centuries later in our modern life income gifts.

---

8. Matthew E. Smith, "The SECURE Act: Trust Planning for Inherited IRAs," *The National Law Review*, January 17, 2020, *https://www.natlawreview.com/article/secure-act-trust-planning-inherited-iras#:~:text=Under%20the%20SECURE%20Act%2C%20these%20trusts%20present%20a,IRA%20by%20the%20end%20of%20the%2010-year%20period.*

9. John Csiszar, "How to Leave a 401(k) to Charity," *The Nest*, accessed August 8, 2021, *https://budgeting.thenest.com/leave-401k-charity-24927.html.*

10. *Rule of St. Benedict, Chapter 59*, accessed July 8, 2021, *http://archive.osb.org/rb/text/rbeaad2.html#59.*

The vast majority of congregations, and even many of their judicatories, do not sponsor these LIGs directly. Much of the time, the set up and holding of these gifts is done by a central sponsoring charity like a national denominational or regional foundation like many Jewish Foundations, or one of the multifaith options in this book's resources. That separation is quite beneficial for individual charities, as managing these gifts is more complex and involves the regular sending of income as well as annual tax reporting documents to current income beneficiaries. Additionally, there are state by state regulations in the United States governing some of these gifts which require expertise that is better handled at a national or regional level. Larger religious organizations may have the capacity to oversee their own LIG programs, but many will seek access to those provided by a sponsoring charity such as their denominational foundation.

Those who know me, know that I could talk on and on about LIGs and their usefulness to both charities and donors. Please review the appendix and online resources to help with this part of your planned giving efforts. I would encourage you not to try and become expert in each type of LIG but do suggest it would be useful for a planned giving leader to understand the basics of each type of gift and the types of individuals who would most benefit from each option. These gifts can provide a substantial donation in the future to the charity as well as income to persons the donor designates. However, as cautioned at the beginning of this chapter, donors must understand that these are true gifts and cannot be returned, even in dire circumstances.

There are three basic kinds of life income gifts, but they all normally follow a typical pattern. That pattern is that after a donation is made, the donor receives a significant tax deduction in the year they make it, varying based on the amount donated and other issues. Following that, the gift is invested as appropriate (some religious traditions will require specific investment guidelines) and typically a stream of income is provided to the designated income beneficiaries (who may be the donor[s]). And three, normally at the death of the person(s) designated to receive income, or at the end of a prespecified term, the remaining value of the gift is paid out to the various charities which the donor chose. These aspects are the most important things for a leader to remember and to share with someone who expresses interest in any vehicle. LIGs are very appealing to people at retirement age as constituents may hold assets that they would be willing to donate, but they cannot currently give that asset without receiving a flow of income in exchange. After a supporter has identified the possibility of interest in such a vehicle, then the potential donor needs to determine the best choice for themselves, from the options available.

Charitable Gift Annuity

The most popular LIG is the Charitable Gift Annuity (CGA); from my experience and review of various private materials, nearly 90 percent of LIGs are done using CGAs. Charitable Gift Annuities are enticing, as they produce a fixed amount of income based on the age of the income beneficiary and the amount of the original gift. (See Stacy Sulman's case study following chapter 1.) And the annuity amount paid to income recipients is contracted by the sponsoring charity. Although income to designated individuals may be assured by the sponsoring charity's assets, depending on how long the income recipient lives beyond their average life expectancy and the performance of investments, the ultimate charities normally receive approximately 50 percent of the original gift. However, that amount is not certain. Since payments to income beneficiaries are made out of the gift assets, it is possible that CGA value will be exhausted (due to income recipients exceeding their life expectancies and poor market performance), leaving nothing for the ultimate charity, even though the sponsoring charity will continue to pay the income recipient out of their own assets. (Another reason to use a separate sponsoring charity.)

Though most large secular charities will create their own CGAs, since religious charities are often smaller, many will seek the assistance of a sponsoring charity. The sponsoring charity will likely be the party in the CGA contract that becomes liable for paying the income beneficiaries if the CGA payments exhaust the value of the gift. Several denominational and regional religious foundations will serve in this role of sponsoring charity. Those belonging to the denomination or religious tradition can often enroll or simply send donors directly to the sponsoring charity. The sponsoring charity also will typically fulfill all necessary state filings, payments to income beneficiaries, reporting and tax documentation as well as the task of investing and monitoring the assets of the CGAs.

The vast majority of US charities use the rates recommended by the American Council for Gift Annuities (ACGA) and you can view their site and resources from their website as referenced in this book's appendix. However, due to some state regulations and other reasons, including decisions made by the charities to limit risk concentration on individuals with large gifts from perceived high annuity rates, other rates may be used. These aspects of CGAs and the numerous regulations imposed on these annuities for charity registration, investment allocations, and reserve requirements are additional reasons to work with a sponsoring charity who will handle the numerous back-office requirements that would be too burdensome for most small organizations and congregations. Though CGAs are available in Canada, there are additional important issues to be reviewed with advisors before creating one. As always, a potential donor should review what is best for them and their family before finalizing any gift.[11]

Charitable Remainder Trust

The second type of LIG, the Charitable Remainder Trust (CRT), is familiar to many, but it can take many different forms based on choices that the original donor makes when creating the trust. These trusts can be created to provide income for a fixed number of years or for the life of multiple income beneficiaries.

Charitable Remainder Trusts have numerous variations, but the alphabet soup of NIMCRUTs and other options fall into two basic categories: Unitrusts, which pay out a variable amount to income recipients based on a fixed percentage multiplied by the current value of the trust as of a particular date, and Annuity Trusts (CRATs), which pay out a fixed amount to income recipients based on a fixed percentage and the original value of the trust assets.

CRTs, especially Charitable Remainder Unitrusts (CRUTs), are quite flexible in their set up for donor and income beneficiaries' needs. In fact, Islamic investment expert Bashar Qasem, founder and CEO of Azzad Asset Management, told me that CRTs can also be used creatively to help donors meet their charitable giving goals while also complying with Islamic inheritance guidelines. They are good options for individuals with significant assets, especially people who may own a second or vacation home, which they and their family may be ready to sell. As a leader of your charity, you could become a hero to your donor by suggesting they use their rarely visited property as a gift to an income producing CRUT, which eliminates

11. Gift Funds Canada, "Tax Advantages of a Charitable Gift Annuity," *Gift Funds Canada*, June 24, 2019, *https://www.giftfunds.com/blog/tax-advantages-of-a-charitable-gift-annuity/*.

the burdens of upkeep and property taxes. (See Randall Nyce's case study which follows.)

There is a new trend of creating Testamentary CRTs and CGAs from the assets of tax deferred accounts, due to the recent US tax law changes in the SECURE ACT of 2019.[12] This may be a growing trend in future years as an alternative to distributing retirement account remainders to children and grandchildren, since required withdrawals must be done on a shorter schedule than prior to 2020.

Pooled Income Fund

The last option that may interest donors in the United States is a Pooled Income Fund (PIF). Although this type of LIG is less popular than in years past, several sponsoring charities (like ECF) still offer them even though income to the designated recipients is usually less than other LIG options. This may be an ideal gift for a donor who is not as concerned with receiving consistent income but needs a larger charitable deduction this year and/or wishes to leave a larger ultimate gift to charity. For a PIF, after the donor has made their gift and received a charitable deduction, their gift is pooled with similar gifts and the designated income beneficiary (usually the donor) receives a pro-rata share of the yield (interest and dividends earned) produced from their gift. Since it is only the yield paid to income beneficiaries, typically the value distributed to the ultimate charities is close to the original amount given by the donor.

In summary, LIG options provide unique ways to make a gift during lifetime that will ultimately benefit one's favorite charities. They are also very beneficial tools for donors and the people they wish to provide income. Although some planned giving leaders will become entranced by them and their potential, please know that not everyone will be interested in creating them. However, as they can be extremely beneficial to retirees and to charities, if you have a large contingent of people over seventy, many would greatly benefit from knowing more about them.

---

12. Kenneth H. Dike, "Goodbye to the Stretch-IRA and Hello to Testamentary Charitable Gift Annuity and Testamentary Charitable Remainder Trust," *Clifford Swan*, November 17, 2020, *http://www. cliffordswan.com/blog/goodbye-to-the-stretch-ira-and-hello-to-testamentary-charitable-gift-annuities-and-testamentary-charitable-remainder-trusts.*

Life Insurance

Life insurance is often used as a "wealth replacement" tool for heirs if individuals provide inherited assets through tax-free insurance proceeds and/or use other appreciated assets for donations. As of the publication of this book, life insurance proceeds to beneficiaries, both individuals and charities, remain untaxed.[13] However, as leaders you can raise awareness of several other options for making life insurance as a planned gift option. The simplest option of which you can raise awareness would be to suggest supporters make your congregation or organization the ultimate, or a contingent, beneficiary of an existing policy, and that would work for most types of policies, including term insurance, unless the contract forbids gifts to charities.

It is also possible to make the charity the owner and beneficiary of a policy with cash value, if the original purpose of the insurance is no longer necessary, such as a policy purchased to provide for a child in case of sudden parental death. This can be a complex transaction and an insurance professional should be consulted if this is something that may work for a donor. Such a gift transaction may provide a charitable deduction from the cash value of the policy. There may also be possible ways for someone to make ongoing gifts to a charity to cover future policy premiums. A good real-life example of the use of insurance can be found in the case study by Davida Isaacson following this chapter. As will be mentioned again later, it will be important for ultimate beneficiaries of life insurance to have documentation confirming their status, as they will need to reach out to the insurance company to process the payout from a policy by filing a claim. The insurance company is not obligated to seek out ultimate beneficiaries in most cases.[14]

Life Estate

One very interesting gift that supporters can make during their lifetime, which will transfer to your congregation or organization after a fixed term

---

13. "Life Insurance and Disability Insurance Proceeds," *IRS*, accessed August 8, 2021, *https://www.irs.gov/faqs/interest-dividends-other-types-of-income/life-insurance-disability-insurance-proceeds#:~:text=Generally%2C%20life%20insurance%20proceeds%20you,report%20it%20as%20interest%20received*.

14. Investopedia Team, "How Does Life Insurance Work?," *Investopedia*, January 24, 2021, *https://www.investopedia.com/articles/personal-finance/121914/life-insurance-policies-how-payouts-work.asp*.

of years or at the donor's death, is called a Life Estate gift. (See Stacy Sulman's case study.) Most of the time, these are gifts of real estate where a donor makes the charity the ultimate owner of the property but retains the right to live in or receive income from the property for a term of years or until death. They may provide a significant tax advantage for the donor, but if such a gift is offered to your congregation/organization, I recommend you review it all carefully with your charity's attorney and the donor, and then draft a letter of agreement. Good planning and documentation ensure that all parties will be well informed and satisfied. I have often recommended that the letter of agreement include clarification that if the property needs significant cash outlays to make it immediately marketable or to settle any debts, that those expenses would be paid by the donor, either from a separate account or through their estate. This will help ensure that your charity will receive a beneficial gift ultimately and not a dilapidated property in need of tremendous repair or having extensive back taxes due before the charity can sell it.

Charitable Lead Trusts

A rare vehicle used by typically only the wealthiest donors is known as a Charitable Lead Trust, which is defined below.

> A charitable lead trust is a type of irrevocable trust designed to reduce a beneficiary's potential tax liability, upon inheritance. . . . A charitable lead trust works by donating payments out of the trust to charity for a set amount of time. After that period expires, the balance of the trust is then paid out to the beneficiary. While this reduces the taxes owed by the beneficiary, once they inherit the remaining balance, it also presents them with other potential tax benefits, such an income tax deduction for charitable donations and savings on estate and gift taxes. Additionally, it sets up a continuous way for the beneficiary and benefactor to make charitable contributions, without having to manually issue monthly payments.[15]

These complex trusts make payouts to charities over time and then terminate to provide assets to heirs or the original grantor. Though only a small number of these trusts exist in the United States, there are many

---

15. Julia Kagan, "Charitable Lead Trust," *Investopedia*, July 19, 2020, *https://www.investopedia.com/terms/c/charitableleadtrust.asp*.

who believe due to current low IRS discount rates, high asset values, and pending estate tax legislation, they may become more popular again.[16] More extensive reviews of this option are available in this book's online resources. Many readers may recall that the late Jacqueline Bouvier Kennedy Onassis sought to use a Charitable Lead Trust to make significant gifts to charities for twenty-five years and then pass on significant assets to her grandchildren. Additionally, Bashar Qasem of Azzad Asset Management has worked with Muslim donors to create these unique gifts to satisfy specific needs for annual *zakat* giving during lifetime while aligning with tax and gift planning. See this book's online resources for more information.

Planned Giving—Adjacent

Giving financially to charities has been evolving for centuries and continues to develop and change in the United States, Canada, and elsewhere. Although the following is not meant to describe every new option or innovation in giving, several of these options have been altering how people create their planned gifts both now and in the future.

Donor Advised Funds

Donor Advised Funds (DAF) are one of the fast growing charitable options in the United States and Canada.[17] DAFs are defined by Investopedia as "a private fund administered by a third party and created for the purpose of managing charitable donations on behalf of an organization, family, or individual."[18] DAFs are held by a sponsoring charity who receives the original and subsequent donations and then makes grants to a variety of charitable organizations as advised by donors or others designated as the advisor to the fund. In many cases DAFs assist donors for timing significant current gifts in a tax-efficient way since the donor receives the tax deduction in the original year and as subsequent donations are made to a

---

16. Bill Laskin, "This Could be the Year of the Charitable Lead Trust," *PG Calc*, May 14, 2021, *https://www.pgcalc.com/support/knowledge-base/pg-calc-featured-articles/year-of-the-charitable-lead-trust*.

17. Mark Blumberg, "Donor-Advised Funds Can Have Greater Secrecy—It Can Also Be a Problem," *Canadian Charity Law*, December 9, 2019, *https://www.canadiancharitylaw.ca/blog/donor-advised-funds-can-have-greater-secrecy-it-can-also-be-a-problem/#:~:text=Donor%20Advised%20Funds%20are%20registered,both%20Canada%20and%20the%20US*.

18. Will Kenton, "Donor-Advised Fund," *Investopedia*, July 13, 2021, *https://www.investopedia.com/terms/d/donoradvisedfund.asp*.

DAF. This enables a donor to distribute grants from the DAF to a variety of charities over many years, while receiving the maximum deduction in the year(s) the gifts were made to the DAF. A few important points: these grants cannot satisfy donor obligations (like an obligatory pledge) or provide benefits to the donor or advisor in exchange for the grant (like tickets to a gala or gifts).[19]

Though normally used as a way of making current gifts and grants, DAFs can also be a part of one's planned giving. Sponsoring charities can allow for gifts to be made in the ultimate distribution of the balance of DAFs to charities following the original donor's death. Additionally, DAFs normally allow for the continuing distributions of grants by appointing successor advisors on DAFs following the original donor's death. If coordinated with other planned gifts, instructions left to successors could continue to provide to a person's favorite charities far into the future.

DAF gifts can also be an indication that donors are more sophisticated and may be interested in considering other types of planned gifts. Planned giving leaders should be made aware by administrators when these grants come in from DAFs so that record can be made in necessary databases and potential future follow up planned. (Another reason to bring administrators chocolates from time to time.) Many DAF donors create that fund for simplicity in place of a family foundation. For some, this is clearly a planned gift, as grant making may continue with a subsequent generation of advisors, similar to many family foundations.

There have been some concerns and discussions raised in the media that DAFs are simply storing up tax deductions and not getting distributed to charities. Actually, DAFs pay out higher percentages of their assets than private foundations, typically over 20 percent, as was again confirmed by the fundraising firm CCS in 2018 and 2019.[20] Personally, I think that any tool that helps supporters to be more philanthropic is a benefit to all regardless of when allocations are made. I encourage planned giving leaders

---

19. For more information see the following: Elaine Gast Fawcett and Audrey Haberman, "What Are the Important Limitations and Restrictions for Using a Donor-Advised Fund?," *National Center for Family Philanthropy*, March 12, 2019, *https://www.ncfp.org/knowledge/are-there-any-important-limitations-to-using-a-donor-advised-fund/#:~:text=Donors%20also%20cannot%20recommend%20grants,satisfy%20a%20legally%20binding%20pledge.*

20. CCS Fundraising, *Snapshot of Today's Philanthropic Landscape (10th Edition)*, accessed September 18, 2021, *https://go2.ccsfundraising.com/rs/559-ALP-184/images/CCS_Philanthropic_Landscape_2021.pdf?aliId=eyJpIjoid2ZQbDB1amxZR0FGc3lkeSIsInQiOiJTeWN4dG5lSXRSWkZOdmZuTWNabEp3PT0ifQ%253D%253D.* Registration required to view this document.

to accommodate their supporters where they are at present, and DAFs can help achieve this.

Qualified Charitable Distributions

Although there have been some recent changes in these options, more and more people are using their Traditional IRAs to make significant and sometimes regular contributions to their favorite charities using this option. More and more people will use qualified charitable distributions (QCD) from Traditional IRAs for making direct current gifts to charities for convenience and, if one is over 70.5 years old, those charitable distributions are not taxed as ordinary income (under current law up to $100,000 as of the writing of this chapter). Also, after required minimum distributions (RMD) are assigned for Traditional IRA holders (currently as of seventy-two years old), the QCD will count toward RMDs.[21] QCDs can be used for satisfying a pledge, special donations, or go toward any number of special projects. (See Stacy Sulman's case study for an example.)

Like DAFs, QCDs are normally used for current giving, but planned giving leaders should carefully coordinate with administrators who tally and track gifts received from QCDs so that records may be kept and proper follow up done in the future. Unfortunately, current tax law does not provide a QCD option from 401(k) or 403(b) accounts. As previously noted, tax deferred accounts like an IRA, 401(k), or 403(b) can be excellent planned gifts to charities when charities are named as ultimate beneficiaries. Charities receive those remaining balances without needing to pay any of the deferred taxes, unlike people who receive those funds who must pay ordinary income tax on withdrawals.

Money Changes Everything?

Many of you may be thinking that there are no people of great means in your congregation, expecting that no one will be leaving any of these gifts to your institution. However, reflect for the moment on the many surprise gifts you have heard about in the news, of janitors or schoolteachers leaving their life savings to charities they believed in or may have even worked for.

---

21. IRA Faqs—Distributions (Withdrawals), *IRS*, accessed August 16, 2021, *https://www.irs.gov/retirement-plans/retirement-plans-faqs-regarding-iras-distributions-withdrawals*.

Among your supporters there are many individuals who have been loyal and consistent donors of small gifts over the course of many years. They are your most likely planned givers.

The obviously and publicly wealthy will not typically be your significant planned giving donors; your most loyal and consistent donors will be. Churches, synagogues, and various institutions across the United States and Canada have endowments because of these dedicated individuals who may have not displayed their wealth or drawn attention to themselves through large gifts during life but leave very substantial allocations after they die. (See the many examples in the case studies of this book.) For many of them, they may have simply planned well for retirement, or had become savvy investors in secret, not wishing to draw attention to themselves. Others may have received a windfall themselves which they kept as a nest egg in case of illness or other radical changes in circumstances. These dedicated members can be the source of significant planned gifts if they are aware that they may make them to benefit your congregation/organization.

Of course, the money should never be the main focus of your planned giving efforts. Some people must spend down savings for any number of reasons, from health care or changing family circumstances. A percentage of one's estate or its residuum relates directly to real life circumstances, and everyone must be celebrated, even if the eventual gift is not significant dollar wise. Their commitment was just as great.

Take the Next Steps Forward

The natural next steps, once leaders have been educated on the many different types of planned gifts and other special gift options, is to raise awareness about these many kinds of gifts to your constituents. Some may be concerned that educating existing and potential donors on the diversity of possibilities is going to be too confusing. Many leaders only wish to raise awareness of giving through bequests included in wills, trusts, and at death designations. Although it is true that most planned gifts come from bequests, I encourage leaders to discover the best ways in their context for raising awareness of as many planned giving options as possible; many individuals who might personally benefit from some of the less common options may not consider them if they are not presented. For example, numerous retirees could benefit both themselves and their favorite charities through the creation of a Charitable Gift Annuity (CGA) or other Life Income Gift.

Evaluate Your Efforts from Time to Time

There is no doubt, planned giving programs are more complex than other fundraising efforts. Please do not feel overwhelmed, feel empowered. Consider what resources your faith tradition or denomination makes available to you. In addition to the resources of this book and its companion website, www.murphyjw.com, I also encourage you to reach out to other communities of faith or religious organizations to compare your efforts. You may find some innovative new ideas that may work within your context.

Although the cost can be high, if you have the means, having a professional fundraiser work with your organization or congregation to evaluate your efforts can be quite beneficial. There may be opportunities for reasonable fee-based work with one of the many denominational or faith-based organization in this book's resources. These professionals may be able to offer their feedback on how you could expand your efforts and guide you well. To underwrite the expense, perhaps a donor exists who may be interested in sponsoring your planned giving efforts. (This was also a suggestion in *Faithful Investing* for a congregation/organization starting socially responsible investing efforts through a supportive donor.)

Summary of Main Points

- Learn the basics of different types of gifts but focus on where the majority will come from: "bequests" in wills, trusts, and designated account allocations.
- Do not only focus on the "money" and generally (unless it is truly a part of cultural tradition) do not ask, especially in congregations, the amount of the planned gift.
- Focus on building a relationship based on trust and appreciation.
- Seek affiliation with denominational or others available resources so that you have access to a "back office" for more complex gifts. LIGs and DAFs are better options with a sponsoring charity. (If you are within the Episcopal Church and chose to do this on your own, please let me know so that I may add you to my prayer list. Those are not easy gifts to handle independently.)

CASE STUDY

Insurance as a Planned Gift for Your Congregation or Religious Organization

Davida Isaacson

Gift planning is the most satisfying—and fun—of all types of fundraising. What sets it apart is the relationship-building aspect of the planning process. Gift officers/planned giving leaders often learn intimate details about a person's life, family, spirituality, and financial health. The ultimate confidentiality and discretion must reign supreme for the gift officer. But as with any fundraising initiatives, there are risks and rewards. In the best of circumstances, the rewards far outweigh the risks. Facing the challenges and applying techniques to mitigate them will lead to a great benefit for the organization—without jeopardizing donor relations.

The use of assets, not income, is the means by which most planned gifts are made. As you can imagine, this opens a great realm of possibilities for the gift planner. As most individuals' assets exceed their income to a large extent, it becomes important when working with a potential donor to discuss the assets at their disposal that could be utilized to make a gift. While many of these are apparent—real estate, stocks and bonds, bank accounts, retirement assets, art or coin collections, and even personal property—an oft overlooked asset is life insurance. This can become a useful gift for a congregation or religious organization in multiple ways.

The Simple Beneficiary Designation

Individuals purchase, or are provided, life insurance at different stages of their life. The timing often dictates who the beneficiary of the proceeds of the life insurance is when the insured passes away. A typical scenario is that a couple purchases a home with a mortgage. Life insurance is purchased on each of the individuals named to provide a death benefit that would pay off the mortgage. Premiums are paid on the policy to keep it in effect. At some point, the mortgage is paid off, but the life insurance policy still exists. The homeowners realize that the initial need for the insurance is no longer applicable, but that the policy (which has now been fully paid) is an asset. Should this couple be members of your congregation or organization, you may have established a relationship with them so that they are ready to make a commitment above and beyond their usual annual gift. A legacy gift (planned gift) is now being considered. As you discuss assets that can be used to fund the legacy, be sure to ask about life insurance holdings. A simple way for them to convert the life insurance policy to a gift is to remove the original beneficiary and replace it with the name of your congregation/organization (they will need the organization's legal name, address, and tax identification number). This gift can often be accomplished online by accessing the beneficiary form and inserting the new information.[1] This sort of plan can also be employed for a policy that is not paid up, but one on which the donor will continue to make payments while retaining ownership of the policy.

Life insurance provided by an employer, though it is generally term insurance for the period within which you are an employee of the company, may also be used to plan a future gift. As indicated above, simply name the charity you care about as the beneficiary of the policy. This is especially useful in the case of single individuals that may want to provide a legacy gift. (Yes, there is certainly a chance that you will never see the fruits of this plan, but you have planted the seed for a culture of philanthropy.)

So, what is the caveat here? You must continue to steward this relationship. This beneficiary designation is revocable—your organization is at risk of losing beneficiary status if you do not nurture the donors to the extent possible. Always be sincere, but also be vigilant.

It should be noted that there is no tax benefit (under current law) to the donor(s) for naming a charity as beneficiary of a life insurance policy of which the donor(s) is the owner.

The Not-as-Simple Owner and Beneficiary Designation

This second version of a legacy gift using life insurance is not as simple as the previous example, but still relatively easy to accomplish. In this scenario a donor's life insurance policy is not yet a paid-up policy. In this case there are life insurance premiums payable on the policy on a schedule that has been established between the owner of the policy and the insurance company. Your gift prospect may have entered into the agreement without considering

---

1. Please note the importance of seeking the advice of a professional insurance advisor before finalizing any gift.

how the asset could be used to make a gift. Once it is determined that this policy would be a good asset to use to make a legacy gift, the donor conveys ownership to your congregation/organization. As owner of the policy, the organization/congregation/charity may now be named as the beneficiary of the life insurance proceeds upon the death of the insured, i.e., your donor.

Note: there may be positive charitable tax implications for the donor at the time the policy ownership is transferred to your organization. Do not give tax advice: Your donor should consult with his/her own tax advisor and professional insurance advisor directly.

Now that your charity is irrevocably the owner of the policy, you have taken on certain responsibilities, the most significant one being the payment of premiums. Do you want your congregation/organization's financial resources being used to fund the premiums? Probably not. Here is where the gift planning gets even more interesting. The donor that provided the policy agrees to continue to make the premium payments when they come due. In most cases the owner (now your charity) will receive the invoices for payment. At that point the donor normally makes a gift to the charity in the approximate amount of the premium due, and will normally account for it as a charitable contribution, under current IRS law. (Donors should always consult with professional advisors before finalizing such a plan.) This process is designed to continue until the death of the insured, at which time the death benefits would be paid and create the legacy gift, or until it is deemed by the insurance company that no further premiums are required to keep the policy in force.

A cautionary tale: you may have guessed this hitch in the plan. What if your donor refuses to make the donation to your congregation/organization, which in turn will be used to pay the premium? That is the proper question to take into consideration when entering into this form of gift arrangement. Let me tell you a story about such a situation, the discourse it created, how it was resolved, and how to take precautionary steps to try to avoid this from happening.

A gentleman prominent in the community wanted to make a meaningful legacy gift. He learned he could leverage low levels of income in favor of a substantial payout to the umbrella organization upon his death. The way to do this is with life insurance. (This may be particularly attractive to younger donors with a commitment to your organization because insurance products are quite affordable at younger ages.) A life insurance agent was contacted with the purpose of issuing a policy on the life of the gentleman (the "insured") with the organization being the "owner" and "beneficiary" of the policy. The insured was told that the policy issued would have "vanishing premiums," which meant that after a certain number of years, the cash build up in the policy based on then-prevailing interest rates would cover all future premiums and no payments by the owner would be necessary. And so, the years passed without incident. Each annual premium payment was paid with an offsetting donation by the gentleman to the organization. And then it happened. The magical year in which the premiums were expected to vanish, an invoice came to the organization. The donor was contacted for his contribution. He relied on the original assumptions at the time the policy was taken out—no more premiums would be payable and declined to make the donation. By this time, the gentleman was not in good health. While there was some cash value in the policy that could support the premium payments for a period of time, there was also the option to use other organizational funds to continue paying or cash in the policy for a much-diminished value compared to the death benefit. There was much conversation around the situation, including a horrifying discussion pursued at a board meeting which essentially had members speculating on the gentleman's life expectancy. What resolution would be best? It was decided to use the cash in the policy to pay premiums as long as that would be sustainable. The decision was thus put off. When decision time came again, the organization sold the policy and received a reasonable amount of cash to create the legacy. Meanwhile, the gentleman lived to be ninety-one, well beyond his age at the time of the premiums that didn't vanish.

How this situation could have been avoided is the real reason for the telling. Appropriate documentation setting forth the obligations of the donor and the organization should have been prepared and signed at the time the gift plan was initiated.

In the world of gift planning there is always an antidote to the cautionary tale. A lovely, philanthropic woman wanted to leave a legacy for an educational institution that assists disabled individuals. She applied for a life insurance policy with the organization to be owner and beneficiary. This donor continued to faithfully donate the premiums for which she received a tax deduction, and the organization had the funding for paying the invoice to the life insurance company. Her total outlay for the policy will reach over $147,000 (if she lives to be one hundred or more), but the death benefit to the school will be over $400,000, making the leveraging of relatively low dollars for a large payoff such good gift planning.

We must always approach gift planning with humility and kindness. What makes it so magical is the confluence of a donor's philanthropic goals and a congregation/organization's needs. The basic question that needs to be answered by a donor is: Do you want to make a gift? If the answer to that question is "yes," we can find a way through thoughtful gift planning to make it happen. Leaving a legacy for an organization one cared about during his/her lifetime is the ultimate satisfaction. As we discuss gift options with our donors, we must never lose sight of the fact that we are helping them do something very special—for themselves and the religious charity.

CASE STUDY

Stewardship of Real Estate–Mutual Benefits and Opportunities for Generosity

Randall Nyce

Gifts of real estate may sound like the playground of the rich. The reality is that for the many of modest means, making a charitable gift of an investment property or generationally owned land makes sense not only financially but also as they consider God's call to stewardship and generosity. This case study will tell the stories of a family living in a community transitioning from rural to suburban and how they decided to make a gift of real estate.

For the first Mennonites who arrived in Philadelphia in 1683, the pull of land ownership was a key factor. Just a year earlier, William Penn founded Pennsylvania in what he described as "a holy experiment"[1] centered on his Quaker ideals and summed up in his bold statement, "Let us then try what Love will do."[2]

For over a century prior, the Mennonites of Europe faced religious persecution that also had economic implications. Birthed from the "radical reformation" of the 1520s, Mennonites were at odds with both the Protestant and Catholic authorities of Europe. Their practice of adult baptism and confession of faith created a church based on belief rather than the mandate of the state. With peace at the center of their faith, an unwillingness to "take up the sword" or to swear oaths of commitment to civil and religious authorities branded them heretics subjected to persecution and execution.

It's understandable, then, that the affection and attachment to their new homeland ran deep. That connection to the land was enhanced as they worked their farms, grew their families, and deepened their faith in a God who had brought them to this new land. While the first permanent Mennonite settlement in America took root in Germantown, Pennsylvania, in

---

1. Wikipedia, s.v. "Holy Experiment," last updated December 9, 2021, *https://en.wikipedia.org/wiki/Holy_Experiment*.

2. Modern History Sourcebook, "William Penn (1644–1718): Some Fruits of Solitude in Reflections and Maxims, 1682," Fordham University, quote 545, accessed April 22, 2022, *https://sourcebooks.fordham.edu/mod/1682penn-solitude.asp*.

1683, by the early 1700s a larger Mennonite community was established twenty-five miles north.

Combine their stories, that history, and a faith that places at its center simplicity and stewardship then fast forward three hundred years to a people living in an evolving place and finding themselves changing. Though the words of Psalm 24:1 (KJV), "The earth is the Lord's and the fullness thereof" still rang in their ears, the gravity of the family homestead was diminishing. What in past generations may have been a decision as to which child should inherit the farm pivoted to the difficult conversation of what to do when none of the kids wanted the farm.

Coupled with the evolving farming dynamic was a change in population density and a shift from a rural to a suburban community. The challenges of consumerism and affluence were suddenly more acute in a community that had emphasized a biblical simplicity of life, both materially and spiritually.

The couple in this case study who worked with the Mennonite Foundation (now known as Everence®) maintained a simple life on their family farm in the rolling hills of Pennsylvania. Like so many farm families, cash was always tight even while their net worth on paper continued to grow with the escalating value of the land beneath their feet. As the community began sprouting housing developments where cornfields once grew, the value of their seventy-six-acre farm grew beyond what they ever could have imagined.

Their four sons loved the land too, with fond memories of their child-hood roaming the fields and wading knee deep in the creek and prowling for crayfish. Those good memories tempered the harder memories of sweat, aching muscles, and sharp words that rose from the daily tasks of baling hay, feeding livestock, and cleaning out chicken coops.

When the time came for the couple to retire from the farm life, it became clear that it was time to sell the farm. Even though they knew that it made the most sense to sell to a real estate developer, the numbers surprised them. They had bought the farm for $21,100. Those seventy-six acres were now valued at $5.3 million, staggering figures for a family who for so many years felt like they were just making ends meet.

The couple struggled with their sudden wealth. They felt a burden to steward this in the same way that they had been stewards of the land for so many years. Having worked hard for what they had earned over the many years, it was unnatural for them to profit from the land sale that they had done nothing to produce and, in their ears, echoed the psalmists' words, "The earth is the Lord's and the fullness thereof."

As they met with the advisors from Mennonite Foundation, they described their goals: to have funds to sustain them through their retirement years; to leave something to their sons; to plan appropriately to navigate what could be a big tax bill; to respond with gratitude to God, offering back to God an appropriate share of what he had given them.

The solution for the couple came in the form of a financial tool called a Charitable Remainder Unitrust (CRUT). A CRUT is an effective tool for those who want to be charitable, create an income stream, and navigate the sale of an asset that has appreciated in value. When a donor gifts an asset in this way, they also mitigate the tax bill. Since the CRUT is a tax-exempt entity, that tax is not immediately due against the asset's sale.

For the couple, their solution was a charitable remainder unitrust that was funded with a gift of 72 percent of the farm. A 28 percent interest was retained to fund their retirement. When the farm was sold for $5.3 million, the CRUT received $3.8 million, and they received $1.5 million.

CRUTs are a split interest or mutual benefit gift. As a charitable tool, the donor retains the right to income from the assets during their lifetime, with the ultimate value given to charity. This takes the form of a regular distribution (normally quarterly or annually) paid out to the donor. IRS regulations require that distribution be, at minimum, 5 percent of a year-end value.[3] The couple's CRUT was structured as a 6 percent CRUT, meaning that each year they would receive a payment of 6 percent of the year-end value of the CRUT. In the first years, that provided a yearly income of approximately $228,000.

That was far more than they needed for their own living expenses, and more than they had ever earned in their working years, allowing the couple to make significant gifts to their church and to several charities that were important to them. So, while a CRUT is a deferred gift for congregation or charity, the income generated facilitated the opportunity for giving while they were living. After many years of wishing they could give more, this new reality created an immense amount of joy for them.

Though most CRUTs will provide income to the donors or those whom they designate for the rest of their lives and then be distributed to charity, they can have another feature that allows the donors to choose successor income beneficiaries for a term of up to twenty years.[4] In that

---

3. "Audit Technique Guide for Charitable Trusts—IRC Sections 4947(a)(1) and 4947(a)(2)," *IRS*, accessed July 17, 2021, *https://www.irs.gov/pub/irs-tege/atg_charitable_trusts.pdf*.

4. "Audit Technique Guide for Charitable Trusts."

way, the income from the CRUT can be designated to others as a sort of inheritance by another name. This was the perfect solution for the couple. Sometimes called a "give it twice trust," that provision allowed the couple to first give a significant income to their four sons and then, at the end of that twenty-year term, provide a significant gift to their congregation and to charity.

The couple's third motivation was navigating what could be a very large tax bill. They faced a unique challenge as farmers. Unlike typical home-owners who are often exempt from taxes on the sale of their primary home, farmers have a much more complicated tax equation to calculate. With a staggering appreciation in the value of the farm, making a charitable gift of the farm allowed them to zero out their initial tax bill. In their case, the total capital gain taxes were initially avoided on the 72 percent portion that they transferred to the CRUT.[5] While they did owe immediate taxes on the 28 percent they maintained, that was offset with a charitable deduction that they received from their CRUT.

Of final, though in many ways primary, importance to the couple was the commitment they had to a life of stewardship. They had spent their lives as caretakers for the land that they had experienced as a gift from God. They witnessed God's faithfulness in the bounty of the land. The lean years taught them that their trust could only be in the Lord. The abundant years taught them to live with open hands offering back to God what had been given. Through rich and poor years, they had learned the importance of mutual aid and of giving and receiving according to their abundance or need.

As they considered their options, those familiar words of the psalmist "the earth is the Lord's" continued to come to mind. The husband's favorite hymn, "How Great Thou Art," reminded him of the awesome wonder he had in considering "all the worlds Thy hands have made."[6]

Paul Schervish, professor emeritus at the Boston College Center for Wealth and Philanthropy, identifies giving as an exercise in authoring our moral and spiritual biography. Our moral biography works to combine our personal capacity and our moral compass. For the faithful, that moral biog-raphy also becomes a spiritual one, allowing us to respond in faithfulness to a faithful God. Schervish extends that to include philanthropic identification

---

5. Due to the tier structure of income payments from the CRUT, capital gain taxes are delayed and paid out over time in a more tax efficient manner. See *https://www.irs.gov/pub/irs-tege/atg_charitable_trusts.pdf* for more information.

6. Herald Press Editors, *The Mennonite Hymnal* (Harrisonburg, VA: MennoMedia, 1960), #535.

as a key driver. People give to that in which they can see themselves in those who are benefitting from their gift.[7]

Russell James, professor at Texas Tech, calls it our visualized autobiography. James's research used brain imaging to identify motivations for planned givers. As they spoke of their decision to give to a specific organization, James noted that the area of the brain that is activated is known as "the mind's eye" and is used in taking a third person view of oneself. As people visualize their own lives, they consider their own legacy and those organizations that are central to their own story.[8]

For the couple, this was very clearly true. Their decision to give and where to give were inextricably tied to their life stories. The chapters were few—faith, family, and the farm—but the stories in those chapters were deep and meaningful. As they looked back, they asked important questions of what their lives had offered and how they would be remembered.

Faith communities would do well to lean into these conversations. What better opportunity for pastoral conversation and engagement than in helping people consider these important life questions? As both Schervish and James demonstrate, planned givers are doing important work as they reflect on their own stories.

Faith communities would also do well to lean into these conversations as a way to invite planned givers to include them in their giving. This is a difficult step for some clergy for whom the giving conversation may feel like holding a sign that says, "Will preach for food." While there are certainly voices within faith communities that perpetuate this mercenary mentality, clergy who navigate past that can open up opportunities to guide the parishioners into meaningful and faith deepening conversations.

These conversations need not be forced. In ordinary pastoral care and conversations, clergy with ears attuned will naturally discover opportunities. Pastors are skilled in recognizing needs and helping people make connections to work toward growth. Every day they offer tools, advice, and encouragement with a goal of strengthening faith and the community. Conversations about wealth, generosity, and legacy are opportunities to connect people with means to the work that God is doing in the world.

7. Paul G. Schervish, "The Moral Biography of Wealth: Philosophical Reflection on the Foundations of Philanthropy," *Nonprofit and Voluntary Sector Quarterly* 35, no. 3 (September 2006): 477–92, *https:// www.bc.edu/content/dam/files/research_sites/cwp/pdf/moralbioref.pdf*.

8. Russell N. James, "Charitable Estate Planning as Visualized Autobiography: An fMRI Study of Its Neural Correlates," *Nonprofit and Voluntary Sector Quarterly* 43, no. 2 (April 2014): 355–73, *https://schol-ars.ttu.edu/en/publications/charitable-estate-planning-as-visualized-autobiography-an-fmri-st-10*.

In *A Spirituality of Fundraising*, Henri Nouwen says it this way: "We do not need to worry about the money. Rather, we need to worry about whether, through the invitation we offer them (the donor) and the relationship we develop with them, they will come closer to God."[9]

This does not mean that clergy need to become planned giving experts. Instead, they should build a strong relationship with trusted planned giving professionals, either from their denominational foundation or other resources, that would add a unique component to a spiritual leader's ministry. A great place to start is with your denominational resources or possibly with many local community foundations. (Clergy, please see chapter 3.)

Navigating gifts of real estate can be tricky and small procedural missteps can jeopardize the tax advantages, both proper handling of capital gain and tax deductibility. The timeline for giving can be rigid and executing certain actions can likewise create issues should the gift be scrutinized. One of the most common mistakes that would negate the tax advantages is setting up a "prearranged sale" before a property has been transferred into the Trust. Be aware that planned giving is a specialty that not every tax professional or attorney has the necessary knowledge or experience to oversee. Collaborating with charitable experts at your denominational or a Community Foundation with experience in real estate will coordinate and guide the tax professional, attorney, and realtor who will need to be in consultation.

Gifts of real estate may seem intimidating and out of reach, but they are more common and can serve regular people more than is currently realized. This is not the playground of the rich but a practical tool for the member who owns a farm, houses they rent out, or a building they are leasing to a small business.

Like the couple the Mennonite Foundation professionals and I worked with, planning well gives peace of mind and the opportunity to respond in generosity to a loving and giving God. Considering what God was calling them to as they considered wealth that they had not earned was important work as they reflected on their own faith journey while planning for their own financial security as well as their sons.

"The earth is the Lord's and the fullness thereof." The more I work with planned givers, the more I am convinced that spiritually healthy people are generous people. They understand what it is to be grateful and that their spiritual biographies are being written well as they respond in gratitude to a generous God.

---

9. Henri J. M. Nouwen, *A Spirituality of Fundraising*, The Henri Nouwen Society 21, accessed July 17, 2021, *https://www.perceptionfunding.org/uploads/1/6/8/9/16891606/spiritualityoffundraisingbyhenrinouwen_267.pdf.*

CHAPTER 5

Raising Awareness

Know Thyself

Based on my experiences and from others doing this work, what keeps individuals from making planned gifts to a congregation or religious organization is often the lack of awareness of planned giving and its options. Since so many congregations and religious organizations do not spend much time (and some avoid it completely) raising awareness to their various supporters, many potential donors don't realize it's a possibility to consider. By educating people about the different ways that they can make a gift to support their congregation or an organization they treasure, people can be inspired to take actions that will benefit a charity they love, and many times benefit themselves too. Most religious organizations remain focused on annual giving alone (religious giving remains the largest portion of giving in the United States),[1] even though extremely deep connections exist for one's community of faith or favorite religious charity. Secular charities regularly raise awareness of planned giving opportunities and are grateful for the lack of potential competition from such a formidable sector of charitable giving.

As a leader, are you willing to raise awareness of the different types of planned gifts? One certainly does not need to be a fundraising expert or an attorney to share basic information. Are you willing to share information from this book as well as from your denomination or other resources to raise this awareness for your constituents to consider? Are you willing to work with other leaders at your congregation/organization to thank and demonstrate appreciation for donors raising your charity to the level of family in their estate plans? You do not need to do this on your own, but organizational leaders will need to support these efforts and commit to thanking and

---

1. *"Giving USA 2020:* Charitable Giving Showed Solid Growth, Climbing to $449.64 Billion in 2019, One of the Highest Years for Giving on Record," *Giving USA,* June 16, 2020, *https://givingusa.org/giving-usa-2020-charitable-giving-showed-solid-growth-climbing-to-449-64-billion-in-2019-one-of-the-highest-years-for-giving-on-record/.*

celebrating these gifts so that leaders can build trust and sustain the awareness of what is possible for individuals to consider.

While a concern for a lack of mastery of details can hinder a charity's
forward movement on planned giving, it is not necessary to know everything to be able to raise general awareness. Additionally, for clergy, raising
the possibility of making a planned gift through estate planning can be a
very natural conversation to have when discussing end of life issues and the
importance of planning to ensure that individual wishes are fulfilled. (See
chapter 6 on personal planning.)

Although many clergy are eager to enhance opportunities for supporters to give, that is not always the case. If you are one of those clergy that
has avoided (or in the past not supported) implementing a planned giving effort, I welcome you wholeheartedly into this endeavor. (If you are
a bishop, priest, or deacon in the Episcopal Church, you must do this.
Look at page 445 of our Book of Common Prayer. Though its location in
the BCP has changed since 1549, a version of that direction to clergy has
always been present.)[2]

Know Your Constituents

A note here about privacy for your constituents. Most people do not want
others to know their personal financial situation. Although some cultures
may be more willing to share financial status and to allow people to know
their successes, those contexts are increasingly more limited. Naming opportunities for buildings and physical spaces are most appropriate with current
major gifts, but do not fit as well with planned gifts, especially for all the
reasons already reviewed. However, there may be tremendous opportunities
for planned gifts to create or add to funds in memory of a loved one or to
celebrate a family's legacy. (Please see chapter 8.) Remember, the largest gifts
will typically not come from the obviously wealthy. Focusing on inclusivity
and accessibility will benefit all your planned giving efforts. You will learn
much more about my favorite tool to build and maintain your planned giving program in chapter 7 on legacy societies.

One other constituent issue. We have noted the importance of encouraging your supporters to seek their own legal, tax, and financial guidance
on their estate plans. Some congregations report that their members lack

---

2. "Ministration of the Sick," *Book of Common Prayer 1549*, http://justus.anglican.org/resources/bcp/1549/
BCP1549.pdf.

knowledge of professional advisors and ask me if they should put a list together of potentials. Although I do know of a few congregations, judicatories, and organizations that have done this, I normally recommend that leaders suggest inquirers first ask other family members who may have already done estate planning. A "preferred list" of advisors creates the risk of misperception that the professionals may be working on behalf of the charity and that the individual won't be properly represented. Your context and culture will better inform this. Public resources are noted in this book's website.

Although not every member of a congregation or every supporter of a religious organization will make a planned gift, as a leader you can easily raise awareness of the most basic options. There are many ways to do this, but the best way is to outline a plan covering the course of several years. This is *planned* giving, after all. (See Karl Mattison's case study to follow and Arlene D. Schiff's review of the Grinspoon Foundation curriculum.)

Know the Basics

Getting started on planned giving is always a challenge, especially for tightly staffed small nonprofits. Fakhir Ahmad, director of business development at F.A.I.T.H. (a grassroots organization that focuses on providing humanitarian aid to individuals and families in need living in the Northern Virginia area), told me:

> There are always so many immediate needs to focus on for fundraising. We continue to try and develop a planned giving program but have not yet been able to fully implement one. We hope in the near future to begin creating brochures or other material to raise awareness of the many ways that our current supporters might create a planned gift. We also anticipate imitating what a few other institutions like mosques and other nonprofits have done by hosting online or in-person events to raise awareness about legacy giving. The COVID pandemic has made mortality apparent for all and has also been a wake-up call for many people to take steps to put their ultimate plans in place. We hope that many of our supporters might include us in those plans. However, we know we need to take the necessary steps to raise that awareness first. [*Does this sound familiar for your context too?*]

As a planned giving leader, please be sure to understand the concepts in chapter 1 on raising one's congregation/organization to the level of family.

This is the starting point and cornerstone understanding that will help you to plan your efforts at raising awareness. Although these gifts will often be the largest gift that someone will make, overfocusing on the money aspect will work against your efforts. Maintaining the trust of donors is crucial as will be the practices that charities will use to invest the donation well. A significant part of your awareness raising efforts will focus on thanking, appreciation, and affording opportunities for individuals to feel a part of your charity's work and ministry. Those who will give a planned gift are devoted to your charity as if you are part of the family. They want your congregation/organization to continue and succeed in the future. These same supporters will be forgiving of some missteps due to their love of your congregation/organization, but if they lose trust and confidence or do not feel respected and appreciated, they may elect to change their planned gift designation to another.

Gently Raising Awareness with Donors

Remember that your awareness raising should always be gentle. Being aggressive with individuals, especially in the congregational context, will work against you, as all planned gifts require the donor to spend time reflecting on what is best for them, their family, and their context. Allow for sufficient time for individuals to consider their best options for their current plans and to have their questions answered. For supporters to make appropriate decisions, they need to have reviewed their plans with family and especially with appropriate professional advisors. Planned giving leaders should not be appearing to give legal, tax, or financial advice, but focus on raising awareness of various options.

Given the very personal nature of planned gifts, not everyone will believe that certain options are right for them or their circumstances even if leaders think they are. I have known leaders who became so excited about Charitable Gift Annuities that they solely focused on them for their retired constituents, to "benefit exactly as they did." Their excessive enthusiasm turned off their constituents and caused their efforts often to be dismissed. (Knowing what you would do was the starting point of this book, but don't try to impose your personal situation onto everyone else.) An overly aggressive or impatient leader may well offend many supporters, especially in the congregational context where relationships are more intimate.

Planned giving is a long-term ministry for leaders, so remain patient. No one wants their treasured supporters to die early, and it will hopefully be many (many) years before they pass away. However, maintaining relationships with your supporters who have made this commitment is crucial for staying in the minds of your donors when they revise their estate plans in the future. Please refer to chapter 2 and see Peter Misiaszek's case study which follows.

Recording and Tracking Information

As one Lutheran pastor told me many times, "good administration is good ministry." There are some very basic practices for remaining faithful in your planned giving efforts but especially: keeping track of any confirmed legacy gifts and of those constituents interested in learning more. Planning events to maintain these important relationships to thank these special donors are vital for increasing awareness. Good record keeping of constituents in many congregations remains an ongoing challenge but is extremely beneficial even with the strained resources so commonly reported by volunteer leaders. Organizations with paid development staff typically do a better job in this area, but all charities need to be diligent and careful in maintaining records when planned gifts have been confirmed or inquiries about new potential gifts are made to leaders.

Keep careful track of information. I realize this may be stating the utterly obvious for some, but I have been amazed by the many congregations (and some otherwise very sophisticated organizations) that have lost information about supporters' confirmed planned gifts or interest in making one. The main problem from allowing information to go missing is that you need to ask supporters again if they made these plans. That communicates a lack of concern for this personally important gift and will break down that crucial trust which had been so difficult to build. If records do go missing, and there is no backup in paper or electronic form, there will be no choice but to be honest and start over again. Maintaining records properly makes this entire process easier.

When choosing a system for such record keeping, I will encourage all leaders to ask questions about how data is stored and what donor-specific reporting can be done from systems. Your goal as a planned giving leader should always be to ensure that this important information on donor choices will be maintained long-term as bequests and other gifts may not come to charities for quite some time, possibly decades. Good record keeping, especially on types of gifts revealed, or interest expressed in certain gifts and other information gained over time can also help leaders connect better with planned givers. Due to their naturally high commitment, planned giving donors typically want to deepen their relationship to your congregation/ organization and become more involved. Not maintaining information eradicates opportunities to continue developing relationships through communicating the impact of other gifts, as well as your charity's appreciation to those already committed.

Commitment of Planned Giving Donors

As reviewed in chapter 4 on types of planned gifts and chapter 6 on personal planning, the majority of planned gifts will come from bequests: wills, trusts, and designated allocations from various accounts. However, many planned givers who have already revealed this preference for your charity with one planned gift may be very open to additional types of planned gifts also reviewed in chapter 4. In addition to the proven commitment of increased annual giving by planned givers,[3] remember that based on the deep affection for your congregation/organization, your confirmed planned giving donors may well wish to be involved in other ways, possibly even participate in leadership roles at your organization. Beyond just financial support, engagement with planned givers will reveal those potentially dedicated volunteers or board members seeking a significant relationship with your charity. Take the opportunity to draw them in. This will enhance your congregation/organization's work and ministry. (See Peter Pereira's case study following chapter 7.)

Identifying Planned Giving Donors

Who are your most likely planned giving prospects? Consistent, loyal donors. Regular giving over many years indicates that deep emotional connection required to make a planned gift commitment. Although leaders should invite and raise awareness to everyone regardless of age or perceived circumstances,

3. Steve Ozinga, "Planned Gifts Increase Annual Gifts, Study Finds," *Kennari Consulting*, June 18, 2015, *https://kennariconsulting.com/planned-gifts-increase-annual-gifts-study-finds/#:~:text=James%20found%20that%20after%20arranging%20the%20planned%20gift%2C,before%20and%20immediately%20after%20adding%20the%20charitable%20beneficiary.*

by age group, the best targets for further education about types of gifts are those from forty to sixty years old.[4] When one reflects on this age range, the reasons should be clear. It is during these years that most people begin to get more serious about retirement planning and what has mattered the most to individuals in their lives. This is the ideal time to share documents for planning and introduce a variety of different gift options for consideration at various online and in-person forums. Many congregations who have education hours before or after services have a great opportunity to do this. (See chapter 6 and this book's website for planning such an event. Many charities host educational events in October, which has recently become "Estate Planning Awareness Month" in the United States.)

Know the Basics: Special Notes for Congregations

Congregational leaders, if you have not realized already, you have opportunities in a congregation that most secular nonprofits can only dream of. You have people coming to your place of worship (and due to the changes of Covid, returning online) on a regular schedule. Such opportunities are unavailable to most organizations. Additionally, congregations create the deepest connection that people make through significant life events, from the birth of children, baptisms, bar mitzvahs, marriages, funerals, and memorials (as previously noted, record these details in your database). Regrettably, many congregations squander these special opportunities and allow thanking and awareness raising efforts to languish quickly. Vibrant congregations can take advantage of these opportunities to continue to thank their donors and raise awareness of additional ways to support the congregation.

Awareness raising events can be an opportunity for working with other congregations. This can create more opportunities for being more inclusive of other faith traditions than you ever imagined and your congregation/ organization could become all the stronger for it. However, those working in congregational settings may discover resistance to inclusive ecumenical or interfaith opportunities. Additionally, among many congregations, there

---

4.Indiana University Lilly Family School of Philanthropy, *The 2016 Planned Giving Study* (Indianapolis, IN: IUPUI, 2016), 8, *https://scholarworks.iupui.edu/bitstream/handle/1805/11006/planned-giving-study2016.pdf?sequence=1*; Dr. Claire Routley, Professor Adrian Sargeant, and Harriet Day, *Everything Research Can Tell Us about Legacy Giving in 2018* (Plymouth, England: University of Plymouth, 2018), 29, *https://legacyvoice.co.uk/wp-content/uploads/2018/05/Legacy-Voice-lit-review_full-report_03.pdf.*

can be distrust or dislike of judicatory or denominational authority structures or regional foundations and federations. Even when valuable resources and services are offered at low to no cost, some congregations will choose to "reinvent the wheel" to retain complete autonomy. If you encounter any of these challenges from others within your setting, I encourage you to ask protestors to explain what they think will happen if collaborations are sought. Generally, the arguments will break down when discussed openly and with compassion. (See more in chapter 6.)

Take the Next Steps Forward

Effective communication is central to your planned giving efforts. As a leader in your congregation/organization, one of your main tasks will be making people aware of how they can "raise to the level of family" your congregation, mosque, or institution. If you do not make people aware of all the ways that they can make a planned gift to your cherished organizations, other charities (especially large secular ones) will fill that gap and let your donors know that they can make that transformational donation to them. Whether donors have worked in your parish soup kitchen for decades or been a loyal supporter their entire life, they may not realize that they can make a planned gift. Although there are many ways to raise this awareness, taking some simple initial steps will be the most effective.

Creating Resources for Raising Awareness

A very important and fairly simple initial step is to create a document/ brochure to share with constituents to educate them about what is possible. (Make sure that you post whatever material you create or a version of the document on your website.) Setting up an attractive brochure with basic information featuring pictures from your congregation or from the important work you do as an organization will function fine for stirring the emotional connection to your charity.

When considering what to include in materials, you will know your congregation or organization best, and the pictures and scripture passages that will move people's hearts. One can easily find many samples of booklets and brochures, but to create one that will work best for you may involve collaborating with office and communication staff, if you have them. If not, another possible method is simply to collect website examples or brochures you are being sent on the topic (if you have not seen too many, visit websites of larger charities or those of congregations in your area) and imitate (giving credit as appropriate) those which seem the most helpful for your own context. Many denominational foundations also have template documents for your downloadable use. There is a fine example of an extensive "case for support" sample provided by the Roman Catholic Adrian Dominican Sisters, in addition to other examples and congregational websites in our online resources. (Do not use images of individuals—particularly children—on your website or on your printed materials without first asking permission.)

It is also important to keep your websites up to date with planned giving and other information. Online sources are how many people review congregations as well as nearly all organizations. Not keeping your sites and social media accounts current sends a negative message and may also break down trust over time by demonstrating a lack of care. Provide endowment/designated funds and gift acceptance policies online as well. This not only guides donors and helps keep leaders accountable, but also demonstrates transparency.

Giving Tools for Donors and How They Guide Leaders

Once you have a brochure or document (and have posted an electronic version or matching text on your website), you can also take another step to set up two key building blocks in your planned giving effort. On your donation card or online giving device used for encouraging regular donations and gathering constituent information, please include two basic planned giving questions consistently: "Please check here, if you have already made a gift in your estate plans to _____" and "Please check here, if you would like more information about planned giving opportunities." These two lines will be the building blocks of your future planned giving efforts. They will identify who has already made this commitment and who would be interested in learning more. I use the phrase "estate plans" so that you are expansive and do not simply refer to a will. (See chapter 4 on the reduced assets ending up in probated wills.) You can share the brochure with anyone who asked for more information from the giving card or other tools with a friendly letter thanking them for their consideration. Be certain to record in your database these notices from supporters as well as send a handwritten note to those who have confirmed a planned gift.

For many congregations, this giving device is often called the pledge card, though more congregations are moving away from a commitment concept given their constituents' circumstances. I have been made aware in recent years of a trend away from the "pledge" term overall. (You may download a template giving card from this book's website.) That change may be due to a perception that constituents receive less predictable income from irregular work in the gig economy or from a growing tendency away from financial commitment by younger generations. You may also have certain cultural issues on terms in your context, such as many Asian congregations avoid the term "pledge" as there is an ingrained prohibition on owing debts, even to one's congregation.

There will also be added benefits to gathering this planned giving information. If you have done little to nothing on planned giving and supporters still confirm they arranged this allocation, those individuals may be great potential planned giving leaders for your congregation/organization in the future. Even if they are not ideal for the main planned giving leader role, they may be good choices for serving on a future committee or assisting with the legacy society (or similar) efforts. Or they may simply be a great person to provide a testimonial about why they chose to make a legacy gift.

If people indicate that they want more information, this can allow for an opportunity both to provide basic information about a gift option for them to consider and also to become a part of the ministry of planned giving by offering resources on planning for the end of life, to ensure that their particular wishes will be fulfilled. Webinars are an easy way to educate your constituents about what is possible. Several useful webinars from various denominational foundations and other resources are available through the various links in this book's appendix and through the other online resources. Even taking these small steps will greatly enhance your planned giving efforts and lead to more opportunities for raising awareness in the future.

Evaluate Your Efforts from Time to Time

Planned giving leaders should confer regularly for reflection and improvement. Consider what appeared to get the most traction or interest. If few people responded to education events, do not be discouraged. Not everyone will be interested immediately, and it will take time for people to become more comfortable with accessing that knowledge. As you continue raising awareness of planned giving and begin to put a legacy society (or equivalent thanking opportunities) in place, people will slowly become more interested. Meanwhile, reflect if there was any aspect of your efforts that seemed uncomfortable or off-putting to your constituency, as this can be very helpful as you plan future events.

An insight to share: complaints about the two additions to your giving card or online device regarding planned giving may provide revealing feedback. This negative feedback may be from the wealthier members of your constituents who do not wish to include the congregation/organization in their estate plans. In my experience, these wealthier members do not want to be "outed" for this choice. Continue to assure members of your congregation or organization that dollar amounts will never be requested and that anyone who wishes can always remain anonymous. In time those individuals may have a change of heart and choose to confirm a gift in the future.

Another useful method of evaluation can be a survey to identify the types of planned gifts which have been put in place by confirmed planned givers. Though privacy and a desire for anonymity must be respected, learning the types that supporters have selected will offer insights on what else you should be educating your members in the year to come. For example, if numerous donors created a CGA, you certainly need to educate about more common forms like bequests.

Cultural reasons may also impede your progress; keep at it and build on what has been accomplished over to time. Dr. Singh Brar's case study which follows this chapter focuses on how a Sikh congregation was able to build on their tradition and expand it, with an eye toward implementing planned giving from estates in the future. Progress is achieved not only from raising awareness and building on existing traditions, but also focusing on future possibilities. Gentle and incremental change can help move constituents into a new level of comfort with new ways of donating, including planned gifts.

Planned giving leaders should evaluate awareness raising efforts at least annually. Formal evaluations are not necessary: planned giving leaders and others can simply gather for an hour or two to discuss the success of responses and the issues that might have been raised, both positive and negative. You can also address those practical challenges for record keeping/coordination and plan to maintain and secure data records for the long term.

Summary of Main Points

- After a lack of trust, the biggest obstacle to individuals making a planned gift to your congregation/organization is a lack of awareness.

- Raise awareness of the different types of planned gifts among everyone regardless of perceived circumstances, age, or wealth. Though not everyone will make a planned gift, they may choose to make one for you if an option appears beneficial. Remember to focus on those in the forty to sixty age range.

- Take advantage of when many other charities raise awareness of estate planning, such as in the month of October which has recently become "Estate Planning Awareness Month" in the United States.

- Slow and gentle is the best pace for planned giving. If people feel rushed or pressured, it will work against your efforts. You want constituents to take their time to choose what is best for them and their family, as well as suggest the use of appropriate legal/tax/financial advisors and to notify family members of their intentions.

- Set up an informational and evocative brochure and adapt your regular giving device to ask about planned giving; be sure to record useful constituent information to set the stage for future thanking efforts.

CASE STUDY

The Spirit of Sacha Sauda: Five Centuries of Sikh Giving: From Charity to Philanthropy

Rupinder Singh Brar

"I was looking forward to meeting you today, for there is something I want to give you," said the thirty-something stranger in front of me. With that, he handed me an envelope containing a cheque for twenty-five thousand dollars! I was taken aback, for we had just met at a formal function organized by the local hospital. He smiled at my puzzled expression and introduced himself—he was a well-known local businessman, and the money was an unrestricted charitable gift to the hospital. He said he had sought me out because he felt that as the director of the cardiovascular program, I would be best person to direct the money to a suitable cause. Though I was familiar with the institution of *Langar*, a five-hundred-year-old tradition of providing free meals to all comers at the Sikh shrines, this was my first brush with the modern idea of Sikh philanthropy.

I later learned that he was a third-generation American from a devout Sikh family that had arrived from India many years ago. Over the years his family had built an impressive business enterprise. As their fortune grew, so did their expression of faith and charitable giving even as they assimilated into the American culture. The first generation sent money back home, to relatives and Sikh shrines. The second generation helped build a local Gurudwara at Yuba City, California, and regularly donated money for its *Langar*. Now the third generation before me, a graduate from the University of California, had decided to bring one of the most important tenets of his faith in line with his American upbringing, by sharing his wealth with the larger community. Much later I realized that he was not alone, for all across North America a whole new generation of Sikhs are growing up similarly and engage in charitable giving for worthwhile secular causes.

For example, a few years ago, a relatively small (only three full-time volunteers) nonprofit organization called The Sikh Coalition raised more than $127,000 over a single twenty-four-hour period as a part of a philanthropic drive. The Sikh Coalition, headquartered in New York, was first formed in response to the violence suffered by Sikh Americans in the wake of the terrorist attacks of September 11th. Over the years, it morphed into a full-time philanthropic organization. Today, up to 80 percent of the group's $1.6 million budget comes from small individual donations, mostly from fellow Sikhs persuaded by e-mails and phone calls made by its volunteers.[1]

On a doctrinal level there is nothing unusual about this kind of faith-based effort because giving and community service are an integral part of the Sikh faith that was founded in fifteenth-century India. Its founder, Guru Nanak (literally meaning The Teacher Nanak), encouraged his followers to be meditative householders but also productive members of the society. As with Jesus of Nazareth, few historical details are available about Guru Nanak's life, but that deficiency is more than made up through hundreds of *Janam Sakhis*, literally meaning life stories, that are narrated accounts of the Guru's life. Like the parables of Jesus, each of these stories carry a moral lesson within. The *Janam Sakhis* are an important component of the Sikh faith, for it is through these that the devout try to imagine what their founder would have them do.

One of the most popular *Janam Sakhi* is titled the Sakhi of the *Sacha Sauda* (fair trade). It tells the story of the teenage Nanak sent by his father to a nearby town with some money to try his hand at trade with the advice that he use the money wisely. The young boy dutifully headed for the town but along the way met a group of starving ascetics. Moved by their plight, he decided to buy some provisions and cook a meal for them, arguing that there could be no better use for the money than feeding the hungry. According to the story, Guru Nanak returned home to face the wrath of his obviously upset father but even here there was a message, that though an act of giving may sometimes involve personal sacrifice, it is still the right thing to do.

That original charitable impulse carried on as a part of the Sikh psyche even after the community turned militant in the face of Mughal tyranny. Accordingly, another such story came to be told about a seventeenth-century soldier saint named Bhai Kanahiya who went around the battlefields

---

1. Heather Joslyn, "Tiny Advocacy Group Reveals Secrets of Giving Tuesday Success," *The Chronicle of Philanthropy*, December 4, 2015, *https://www.philanthropy.com/article/tiny-advocacy-group-reveals-secrets-of-giving-tuesday-success/?cid2=gen_login_refresh&cid=gen_sign_in.*

ministering to friends and foes alike. He was reportedly hauled before the tenth Nanak, Guru Gobind Singh, who asked him for an explanation. Bhai Kanahiya replied he was only doing the Guru's bidding by practicing charity toward one and all. The Guru was highly pleased and told Bhai Kanahiya to continue doing God's work. In the twentieth century, a poor orphan boy named Bhagat Puran Singh grew up to set up one of North India's best-known networks of orphanages and came to be hailed the Sikh equivalent of Mother Teresa by the grateful nation.[2]

As the Sikhs spread out in the world during much of the twentieth century, they took their traditions with them wherever they went, but for a long time their charity remained limited to sustaining the daily *Langars* at the nearby Gurudwara. More recently, that pattern has begun to change. Several Sikh charitable organizations have come up in the recent years that pool small individual contributions during a crisis to provide relief efforts far from home. One such organization is the Khalsa Aid that has sent volunteers and material aid around the world during the times of need. For example, they carried out valuable relief work in war-torn Syria in 2015 and again during the Rohingya refugee crises in Bangladesh in 2017.[3]

Nevertheless, all such efforts, noble as they are, fall under the category of charity, not philanthropy. The two are closely related but separate concepts. Charity is considered a spur of the moment decision, driven by the need to relieve immediate suffering. It is an impulsive decision, made from the heart. Philanthropy, on the other hand, is a more measured, strategic decision, motivated by a need to make long-term change, which requires critical thinking and planning, a decision making from the head.

This kind of "giving" is still a relatively new concept among the Sikh community, though there are some honorable exceptions. One of the first Sikhs with the vision, foresight, and the means to engage in philanthropy in a big way was Dr. Narinder Singh Kapany, a physicist inventor known among his peers as the father of commercial fiber optics.[4] As early as 1967 he set up The Sikh Foundation International to promote and preserve the Sikh cultural heritage.[5] Over the years, he poured millions of dollars into other

---

2. Sikhwiki, s.v. "Bhagat Puran Singh," accessed July 18, 2021, *https://www.sikhiwiki.org/index.php/Bhagat_Puran_Singh*.

3. "About Us," *Khalsa Aid*, accessed July 18, 2021, *https://www.khalsaaid.org/*.

4. Wikipedia, s.v. "Narinder Singh Kapany," last updated March 11, 2022, *https://en.wikipedia.org/wiki/Narinder_Singh_Kapany*.

5. The Sikh Foundation International, accessed July 18, 2021, *http://www.sikhfoundation.org/*.

similarly strategic projects, notable among them was the setting up of a chair of Sikh studies at the University of California at Santa Barbara.[6] Following his example, several others came forward and made similar contributions, but these were limited to a select few high profile and wealthy individuals who understood that such giving not only benefited the society but also themselves by way of enhanced social standing and prestige.

New Opportunities

The kind of relatively anonymous, grassroots philanthropy by community leaders targeting local well-being as described earlier is a relatively new phenomenon in our community. One such initiative was launched by our society called the Punjabi American Heritage Society, an organization that until then was known only for organizing an annual fair and community festival.[7]

Around 2015 about a dozen members within the society, mainly physicians, farmers, and businessman decided to identify and execute a project of lasting value to the entire community. In this way was born the idea of a Sikh Community Center, a resource for the entire Yuba Sutter community but geared toward the very young and the elderly.[8] After some initial planning and a small amount of seed money donated by the members themselves, a vacant commercial building was rented and remodeled as a Sunday school. Volunteers were recruited from within the community to provide adult education classes for newly arrived immigrants and a school was organized for children where Punjabi language and religious studies classes were taught every Sunday. In addition to these regular activities, the center was made available to the community for holding yoga classes and for lectures on various topics of interest to the lay public.

After some initial hiccups, the community warmed up to the idea so that within the first two years the Sunday school grew to over 150 students with more on the waiting list. Soon it became obvious to us that a bigger and more permanent place would be needed for the project to continue.

Fortunately, around the same time a local bank building went on sale that was just the right size and perfect for our needs. However, it came with

6. Accessed May 16, 2022, from *https://punjab.global.ucsb.edu/endowed-chair?msclkid=2aac214fce5511 ec9d57f02db8d33b27*.

7. Punjabi American Heritage Society, *http://www.punjabipioneers.com/PAHS*, accessed April 9, 2022.

8. Sikh Community Center, accessed July 18, 2021, *http://sikhcommunitycenter.com/*.

a price tag of eight hundred thousand dollars. At this point it was decided to involve the larger Sikh community through a major fundraising effort.

It was a novel concept for the Sikh leaders in our town. For five centuries the Sikh social and communal life had revolved around one institution alone—the Sikh Gurudwara. It was one place where people went in good times and bad, to celebrate the birth of a child or mourn the loss of a loved one, to attend a wedding or to meet and greet a visiting dignitary. The Sikh faith required the devout to earmark 10 percent of their earnings for charity but because this was a tenet of faith, many people believed charity began and ended at the Gurudwara alone.

However, the Gurudwara was ill-suited for the kind of activities we had in mind. For example, the Sikh faith treats its scripture like a living body of the Divine, to be worshipped and revered appropriately. Although no one is barred entry, one has to approach the Gurudwara with heads covered and with bare feet. Everyone also has to sit on the floor, symbolizing equality before God. Though food and drinks are allowed in the *Langar* area, meat and alcohol are strictly forbidden. Such restrictions make it difficult if not impossible to create a classroom or a casual, conference-center-like atmosphere at the Gurudwara that is essential to meaningful dialogue and learning, so a separate community center made perfect sense.

Still, the idea of creating a space for social and educational activities outside the Gurudwara was hard for many in the community to understand. Some saw it as redundant. Others feared it would compete with the shrine and perhaps lead to a fragmented congregation. All these issues made the community wary at first and our initial efforts at fundraising met a tepid response. We quickly realized that unless such fears were addressed patiently and in a noncondescending way, we may not have a viable project even if we could somehow raise the money ourselves. Accordingly, the Sikh Community Center board members began to reach out to the community without raising the issue of funds. Several meetings were held to address those concerns. We came up with patient counter arguments and developed talking points in a nonconfrontational way. It was agreed that the Gurudwara was indeed the focal point for the community and that no attempt would ever be made to dilute its importance.

A short, informational video was created to highlight the work already done and the vision for the future. All along it was emphasized that such projects not only were an extension of the charitable Sikh traditions but also the wave of the future. Individual society members reached out through phone calls, e-mails, and personal one-on-one meetings to community members, elders, and others who either had reservations or had never before participated in any faith-based fundraising. Still, the idea of making a significant and planned gift to create a communal legacy other than a shrine was new to many and there were several skeptics and holdouts.

Finally, it was decided to hold a formal function where key people could be invited to an event that would be part entertainment, part education, and devoted to information about the planned Sikh Community Center, its activities, and its future role in the community. I was asked to personally reach out to one very influential individual, a community leader and patriarch from one of the oldest families in the area that was well known locally as well as all over the world among the entire Sikh diaspora. He was also active in the Gurudwara committee and had a personal stake in it, having donated hundreds of thousands of dollars to that institution.

I had known him professionally for years and we had come to trust and respect each other. Not only was he a graduate from a major university in California, but he had also studied philosophy and taken courses in comparative religious studies. In a rare private moment, he confessed to me that he had once wanted to be a professor of philosophy. My fellow board members felt it would be a boost to our cause if he could simply be seen at our function. I accordingly called him up and politely explained our vision, motives, and our financial needs. I did not ask him for any money but simply invited him to our function. He did not promise anything but agreed to attend.

In the meantime, we went ahead and closed the deal on the building. An open house was held, and the community was encouraged to come and check it out. On the appointed day we held our formal function. Not only did the particular gentleman come as promised, but he also surprised me by handing me a check for a thousand dollars at the door. I felt it was his way of telling us that he would not oppose our cause.

The function itself went very well. Our society president showed a brief video and then invited people to come forward if they thought they had benefited from our efforts. Several parents of children attending the Sunday school stood up and spoke. A thirteen-year-old boy, whom I had mentored for two years, stood up to speak about what he had learned there.

He began by quoting a paragraph from the sacred Japji, a poem written by Guru Nanak and revered the world over by the Sikh community as God's word.

"Nights and days, seasons, and dates; winds, waters, and fires he made,
Amidst it all, is a virtuous workshop, this flawless dust—Planet Earth,"

He began. Suddenly, there was pin-drop silence. Good, I thought. People were paying attention.

"Animals and worms, so colorful, with so many names, all wonderful. By
word and deed, all will be judged, for Righteous is he, his tribunal just."

He went on. By now, I could hear some people had started to repeat the verses aloud after him. It seemed like a spiritual moment. A lump came up in my throat.

"The Accepted ones there seek His grace, on sands of time, they leave a trace.
Those ripe or not, too will be discovered, this O Nanak, will eventually occur."

The speaker had come to the end of the stanza, but he went on further to elaborate what the words of the poem meant to him and how he applied its lesson in his daily life. This kind of exegesis was different than the prayer service in the Gurdwara where words are read aloud or routinely sung but the interpretation is left to the individual listeners. People listened to the young man in rapt silence.

By the time he finished his speech, we knew that something had changed, and we had won over the audience. The society chairperson once again took the stage as volunteers began going around the room and take pledges that were announced by the madam president over the speakers. There were about two hundred people in the room, and we hoped to raise close to a hundred thousand dollars that day. Sure enough, pledges began to role in. First in the hundreds then in thousands; a thousand here another there. Several people pledged five thousand dollars each. Each pledge that was announced was received by a round of polite applause. Suddenly there came an announcement that blew everyone away. Our president announced the community leader whom I had invited hesitantly had pledged one hundred thousand dollars!

After a moment of disbelief, the hall broke out in a loud applause. We cleared over three hundred thousand dollars in pledges in all that day—way beyond our wildest dreams. Not only that, but we also earned the trust of some of the most respected and generous people among our community that day. A new era of Sikh philanthropy was thus born in our small community.

Though our community center is closed temporarily due to Covid related mandates, it has been in use from almost the first day that it opened. We have used it to not only host the weekly Sunday school but academic lectures, documentary movie screenings, interfaith symposia, and book release functions. These events are usually well attended and often there is standing room only. The center has plans to add new activities once it reopens because it is now on a solid financial footing—the building loan almost paid off. Next step in our fundraising journey, we have plans to create an endowment fund through faith-based bequests. I believe we will have far less resistance this time and even more community support. All thanks to a new spirit of the future of planned giving, born that magical evening among the Sikh community of Yuba City.

CASE STUDY

Leaving a Gift of Encouragement

Peter Misiaszek

In the weeks following the birth of our first child, my wife and I had our wills drawn up. Being in our earlier thirties we had little in the way of material possessions, but we wanted to be certain that our son's interests would be cared for. Several years later, when we purchased a new home (and with two small children in tow), we amended our wills again to reflect guardianship and to ensure that our possessions would be distributed according to our wishes should something unfortunate happen. Following the birth of our third child, we altered our wills again, making specific provisions for each child. In time, as our children outgrow the need for guardians, we will update our wills again, designating larger gifts to the church and some to charities.

Having a will drawn up was no big deal and yet surprisingly only 49 percent of Canadians have one.[1] In fact, most Canadians are hardly aware of the need to write a will and only do so perhaps when faced with an overseas trip or unexpected illness. Some feel they have inadequate assets to justify getting one, while others think they are too young.

If a person dies in Ontario without a will, the current law determines who is to receive accumulated assets and the amount of any inheritance.[2] The distribution of assets may not necessarily coincide with the wishes of the deceased. For example, no gifts will be made to friends or to the church or a favorite charity, no matter how much it meant to the individual during their lifetime. By making a will, an individual can choose their own beneficiaries based on existing and potential financial needs as well as their relationship. Family heirlooms and items of sentimental value can be given in a will to specifically named beneficiaries, thus avoiding conflict among family members.

---

1. "What 'Will' Happen with Your Assets? Half of Canadian Adults Say They Don't Have a Last Will and Testament," *Angus Reid Institute*, January 23, 2018, *https://angusreid.org/will-and-testament/*.

2. "Administering Estates," *Ontario*, accessed April 9, 2022, *https://www.ontario.ca/page/administering-estates*.

In my Anglican tradition, we are inheritors of a heritage rich in worship, sacrament, fellowship, and service to each other and beyond our faith communities. Throughout the history of the Anglican Church, each generation receives this gospel tradition and is called to steward it for a time and then pass it on to generations that follow. Anglicans are instructed in the Book of Common Prayer to offer money to support the work of the church as part of a Rule of Life.[3]

We are all familiar with the gifts we give to the church through our weekly offering, preauthorized giving, e-transfer, or to some other special offering or fundraiser. These gifts normally come from our current incomes—our substance. We are less familiar with the many ways we can give to the church and its ministry from the assets we have accumulated over the course of our lifetimes—assets such as real estate, stock, collectables, or life insurance.

In our tradition, gifts made from our accumulated assets are called "legacy gifts" or "gifts of encouragement" and they are a wonderful way that we can provide additional resources to expand the mission of the church for generations to come.[4] I use the term "gift of encouragement" deliberately, as it provides an intentional link to scripture. Such a linkage adds credibility to our work as we can draw on the experience of early Christians as they endeavored to found and grow a church. Examples of generosity in the first century are a powerful reminder that giving thanks has been a focus of the church throughout its history and continues to this very day and beyond.

Gifts of encouragement might seem like a relatively new concept in the church, but it is as old as the church itself. In the New Testament, Acts 4 tells the story of a man named Joseph, a native of Cyprus, selling a field that belonged to him and giving the proceeds to the apostles for them to distribute the money as needed.[5] Joseph experienced the joy firsthand of making the gift and bearing witness to how it would be used to further ministry. He made the gift without reservation or specific designation. It was an act of pure altruism. The apostles gave Joseph a new name, Barnabas, which means "son of encouragement" in Hebrew.

---

3. Anglican Church of Canada, *Book of Common Prayer, 1962* (Charlottetown: The General Synod of the Anglican Church of Canada, 1962), 555, accessed April 9, 2022, *https://www.anglican.ca/wp-content/uploads/BCP.pdf*.

4. "About Gift Planning," *Canadian Association of Gift Planners*, accessed June 20, 2021, *https://www.cagp-acpdp.org/en/about-gift-planning*.

5. See Acts 4:36–37.

The good news of legacy giving is that we can be sons and daughters of encouragement through the gifts we give to our communities of faith or religious organizations from our accumulated assets. In fact, many of our Anglican churches can boast that their very foundations were laid through the benevolence of their past parishioners.

Consider the gift of a generous benefactor whose legacy gift to the Anglican Diocese of Toronto in 2004 allowed us to establish our diocesan website. Today, our website has one of the highest traffic flows within the Anglican Church of Canada because of the resources we provide. And it is through our website that we can connect with volunteers and clergy alike. We have even used the website to broadcast Christmas and Easter services live from the Cathedral and during the Covid-19 lockdown.

Indeed, many churches across Canada and elsewhere have benefited tremendously thanks to the generosity of numerous donors over the years. Their names can be found on the beautiful stained glass that adorns the naves in our churches: Each window is a richly colored and detailed tapestry of scripture—a sermon in glass. They are memorials to loved ones and fallen heroes that honor their names and works, teach the viewer, and enrich the church building. Their memories live on and perpetually support the work of the church. Perhaps their example of giving will encourage others to expend their generosity in a similar way.

But I can almost hear you thinking to yourself, "That is all well and good, but your parish and a diocesan website were both funded from large gifts by wealthy donors. The members of our congregation or our charity's constituents are not wealthy. Few have very little worth passing on." But consider this: small gifts can make a tremendous difference if people are inspired. For example, one undesignated bequest of $25,000 will provide a multiyear scholarship for a student studying theology at Trinity or Wycliffe College in Toronto. And $5,000 will provide AIDS treatment to fifty patients for one year in our former companion diocese of Grahamstown in South Africa. Imagine the lives that could be transformed by these sorts of gifts.

I urge all people of faith to make a will if you have not done so, or to review it if you have one. Congregational and religious leaders can encourage their members to prayerfully consider a gift to a congregation, the judicatory, or to another beneficial program, perhaps at the national level or to benefit those in other countries. Even a person of modest means often has a considerable estate when property and insurance are considered. And one's gift will help continue the good work your constituents have supported over a lifetime and enable new ministry to be taken on as a result of your generosity.

I would like to share with you a story that a priest friend of mine told me a few years back. One week Rev. Paul was beset by four funerals. To make the experience all the more draining, these were people who were longtime members of his congregation who had served as churchwardens (primary lay leaders), treasurers, members of the choir, and sides-people (greeters and ushers for a worship service). Four committed parishioners gone in one week.

The experience was made more onerous when he learned some three months later that one of those parishioners donated over $100,000 to a national charity through their will. Sadly, his parish received nothing. This example is not meant to denigrate the efforts of other charities, for they do important work. However, I am discouraged when parishioners overlook the very church that they turned to for the rights of passage during their lifetime, moments of joy that marketed new beginnings and opportunities. When I asked Rev. Paul why this faithful parishioner did not make a similar gift to the church his response was predictable: "We did not ask."

It is an unfortunate reality in my experience as a stewardship educator that many clergy and church leaders from multiple traditions believe that discussions concerning money are somehow dirty and beyond polite conversation in the church. While we know that Jesus spoke about money and those things we make into false gods more than anything in the Gospels, the sentiment persists that members of the church do not need to be constantly reminded of its temporal needs. We continue with this thinking at our peril. If Rev. Paul's experience tells us anything, it is that members of our congregations need to be informed of the ministry needs of their community of faith and giving cannot be left to chance.

I encourage all people of faith to give serious consideration to how you can make a gift of encouragement through your estate to support ministry beyond your earthly lives. Estate planning is something most people approach with apprehension because it forces us to consider intimate details of our lives with lawyers, financial planners, family members, and sometimes our clergy. It is not easy to talk about end-of-life issues, especially the end of our own life.

Grappling with matters relating to our estate inclines us to confront our own mortality and for most of us, myself included, it is something we would rather put off. Ultimately, we all have to deal with the reality that life in this world comes to an end for all of us. For Christians, as for most people of faith, we believe that there is something beyond the here and now. And so, planning for how a lifetime of dreams, hopes, and memories is properly distributed following our passing is an important part of the legacy we leave behind. Our estates, properly planned and distributed, can generously provide for the next generation of families, friends, our communities of faith, and people in need who we may never have met.

Earlier on I mentioned the importance of our weekly offering and differentiated it from the gifts we might leave behind after we are gone. But the current temporal needs of our congregations are important too. On a wall in the diocesan stewardship office hangs an old placard from the Cathedral Church of St. James in Toronto that reads "All Seats in this Church are free. . . . The maintenance of the Church depends on the free-will offerings of the people." This brief statement should be considered by everyone, as it strikes at the heart of the relationship between each one of us and the important work being carried out in the local faith community.

The needs of our communities of faith depend on the generosity of each member of the congregation. For too long, many leaders in Christian churches have made some poor assumptions about giving. We have assumed that people instinctively know what to give, that they have given enough, and that they do not need to be asked. Regardless of your tradition, does this ring true for your context as well?

Unless members are informed of the time, talent, and treasure demands on a congregation, they may never feel inclined to give more than a few dollars a week and we might overlook those opportunities to invite members of our place of worship and newcomers to give generously to our ongoing ministry and capital needs. Each one of us is called to live out our lives as disciples and acknowledge that everything we have—our talents, our wealth, our families, and all those things that we acquire—is actually God's. We nurture and share God's gifts abundantly. We give generously and joyfully of all that we have—including our money—because we have already received the gift of life and its accompanying benefits.[6]

In his book, *A Spirituality of Fundraising*, noted Roman Catholic priest and author Henri Nouwen reminds us of the blessing we receive in making a gift.[7] Rather than being an intrusion, the ask is a sacred invitation for us

---

6. John Westerhoff, *Grateful and Generous Hearts* (New York: Church Publishing, 2002).

7. Henri Nouwen, JM, *A Spirituality of Fundraising* (Nashville, Upper Room Publishing, 2011).

to think beyond ourselves and embrace the opportunity to give to something that is transformative. The very act of giving spare change to a homeless person, for example, is an act of solidarity with Christ who consistently challenges us to do unto the least of these (Matt. 25:40).

Normatively the Anglican Church in the Diocese of Toronto does not make a habit of setting aside a particular Sunday in the liturgical calendar to focus on a special need. The aversion is practical, lest one dedicated Sunday lead to others being set aside for a myriad of purposes.

Last year was meant to mark a departure from that pattern as we established Encouragement Sunday to coincide with the Reign of Christ—the last Sunday in the church year, just prior to the beginning of Advent. Our bishop was moved to introduce a dedicated Sunday as a way of promoting the importance of will preparation and providing for the long-term needs of ministry. The event was postponed because of the pandemic. Perhaps this sort of focus is something your congregation or religious organization could do.

For many Christian denominations, the Reign of Christ provides a welcome opportunity to encourage end-of-life giving. It is the triumph of the cross that provides that model of giftedness that we are invited to participate in. As Christians, we believe that Jesus was made a gift to us. His life, death, and resurrection lay the foundation for new life, grace, and peace. We celebrate this legacy each Sunday when we gather for Holy Communion. It is the *eucharistia* (from Greek meaning "thanksgiving") that empowers us to be living legacies when we go into the world and become examples of Jesus's love for the world.

Like most Christian traditions, the Eucharistic prayer in the Anglican Church repeats the words of scripture: Jesus takes bread, blesses it, breaks it, and shares it with his disciples (Matt 26:26). This same pattern is found in the miracle of the feeding of the five thousand when Jesus takes two fish and five small loaves and multiplies them beyond imagination (Matt. 14:13–21). This act of thanksgiving demonstrates how Christians believe that Jesus transforms human scarcity to divine abundance.

For Christians, gifts of encouragement intimately connect us to the same experience of Jesus. His triumph of the cross, his sacrifice, demonstrates how good overcomes evil and death becomes new life. In the same way, our death can give way to new ministry, new opportunities, and new ways of expanding God's work on earth. This is what grace does—it transforms. It is God's power working in us that creates infinitely more than we can ask or imagine (Eph. 3:20).

A faithful Christian steward reflects on this experience of humility and allows her- or himself to be used as a channel for Jesus in our own world. So, what characteristics of Jesus are going to be seen by what you and I do and speak? How can our gifts of encouragement serve to commemorate the lives we have lived and cooperate in God's plan for humanity?

The Anglican community in the Diocese of Toronto has an extensive history of social outreach. Deeply committed to building communities of hope and compassion, the early clergy and laypeople of the diocese joined together to build hospitals and schools, seeking to help not only its own congregations, but to reach out to the needy, the sick, and the elderly in all walks of life; this work has continued to the present day. I am grateful for the foundation laid by those who have come before us and pray that our current generation will respond with the same energy and fervor.

The American Episcopal Book of Common Prayer includes the following passage in its rubrics:

> The Minister of the Congregation is directed to instruct the people, from time to time, about the duty of Christian parents to make prudent provision for the well-being of their families, and of all persons to make wills, while they are in health, arranging for the disposal of their temporal goods, not neglecting, if they are able, to leave bequests for religious and charitable uses.[8]

Helpful advice indeed, thanks be to God.

---

8. The Book of Common Prayer (New York, Church Hymnal Corporation, 1979), 445.

CASE STUDY

The Essential Phases
of a Planned Giving Program

Karl Mattison

Planned giving in a congregation requires a difficult balance between what's perfect and what's possible. Launching a program feels daunting. To do it right, the work feels too expansive, amorphous, and unknown. So, most congregations push it back on their list of priorities—and never start a program at all. Is it possible to pare it down to just the essentials? Not only is it possible, for 99 percent of the effort it's really the only way to succeed.

Let's learn about those essentials from a collection of congregations who have a strong planned giving program. I focused in on Presbyterian congregations that showed recurring bequest revenue for five or more consecutive years. That is a reliable indicator that planned giving is a part of their congregation's culture.

You might expect these programs to be highly productive and polished with multichannel marketing. Yet, these programs are not flashy or complex. In fact, they are often understated, even low effort, yet their hallmark is a well-built foundation and a sustainable plan. Following are a variety of insights on what is essential. When working with a congregation, we break this out into three phases: **a beginning** to set the groundwork for a solid foundation, **a middle** to generate support and enthusiasm from leaders, and **final phase** to launch a sustained message to everyone.

(Phase 1 of 3) GROUNDWORK

Great programs have laid solid groundwork. It makes a program coherent. It is the glue that helps sustain the program for consecutive years. Without the groundwork, programs struggle to get over the 12–18-month wall. Solid groundwork creates a blanket understanding of why one should make a planned gift to this congregation, and the congregation has a plan for my planned gift.

Without solid groundwork, a program struggles with coherence and at least appears not to have a plan for significant gifts. For most planned givers, this is the largest gift we will ever make. It's our big moment. We want and need to be certain that those we entrust know what to do—and that this isn't too much for the congregation to handle.

Getting started with groundwork: first, get the right people on board.

The Team

Depending on your congregation's size, your team might range in size from just you (and a companion leader as discussed in chapter 3) on up to a cohort of ten committee members. Most congregations are on the smaller side of this scale. Either way—whether it is just you or a wider team—team members thrive with a specific role and are depended on for an area of responsibility. Also set some expectations for time commitment so they can understand the load they carry before accepting the position.

What makes a good committee member? The greatest contributors have been far more notable for their characteristics than their expertise. For example, a team with people like this is going to have great impact: true love of the congregation; enjoy the experience; good role models; strong encouragers/tactful delegators; good collaborators; already made a planned gift. As for experience, though not necessary, consider relevant professional experts—like estate planning attorneys (as long as they are not seeking to use the planned giving efforts to build their client base), professional fundraisers, or marketing experts.

Are the clergy involved? Most definitely. In the most effective programs, you can sense and see the support of clergy. Clergy might not be the hub of activity or monitor detailed minutiae, but they regularly express support and encourage the planned giving team.

The Why—Your Case Statement

Develop a clear focused statement of purpose. What is the underlying purpose of planned giving at your congregation? A good case statement will play into all communications and thereby keep coherence and momentum within the membership of the congregation. Importantly, it helps all leaders to describe it in one voice. (Please look at the simple text of a case statement as well as a fully developed case for support booklet in online resources.)

Without a case statement, the term "planned giving" is likely to get whisked away in the wrong direction—different people will interpret planned giving in multiple directions, using their own assumptions that are often counterproductive. Here are examples of counterproductive directions: "planned giving is for the rich," "the congregation is seeking money when a member dies," "the congregation doesn't know what to do with bequests." These are sour yet prevalent opinions, and it will be important to address them, so that efforts are not derailed or misunderstood from the beginning. Isn't it more exciting when we can reframe it over and over as an opportunity for the giver to keep doing ministry after their lifetime?

Chart a Course

Set a target date to complete your launch. Smaller congregations might aim for nine months; larger congregations might aim eighteen months to complete the full launch. That is not as long as it seems. It is just enough time-space to enable a thorough plan that is evenly paced out for you to build a sound base for the program and enable a deliberative experience for your membership. Working backwards from there, set a plan. Get specific and make it into a calendar.

Articulate objectives.

Say what you want the planned giving program to have achieved in a set period of time. Be specific and realistic so that you can plan your efforts to assure making the objectives.

Example objectives:

- members have created a faith legacy and included a legacy gift to the congregation.
- sermons
- educational events on leaving a legacy
- messages per year on legacy and planned giving.

Setting dollar goals is not an ideal objective; first it is impossible to forecast for such a long-term horizon, and furthermore it can be a very counterproductive prioritizing dollars over the concept of legacy.

Policies and Guidelines

Many want to leap right over this. It is a barrier that we want to get around to move on toward the more satisfying part of a planned giving program. Can't we just skip policies? Well, no. If policies were simply pomp, we certainly should skip it. Rather, a policy is really *the offer* to the planned giver. Effectively the congregation and the giver are making a future agreement— that when the giver makes this planned gift, the congregation will then care for the gift in this prescribed manner. The policy is *the written plan* we the congregation will follow to allow each planned giver to continue their legacy through this congregation. The policy is simply the collection of rules that we pass along to the next congregational leaders so that they understand the agreements made.

The absence of policy leaves the congregation's evolving leadership to decide how to apply the planned gift proceeds. Generally, the default will be based on (1) what the congregation most needs and (2) what the congregation knows of the giver's intentions. This no-policy approach is survivable when planned gift sizes remain small. For large gifts (i.e., the size of the annual budget), it is common for leadership to be divided. For gifts in the range of ten times the annual budget or more, the issue will normally be very contentious. A policy would solve the problem. As a rule, it is far easier to agree on a policy how to handle money before it is a reality than after it is received.

So how do we compose policies? What should policies say? Start by reviewing other charities or congregations' policies. Don't compose yours from scratch. Templates and samples often are a helpful compilation of past learnings. A great source for templates or samples is often your denominational foundation. (Please review the website for this book: www.church publishing.org/faithfulgiving.) Within most of these policies you will likely see these components:

Gift Acceptance Policy establishes guidelines for what gifts can be accepted. It lists easily acceptable gifts like cash and securities, and it might exclude or at least place conditions on more complex gifts, like collectibles or timeshares. Check with your denominational foundation about what types of more complex gifts they might accept on your behalf. (See the appendix for denominational resources and online reference links.)

Gift Purposes or Disposition dictates where gifts go. In this, the congregation establishes what happens once a planned gift arrives. It may say how and when will the funds be spent. It may outline which ministries these gifts are going to support. It may establish endowment funds to appeal to a giver's passion—like a music fund, ministry fund, and outreach fund. It might state conditions for a giver to request a specific purposed (restricted) fund.

Investment Policy demonstrates how we will hold these funds in a responsible manner so that funds will be held and invested prudently and will neither sit idle nor put at unnecessary risk.

Other Guidelines and Highlights. Many congregations establish guidelines to have a specific protocol, like how to record planned gift intentions and acknowledge gift receipts and gratitude. A policy to set a threshold amount for a restricted fund is also advised so that a huge number of small accounts are not created.

This is not everything you can consider in a groundwork phase. Rather these are just some effective essentials that are consistent among highly successful programs.

(Phase 2 of 3) Inner Buy-In: *Your Biggest Fans: Get Them Excited!*

Engage Your Leaders

Rally your leaders around planned giving. Engage those who hold office, those with influence, those who are visibly passionate about your ministries, those who work and volunteer at the congregation. Brief them about the groundwork that's been built, about the planned giving program that is coming. Make it relevant. Ask them questions. Invite them to lead. Invite them to support.

Leader Briefing

At a regularly scheduled meeting, brief your officers on the planned giving program. Include an overview of the case statement, the groundwork, your plan, and simple ways they can help. Invite them to lead by making a public commitment for a planned gift.

Staff Briefing

Whether just a couple of paid people or a few dedicated volunteers with specific oversight responsibilities, staff are the central communication hub of your congregation. Having them aware of the importance of the program is invaluable. When staff are not aware of the program, it feels like it is not a serious program. Givers might perceive the congregation is not prepared for serious planned gifts. Brief the staff on what planned giving is, who it's for, and what are the next steps if a member inquires. Brief them on your plan— and how they might react to questions or comments on planned giving— and how to document intentions or to connect the inquirer with the right point of contact to learn more. (These guidelines can also be maintained as a part of your endowment and gift acceptance policies.)

Pillar Member Buy-In

Expand your concept of leadership beyond those with official roles: Let's include those who can be influential, helpful advisors, and even early adapters of your program. Many highly effective programs seek out a targeted group—to solicit their thoughts, invite their ideas, and consider their own participation. They are the most likely to be (1) the most interested in what happens to your congregation after their lifetimes, (2) your most passionate advocates/or conversely your greatest detractors, and (3) your first round of planned givers. Asking for their thinking early on makes them feel like a part of the effort and minimizes the likelihood of ideas counter-to-your-culture early in the process.

Do we have to do this phase? Many want to jump past this. You can, but those who have taken this phase seriously report that it is the best of all. They shared that these were eye-opening conversations and deep reflections that would not otherwise have happened. They shared that many planned gift commitments grew from within this phase much sooner than anticipated. It is not surprising that these are often the most likely and largest gifts in a planned giving launch. These are the most likely audience to see planned gifts to the congregation as a critical part of their own personal future planning—their own legacy.

(Phase 3 of 3) Broad Invitation

Now tell everyone. Keep it starkly simple so that it is sustainable for the long-term. Many congregations are not succeeding in planned giving, no matter how committed individuals are to their community of faith. Our experience indicates that most planned gifts go to the larger secular nonprofits. They invest significant resources in sophisticated planned giving departments.

They put all of this forth to catch a prospective giver's attention and then establish a relationship to cultivate them as a donor. Most congregations and small religious organizations sit by feeling powerless and watch these planned gifts happen all around them.

Yet as we watch from afar, we seem unaware that we have a planned giving superpower. It's something the large nonprofits would trade for any tool in their belt. Our givers gather here with us in person (or online) every single week, listening intently to what we have to say on their faith, beliefs, and, of course, money. Our givers are already here and listening. Our best communication tools are already in place. Use that. We are already almost there, 90 percent of the way.

The Basics

Closing in on that final 10 percent stretch is the work ahead of us. In my experience, now is a good time to refer back to our most successful congregation programs. The two most effective characteristics are that (1) these congregations all have a noticeable **recurring invitation** (2) sustained **over multiple consecutive years**. This seems to be the key to unlock widespread participation.

The Bare Minimum

PASSIVE—ALWAYS PRESENT: There should be an ever-present yet subtle message of planned giving. With just a few tools in place, each member will regularly pass by the words "planned giving" along with your "case statement" throughout the year. The minimum might be in two places: a brochure on a table (even a generic planned giving brochure from your denominational foundation) and a page on your website.

This recurring and subtle presence will keep a place for planned giving in their minds, so that it emerges at the unpredictable times that your members are planning their future affairs. At the moment they are setting up a retirement account or (re-)writing their will, it will trigger the memory to make a planned gift. It's that **simple**: because most of your members are not opposed to making a planned gift, it just doesn't cross their mind unless they are reminded.

ACTIVE—SCHEDULED ACTIONS: Seek to say something about planned giving more regularly. Start off with a planned giving introduction letter/article. Then consider brief monthly messages, like a blurb in the bulletin or electronic newsletter—or occasional word from the pulpit. Use words of invitation, stories about impact, or a testimonial from a member. Sustain this very simple cadence for three years, and, in my experience, you will easily improve your realization of planned gifts.

That is it. Too simple? It sounds like too little, but it unlocks the most important ingredient: Sustainability.

Want more? For programs that want to go deeper, please do so only after locking in these basics as a part of your culture. Only then should you pursue perfection. Overadvanced or overambitious planned giving programs have an extremely high energy burn rate. Remember they are very difficult to sustain unless a team is fully available and committed to sustaining such a high level. If you would like to review more advanced efforts, you may check with resources provided by your denomination's foundation, or you can review the more advanced planned giving efforts on this book's website.

Donor Planning

Know Thyself

Is our greatest fear death, or that we will not accomplish our goals, or that we did not find meaning in our lives? All faith traditions seek to share deeper truths with their followers. For planned givers, knowing the specific choices that we personally wish fulfilled is the first step, the second is putting those intentions and other end-of-life desires in writing. Though there are many ways to take care of those specifics, recognizing that everyone will have particular and varying desires is often a harder thing to accept, especially if one's personal wishes regarding their future health and death are very different from family traditions. However, your own openness to encourage others to confirm their actual wishes may serve you well in your charity's efforts in planned giving.

Know Your Constituents

Encouraging those with whom one worships or those who support an organization's mission to reflect on their medical, funeral, and estate desires is a key part of what I refer to as the ministry of planned giving. Regardless of your faith tradition, end of life plans are inherently personal and spiritual, as well as an opportunity for you as a planned giving leader to display that you and your organization place personal choices as paramount.

As already said many times, your planned giving efforts are not primarily about raising money for your congregation or organization, they are about creating and sustaining a relationship and thanking individuals for raising your charity to the level of family in their estate plans. Not everyone will choose to make a gift, a few people may outlive their assets and not be capable of leaving what they intended and several, typically very consistent regular supporters, will leave the largest donation of their lives. Remain open to all possibilities while focusing on the basics of trust and relationship development. Creating opportunities to make end-of-life plans and sharing useful resources will enable constituents to do these important tasks and may also lead to a significant allocation to your charity in the future.

Know the Basics

There are many ways to motivate your constituents to plan for the future. I would encourage you to be inclusive in the ways you motivate them to consider their options. It is better that their congregation or favorite charity was the entity that shared with them the necessary planning documents or held an event to promote ensuring their wishes. That generosity afforded to them may cement a relationship that will be remembered and will be a recountable story for that person to tell friends and family of how charity X shared those beneficial resources. It may inspire current donations from friends of the individual to get those same materials that were so well touted.

Many denominational foundations provide materials that you can simply recycle under your own branding and many more are available online either for free or can be purchased; please see the references in the appendix and this book's website. You might also make use of resources like Jody Giles's *Missing Pieces Plan* on end-of-life and estate planning, the many resources of FreeWill.com, or others. Although your organization should always recommend that people seek their own legal/tax/financial advice, there are some organizations like Islamic Relief USA that chose to take a more proactive stance. (Please see Anwar Khan's case study which follows.)

Remember the reality of our shared discomfort with talking openly about death and fear of making end of life plans. Whether from superstitions of calling death to you by making these plans or by causing yourself to admit to one's own mortality, taking the steps to put arrangements in place remains a challenge for many. Gentle prompting is usually appropriate. However, if you were to ask people after they have completed their plans, most would say it was a relief finally to have it finished and quite empowering to be able to make their particular choices in advance.

Ensuring One's Wishes Are Fulfilled

There are typically three main areas of focus when it comes to end-of-life plans: first, medical directives and other clarifying documents and processes explaining how you wish to be treated medically if you cannot communicate yourself; second, funeral and related memorialization documents; and finally, estate planning documents. I would recommend if you reproduce any downloaded or printed materials, make it clear to the person receiving them that these are intended to be introductory or initial documents, not legal ones. This matches the same principle that you and other leaders do not offer legal/tax/financial advice. Any documents that require specific legal forms, such as many health proxy designations, or specific forms from your state or province or other governmental authority, must remain the responsibility of the individual. Your goal is to share basic information, as you will never be able to determine what is legally correct in every situation. Although many people find legal expenses excessive, it is always better to ensure that one's wishes are fulfilled by using a qualified lawyer or other professional. In summary of the following, leaders should encourage constituents to put their medical care, health proxy designations and alternates, funeral/memorial plans, and, of course, estate plans in writing. Appropriate legal forms and professional advice should be used to ensure that one's particular wishes will be fulfilled when a constituent is no longer able to do this for themselves; clergy who retain funeral, burial, and other wishes in writing can help ensure individual choices as well. Advocates for constituent desires should be carefully chosen as well as designated alternates to those advocates. Raising awareness of these topics is a part of the ministry of planned giving.

Medical Care When Incapacitated

Ensuring that one's wishes are fulfilled regarding medical treatment is an important process for everyone, regardless of age. Although many people designate their spouse or another relative as their health proxy, ensuring that the designate specifically follows one's wishes necessitates clear and precise communication. To ensure that a spouse or other designate will carry out one's wishes, individual desires must be reviewed well in advance and should be detailed for specific potential circumstances. If it is feared that a spouse's resolve might weaken regarding difficult choices, such as avoiding life-prolonging technology when one wishes to pass naturally, perhaps someone else should be selected. Is one's health proxy geographically near where one would normally be? Was appropriate documentation for a state/province or other legal context used? Are documents up-to-date and appropriate for where one currently lives? Not every locality will recognize health directives from other places. All issues need to be considered and can often be clarified with appropriate documentation, including required state or provincial forms.

Thankfully, people in same-sex relationships can now have the same rights as other married couples in the United States and Canada, but if one is in a nontraditional relationship or if a couple choses never to marry, has a specific designation been made which will prevail over local laws and regulations? In my work among the retired in Florida, many widowed and divorced people entered relationships outside of marriage for a variety of reasons. However, few of them had made provisions regarding how their significant other would be involved in their end-of-life plans.

Has an alternate to a primary health proxy been selected? Will one's proxy be able to stand up to family who might protest difficult choices? Has detailed information been shared with a healthy proxy? Given the complexities of modern medicine there are options for care never conceived of a few decades ago. Many people do not want extreme measure taken to prolong life on machines, others do. What is appropriate? Only the individual with the guidance of their faith tradition can decide among these options. Clergy can often assist with putting individual funeral/memorial planning in writing also, to ensure those wishes are fulfilled.

Encouraging Estate Planning and Planned Gifts

Estate planning evolves naturally from all of the other wishes one may have in considering the end of one's life. As leaders of a congregation or organization, recommend that individuals seek proper legal/tax/financial advice and reflect on the different type of assets they have. No one can determine exactly what is right for anyone else, but as leaders, you should always promote that potential donors provide for spouses and family first, before ever considering making a planned gift. Case studies, such as Amy Palmer's which follows, offer beneficial strategies for you to consider as a leader. Even with few current assets, finalizing an estate plan brings relief and helps leaders fulfil the essence of the ministry of planned giving: helping constituents face their own mortality with the confidence of planning and choice.

There is no single way to suggest individuals consider making a planned gift out of their estate and not every lawyer will suggest gifts for charity as a part of an estate plan. I wish that Christian traditions were clearer on guiding people on what to bequeath family, friends, and charity. I found the Muslim traditions for giving, in life and at death, quite heartening in clarity, but even in that wonderful tradition, there will always be opportunities for people to make individual choices. The Orange Catholic Foundation of Orange County, California, is currently doing an outstanding job on raising awareness of estate planning through highly effective end-of-life planning seminars led by local professionals who volunteer their time and expertise. These events, conducted in English and Spanish, both educate local Catholics on estate planning and on ways to support their own parishes and favorite institutions. Readers can view their website in our online resources. Increasing efforts like these will encourage more people to raise the desire to make charitable gifts in an estate plan, even if a lawyer does not bring up the option.

A Note about "Planned Giving While Living"

Occasionally, professional investment managers may react negatively to a client's decision to make planned gifts during life, such as life income gifts (LIGs) and donor-advised funds (DAFs). In fact, some may actively discourage those gifts. If you have constituents who mention this challenge to you, instruct them to be clear with their asset manager on their choices. They are ultimately in charge of their assets, regardless of the manager's investment skill or desire to oversee assets.

Take the Next Steps Forward: Various Suggestions for Events and Collaboration

Many congregations will hold adult forums/educational opportunities or "final affairs" events at appropriate times and will invite constituents to attend. Such an event is a great opportunity to collaborate far beyond the walls of the worship space. Making plans about final affairs while learning about Social Security and retirement planning can be a great draw. This could be a multifaith effort among many congregations, and I would encourage the leaders of religious organizations reading this book to consider underwriting such events along with congregations in your geographic vicinity. By reaching beyond one's own congregation, you may find leaders at other congregations and organizations willing to offer their expertise on estate, end of life, and health care planning. In addition, a panel of various clergy could easily go through a variety of pointers and circumstances for funerals and commemorations. For an outline of such an event, see our book's online resources.

If you are a community of faith, there may be other nearby congregations that are struggling with the same issues you are. This is a great opportunity to learn directly from other faith-based leaders developing their own planned giving programs. I hope that all clergy are in regular contact with other clergy in their area and seek to coordinate efforts, even if they reach beyond their own faith tradition. Use event titles like "Future Planning" or "Retirement Planning and Your Future Choices" to draw the widest age range of people to the event.[1]

Leaders in the United States should find that the Social Security agency will be extremely helpful with sending materials if you request them in advance. A few years ago, I found they were happy to send out staff to help groups learn more about Social Security benefits. However, Covid and other restrictions may have caused this practice to end.

The shared expense and multicongregational experience may prove to be tremendously beneficial and may lead to other collaborations in the future. Be sure to use the best facility available among those you collaborate but make it clear to attendees the many different congregations/organizations which were sponsors. (It's always good to demonstrate how people who worship differently can still collaborate.) Several years ago, I collaborated with a local rabbi and a priest at a large Roman Catholic parish to host a three-night interfaith series of awareness raising events. Due to a sharing of costs and the ability to rely on multiple leaders' contacts, it was a well-attended and extremely informative event. I include a basic outline for such a series in the online resources. As with all the resources, use them as a template for what you might do in your context. End-of-life issues reach beyond faith tradition or denomination and will benefit so many!

Evaluate Your Efforts from Time to Time

Hosting or collaborating on educational events can be a significant step forward for raising awareness. You should be mindful of what parts of the event went well and what could have been done better. Even though the event may be a significant endeavor of coordination among many sponsors, it is certainly going to be more efficient than trying to do an event all on your own.

---

1. Russell N. James, "Inside the Mind of the Planned Giving Donor with Russell James," *World Documents*, January 27, 2015, *https://vdocuments.net/inside-the-mind-of-the-planned-giving-donor-with-russell-james.html*; "An Emotional Connection," *Remember a Charity*, accessed August 22, 2021, *https://www.rememberacharity.org.uk/stories/an-emotional-connection*.

Push your boundaries and incrementally attempt new opportunities so that you may learn from other congregations and organizations.

Summary of Main Points

- When encouraging constituents to put plans in place for estate and end-of-life or medical planning, direct everyone to seek their own legal/tax/financial advice. You and your leaders are simply raising awareness and sharing tools. Constituents should also be encouraged to share their wishes in advance with their family and friends.

- Clergy can also serve as advocates for your members' end-of-life choices, but will often need to possess written instructions for funerals and other memorials if family members are in disagreement.

- Focusing on estate planning is essential to your planned giving efforts and should be thought of as a part of your ministry to constituents. Even if many use your tools or references for their planning, and still do not leave you a gift, consider this an important victory for helping them ensure that their wishes are fulfilled. Give thanks for being a blessing to them and their family.

- Leaders who encourage their constituents to put their various wishes in writing, and in appropriate legal form, as well as appoint appropriate advocates and alternates are doing their part in the ministry of planned giving.

CASE STUDY

Islamic Wills and Islamic Relief USA

Anwar Ahmad Khan

Creating a will is a tradition and act of faith in Islam. The Quran says in verse 180 of chapter two, "It is decreed for you: when death approaches one of you, and he leaves wealth, to make a testament in favor of the parents and the relatives, fairly and correctly—a duty upon the righteous."[1] This reference to when death is near you means that death is a reality for all of us, every moment of our lives.

In one of the narrations from the Prophet Muhammad (recorded in Sahih Hadith Bukhari and Muslim), he said, "It is not permissible for any Muslim who has something to will to stay for two nights without having his last will and testament written and kept ready with him."[2]

In the aforementioned narration the Prophet Muhammad charges every Muslim with the responsibility to be prepared to have their affairs in order, because our departure from this life is truly unknown to us. For Muslims in the West, it becomes even more important. If a Muslim does not write their will, then the local court may decide what happens to their wealth and their children, and this may not be in accordance with their faith, values, and wishes. Islam commands we believe that wealth can be spent on *halal* (approved) actions while we are still alive, but after our death, the bequests must be assigned according to the Quranic criterion. The Quran goes into detail regarding which family members will receive what shares. However, traditionally up to one third can be given to charity at the discretion of the person. Often bequests have funded *waqf* (endowments) in the Muslim world. These endowments are funded by donations when people are living and through their wills. They were a major source of funds for social well-being programs in the Ottoman Empire and the Muslim world. Even today, there are Ministries of Endowments that fund religious programs in some Muslim majority countries. These same wills become resources for

---

1. "Quran," *Clear Quran*, accessed July 17, 2021, *https://www.clearquran.com/002.html*.

2. "Sahih al-Bukhari," *Sunnah*, accessed July 23, 2021, *https://sunnah.com/bukhari*.

living kin, comfort for the impoverished, and a steppingstone for preservation of religion.

Islamic Relief USA is proudly part of the family of Islamic Relief Worldwide, which works in over forty countries around the world to provide humanitarian relief and development. Islamic Relief Worldwide was started by students who wanted to make a change in the world at the University of Birmingham (United Kingdom) in 1984, and Islamic Relief USA (IRUSA) was started in 1993 in California with this same ethos. During 2020, Islamic Relief USA was able to raise nearly $110 million cash to support its programs in the United States and around the world.[3] Its mission states: "Islamic Relief USA provides relief and development in a dignified manner regardless of gender, race, or religion and works to empower individuals in their communities and give them a voice in the world."[4]

Islamic Relief USA is supported mostly by Muslim donors in the United States. It started its activities in humble mosques (with youth groups and women's committees) and in student groups on campuses made up of ordinary people with extraordinary hearts. It is not legally linked with any denomination and is a big umbrella for people from the Muslim community to work together on humanitarian activities. It also works together with secular and other faith-based charities to improve social harmony, while helping those in need. Over its twenty-eight years, it incorporated mosque presentations, university lectures, community dinners, banquets, as well as Islamic concerts, all to raise awareness of its mission and raise funds to pay for life-saving humanitarian aid.

Since IRUSA began in the United States., it has endeavored to blend the traditional Muslim methods of fundraising with the American methods of philanthropy. In Muslim majority countries, often the mosques are supported financially by the state. That is not the case in the United States. Muslims learned how to do strong appeals after the sermons in the mosque, fundraising banquets, and adopted other techniques of philanthropy. At the same time, they were incorporating scripture and prayer into these activities, to give a Muslim feel to these engagements. Islamic Relief USA has not been complacent with how much it has learned, or how much it can raise for those suffering. There is always a hungry child, or one that needs

---

3. "IRUSA Annual Report 2020," *IRUSA*, accessed February 6, 2022, *https://irusa.org/wp-content/uploads/2021/12/2020_Annual-Report_IRUSA_122021.pdf*.

4. "Mission, Vision, and Values," *Islamic Relief USA*, accessed July 23, 2021, *https://irusa.org/mission-vision-values/*.

an opportunity to gain an education that they can support. Recently, they have been doing more to improve the Major Gifts Program and their own endowment (*Waqf*). Endowments are a traditional tool for financing Islamic social well-being programs, and they are sustainable. As part of our new endowment campaign, Islamic Relief USA decided to do more to focus on the estate plans of our constituents.

In our planning, certain decisions were made to our context and goals. The endowment would be funded by planned giving (primarily wills and designated bequests), charitable trusts, capital campaigns, and major gifts. Our investment policy for the endowments would invest in a diverse portfolio of public and private equity. However, all investments would be Shariah (according to Islamic Law) compliant and therefore not invest in alcohol and other forbidden products.

Thankfully, recent fundraising initiatives for current giving proved very successful. However, some of IRUSA's major donors feared that recently increased annual donations were not sustainable in future years and suggested that some current gifts should be set aside for investments. IRUSA leadership believed this to be true as well. IRUSA leadership also agreed that the IRUSA endowments (*waqf*) should be managed by a separate board, and so IRUSA *waqf* was created as a supporting organization to bolster confidence in IRUSA's future humanitarian efforts. As the director of Islamic Relief USA's *waqf*, Faisal Khan said, "People don't give to the endowment because they love the endowment, they give because they love the work of Islamic Relief USA. . . . We know people want to be able to continue to make gifts to support its good work even after they are no longer alive." This demonstrates the Islamic goal of *Sadaqah Jahriyah*, which means "continuous charity." Or to say another way, as long as someone benefits from that donation to the endowment, the one who donates it still benefits with blessings from God long after the donor is deceased, even many decades later! This long-standing tradition is witnessed through the many endowments in the Muslim world which are centuries old. These efforts support both IRUSA's long-term mission as well as its goal to diversify its funding sources.

Like many charities, Islamic Relief USA struggles to discover who has actually decided to designate IRUSA in their estate plans regardless of its regular efforts to raise awareness of planned giving to donors. Even with annual donors exceeding 130,000 in 2020, IRUSA struggles to motivate its donors to reveal their planned giving intentions in significant numbers. Keeping their intentions secret may be a cultural choice for many in our Islamic communities. In fact, IRUSA leadership has become aware that many estate gifts continue to be set up by our loyal constituents through anecdotal evidence. Without revealing their clients' identities, several estate lawyers who are friends of IRUSA notified our leaders that IRUSA was included in many of their clients' wills and estate documents, but unfortunately, clients wanted those gifts to remain secret until their deaths.

Another factor that challenges IRUSA and many Muslim planned giving efforts at present is a demographically positive one. The American Muslim population is a young population, their median age is thirty-five, compared to forty-five for the general public. Only 14 percent of American Muslims are 55+, compared to 36 percent of the general public.[5] This is very good for the future of American Muslims, but also means that they are less likely to feel the need to plan for their deaths in the near future. The long-anticipated transfer of generational wealth, now taking place from the Greatest Generation to the Baby Boomers, and then bequeathed to their descendants and donated to their charities, will have less effect on the younger and more recently arrived Muslim population. However, it will still be a significant transfer of assets for some long-standing Muslim communities.

Even though Islamic Relief USA has found it difficult having this conversation in the many ethnically diverse cultures of Muslims in the United States, especially those with any cultural bias for avoiding speaking of one's death, religious scripture encourages all to have this discussion, even if their particular culture may cause hesitation. Thankfully, leaders at Islamic Relief USA are finding that due to the various factors, these attitudes are changing to make these conversations easier. Due to education on the topic and access to new resources, more Islamic donors are considering planned gifts.

As previously noted in this book, most planned gifts are done through a will or similar estate vehicle. To overcome both the natural resistance of the young to creating a will and the cultural avoidance of others, IRUSA leadership decided that it would incorporate a tool on its website to make the process easier, both for making a gift to them and to simplifying the initial estate planning process. Although it is still recommended for everyone to seek appropriate legal/tax/financial advice, as a part of its mission, in 2020 IRUSA and its endowment started a partnership with an Islamic Wills website.

---

5. "Demographic Portrait of Muslim Americans," *Pew Research Center*, July 26, 2017, *https://www. pewforum.org/2017/07/26/demographic-portrait-of-muslim-americans/*.

This was a potential win for the charity, for the website, and for the donors, who could find a convenient way to fulfill their Islamic obligations and have a will prepared at a reasonable price. Both IRUSA and their vendor agreed to promote each other's websites. The wills website provided a software platform for people to draft their wills, which could then be reviewed by appropriate personal legal counsel. For Muslims seeking to fulfill their religious obligations, the collaboration was extremely beneficial, including an inheritance calculator and Frequently Asked Questions section to help with any confusion. The inheritance calculator would calculate according to Islamic principles for how much each family member could receive. For those interested in donating part of their inheritance, Islamic Relief USA was the default charity, but other charities could be chosen by the user.

The website collaboration proved to be a success. In the first few months, there were 45 individuals who went through the process and seventeen included Islamic Relief USA as a beneficiary.

The website is licensed in all states and users pay a fee for the service. Islamic Relief USA was hoping to promote this service to people who would otherwise feel reluctant for financial reasons to draft a will.

To encourage greater use, marketing would play a key role and the landing page was enhanced over time. To make it enticing and easy to use, the design was kept simple with appropriate scripture quotes, basic instructions, Frequently Asked Questions to help educate people about the need for a will, how to set it up, and the unique inheritance calculator according to Islamic Family Law. This calculator alone made what may be confusing to some easy to comprehend.

Marketing the site was also done through multiple social media channels, including a *Waqf Wednesday*'s sending messages and posts to encourage our supporters to write their wills and highlighting the new site. IRUSA podcasts focusing on Islamic will writing were also recorded and promoted. Because some IRUSA donors still prefer mail, an inset was also included in the annual Ramadan appeal package to encourage recipients to write their wills and to consider including Islamic Relief USA as a beneficiary.

IRUSA is pleased that the new wills website has provided a new medium for creating wills conforming to Islamic law and obligations, even if not all users included IRUSA in their estate plans. However, this has also helped Islamic Relief USA to raise awareness of its good work and increased our knowledge of the number of bequests naming Islamic Relief USA as a beneficiary. Other religious organizations might consider doing something similar to encourage planned giving overall, while also offering opportunities to support the unique mission of one's organization.

A more concerted campaign is currently under consideration at IRUSA which should not only encourage more planned gifts to the organization over time but will also clarify how we could steward particular gifts if they are done through our wills website. As with many religious nonprofits, coordination among departments is key to success. For IRUSA, we are working between our attorneys, finance department, major gift officers, and the development department, as well as the IRUSA *waqf* to engage directly with trustees and lawyers of the estates of our various supporters. Our strategic team goal will be to ascertain if IRUSA can fulfill its obligations to oversee any new designated-to-a-purpose gifts, while also confirming if the gift is *halal* (religiously approved) and conforming with our own internal endowment. New policies and procedures are being created as more donors are signaling their intentions through the wills website to make restricted gifts directly to Islamic Relief USA through their wills. We are hopeful that our continued engagement with donors through these innovative channels will continue to increase their philanthropy and IRUSA's ability to enable their generosity.

In conclusion, as attitudes have changed in other areas of fundraising over time, Islamic Relief USA expects that will happen with wills and endowment giving. Wills have always been a part of the Islamic faith and can be used to fund humanitarian and social action for future generations in a sustainable and powerful way. Clearly, technology, philanthropy, and religious efforts can work together to make the world a better place for all.

CASE STUDY

Strategies for Planned Giving

Amy Palmer

It was a cold and windy day when I met George and Donna in their home. I was there to thank them for their generosity to our organization and to ask them to consider including the Adrian Dominican Sisters in their estate plans. George and Donna weren't what we consider major donors, but they were longtime givers and had personal relationships with many of our sisters through their local parish. George and Donna were in their seventies, with two children and four grandchildren. We had visited them a few times before and our conversations were always light and easy, and because we knew many of the same people, our visits also provided an opportunity to reminisce about our mutual friends.

However, this visit was a little different because I wanted to talk with them about their estate plan. When we talk about estate planning, we are ultimately talking about what happens when we are no longer of this earth and let's admit it: nobody likes to think about their own demise. We know it's going to happen, but we are so busy living our lives and planning for tomorrow, who has time to think about the end? I'd honestly much rather plan for dinner with friends or think about my next vacation than to think about writing a will or deciding how to divide up my personal belongings after my death.

For fundraisers, asking our benefactors to consider leaving our organizations in their estate plans is pretty much inviting them to think about their death. That seems awkward, but, my friends, it doesn't have to be. I want to give you eight strategies to help you have "the talk" with your benefactors. These tips are written to help any fundraiser, regardless of the size of your organization, whether your organization has been doing development work for many years or if you are new to the ministry of development, and these tips can help longtime fundraisers or new fundraisers alike.

I work for the Dominican Sisters of Adrian, Michigan, a congregation of nearly five hundred Catholic Sisters, serving in ministries around the United States, Dominican Republic, Philippines, and Norway. The Mission of the

Adrian Dominican Sisters is to Seek Truth, Make Peace, and Reverence Life. It is a mission that is lived out by the sisters, associates, coworkers, and benefactors, or as we call them, partners in mission. The Adrian Dominicans have long been known for their forward thinking and for their efforts to protect the integrity of creation as they bring about a more just, peaceful, and compassionate world.

Strategy #1: Build a Culture of Philanthropy

In 2014, our office of development went through a time of transition with a change of location, a new director, a new donor database, and a complete changeover of staff. The transition, supported by two consultants, was a time of renewal as well as time of celebration and acknowledgment for the good work that had happened in years before. One of the first recommendations of the consultants was to "build a culture of philanthropy." In other words, find strategies to make sure that everyone in the organization (sisters, associates, coworkers, and business partners) understood the importance of our development work and felt a part of it. We did that in several different ways, at different times, in different venues. The Adrian Dominicans have a solid communication system in place for sharing information within the congregation. Therefore, we used the sisters' listservs, mission group meetings, intranet and Congregation Communiqué (a monthly e-mail to the sisters and associates from the General Council), and face-to-face campus meetings to share with the sisters our plans for the upcoming year. We also developed a procedure for sending the sisters our mailed publications two weeks before they were sent to donors. This way, when they were talking to their friends and relatives and the publication was mentioned in conversation, the sister would understand the reference. We also asked sisters to share names of potential donors with us and we invited them to become volunteers, helping us call and write to donors. Building a culture of philanthropy is what led us to George and Donna. Several years before our estate plan visit, a sister suggested we visit them because she knew how much they loved our organization.

Strategy #2: Have a Case for Support

As a fundraiser, it's crucial that you understand the needs of your organization, why donations of any size are needed, and how they are used. The best way to do this is to create a case for support. The case can be written to be used only internally, or it can be used as a published document that can be given to donors. With the help of our consultants, we drafted a case and then "tested" it with several people through focus groups. The final product is an external document that we take with us to donor visits. It explains who we are, what we've done with donations that we've received in the past, and why we still need additional donations. It also has a folder in the back where we can put personalized information and up-to-date needs and requests. Since we have created the case for support (see this book's online resources for this piece), we've found that our asks are more clearly articulated, donors enjoy reading the case and looking through the photos for sisters they may know, and it gives us confidence that our talking points are clear and consistent. When we visited George and Donna, we shared the case for support with them with a letter they could read after our visit.

Strategy #3: Rely on Your Personal Experiences to Give You Strength and Confidence

In early 2021, the loss of life from the worldwide Covid-19 pandemic hit me both personally and professionally. At work, we lost fourteen of our dear sisters to the virus. It was devastating. These were women who had given so much during their lifetime. They were my friends, mentors, and women I looked up to for so many reasons. That was quickly followed by the loss of both my maternal grandmother and my wonderful and loving father. I lost my grandma and my dad on the same day, just hours apart. As a believer in God and the ever-after, I relied on my faith to help me navigate those sad, dark days. I've been associated with the Adrian Dominican Sisters for more than twenty years. In those years, they have taught me so much about faith, life, and death. I've watched them mourn the loss of their friends, relatives, and, of course, their dear sisters. While death is always a sadness, the sisters taught me how to celebrate life, how to honor our loved ones, and how to grieve. This knowledge and these experiences have, over the years, given me strength and confidence to deal with my own grief and challenges head-on, while honoring the situation and staying in the moment. I use these experiences from my heart and soul when talking with donors about their own life stories as I help them to honor their life and plan for the legacy they will leave. With George and Donna, I realized quickly that I had so much to learn from them as well. During our conversations, they also taught me life lessons about love and loss, and as they shared their stories of happy times and sad times, I could relate, while also sharing how the sisters have given me strength and courage over the years. Because of their close relationship with our congregation, we shared a common understanding about being taught by such smart, kind, compassionate women. Simply put, my past experiences often help me connect with our donors.

Strategy #4: Know Your Donors

This probably seems like an easy one, but easier said than done in some cases. Before you ask a donor for financial support, it's important that you know as much about them as possible and this is done through relationship building. Even if you have many donors and they live all over the world, this is doable, though it takes time. As with any relationship, there is give and take; building trust is done one phone call, one e-mail, one visit at a time. The other important strategy is to take notes. I know I can't rely on my memory to recall all details about each donor, so we take copious notes after every phone call, we document every e-mail, and every visit gets a long and detailed note. Before I met with George and Donna, I reviewed our previous contacts with them. It helped me to remember their children's names, where they had worked, and some of the sisters they knew. When I walked into their home that day, I was prepared to pick up where we had left off from our last visit.

Strategy #5: Continue Learning

While the basics of fundraising usually remain consistent, there are always new rules, laws, and regulations when it comes to planned giving. The more you know, the better you can answer questions and help guide donors in their decision making. One resource for you is your local Association of Fundraising Professionals (AFP) chapter and your local National Association of Charitable Gift Planners (NACGP) chapter. Their yearly dues are usually affordable and the programs they offer are helpful for fundraisers at any level. There may be other fundraising organizations in your community as well and if you can't find one, talk to other development professionals in your area and start your own. Sharing with and learning from colleagues doing similar work makes you realize that you aren't alone. We all have similar challenges and can support each other. Shortly before I visited George and Donna, I had attended a local AFP workshop where the topic was how donors could leave money for their children and for their favorite charity. The tips I learned at that workshop were a huge advantage during my conversation and ultimately helped our organization in more ways than one.

Strategy #6: Make Building Relationships Your Goal

As you are setting your monthly, quarterly, and yearly goals, it's important to remember to track more than just the dollars raised. By tracking other areas of your work, it is easy to see how relationship building plays a role in the bigger picture. For example, track how many phone calls you make monthly, how many e-mails you send, how many visits you've had. I had taken the time to build a relationship with George and Donna. In between personal visits, I had sent them birthday and anniversary cards, called to thank them after each donation they'd given, and added personal notes to some of the appeals we sent them. When George had knee surgery, I sent a get-well card indicating that we added him to our prayer list and that the sisters were praying for a speedy recovery. None of this took much time or money, but helped George and Donna know that I was thinking about them and that I cared for them. Dominicans are known for their hospitality. It was actually one of the first attributes I noticed about the sisters. When a visitor comes to our campus, they are going to get the red-carpet treatment. The sisters are professional hostesses and they have shared that knowledge and ability with their partners in mission. Building relationships is just what the Dominicans do, so building relationships is an integral part of our ministry of development.

Strategy #7: Use a Little (Philanthropic) Psychology

A lot of this strategy goes back to the idea about knowing your donor. But this takes that notion a tad bit further. We need to know our donors, but we also need to love our donors and invite them to love us back. This is what philanthropic psychology is all about. Yes, it seems a little deep, but as a fundraiser for a congregation of women religious, this comes quite easily for us. If we have a better understanding of how our donors are connected to us, what it is they love about us, then we can better communicate with them and better meet their needs. One simple way to do this is to change the way you write and talk to donors. For example, instead of thanking a donor for their donation, thank them for being such caring, generous people. See the difference!? Encouraging George and Donna to talk about the sisters they loved and our mission that was so close to their hearts helped build trust as we talked about the difference they could make with a legacy gift.

Strategy #8: It's Not about You. It's about the Mission.

My friends think I have the worst job ever. They always say that asking for money must be terrible. In my mind, I'm not asking for money. I'm inviting people to become part of our mission. A mission like "Seek Truth, Make Peace, Reverence Life" is an inspiring message. I'm not asking for people to give me money, I'm asking them to provide funds to a mission that means a lot to me, and it must mean something to them, or I wouldn't be asking. I've been turned down before. I've been told "no," but I don't take it personally. Usually, donors explain their reason for saying "no." They don't have the money; they aren't ready to commit, or they want to support other organizations. I also don't let the relationship end with the "no." There are so many other ways to support the mission—I find another way to keep them connected to our organization.

So, here's what happened. At the end of the meeting that day, George and Donna weren't convinced that they wanted to add our organization to their estate plans. They really worried that they wouldn't have enough left in their estate to support their family and the sisters. We stayed in touch and a few years later after Donna had passed away, George realized that he did have enough funds and, confident that his children and grandchildren would get a proper inheritance, named our organization as the beneficiary of one of his accounts. We are grateful to both George and Donna and we continue to stay in contact with George to ensure that he knows of our gratitude for his generosity and, more importantly, his friendship.

As you use these strategies, remember that it's all about the mission and that sometimes, conversations won't go quite as planned. Be strategic, be confident, and most importantly, be yourself. If you love your mission, that love and that passion will very easily be heard. Take a deep breath, say a prayer, and make that call.

CHAPTER 7

Legacy Societies

Know Thyself

From my experiences throughout the Episcopal Church and from discussions with numerous colleagues in the ecumenical and wider world, most congregations and religious organizations could benefit from creating a legacy society to enhance their planned giving efforts. A legacy society is a designated group that supporters may join after setting up a planned gift. Reflecting for yourself, how would you most like to be thanked for raising your congregation/religious organization to the level of family? Your initial thoughts, and those of your planned giving colleague leader, will be quite valuable. Thanking must always conform to what is appropriate for your culture, your congregation, and your supporters. If you tend to avoid thanking (a problem for many congregations), you may need to consider what are the best and most creative ways to thank constituents who have made this substantial commitment in a planned gift while still being true to your context.

Know Your Constituents

I had several conversations to push a large congregation though their resistance to do any public legacy thanking. Their primary leaders claimed their "very sophisticated" members would never want to be thanked publicly and any ceremony for legacy society induction, even if simple, would be perceived negatively. With some persistence, I was able to move their leaders to try an induction during liturgy and a subsequent "thanking" gathering. Both were successful, to the degree that multiple parishioners revealed to the rector that they would have loved to have been recognized with the others as they had also remembered the parish in their estate plans.

It is my belief that legacy societies are very beneficial to an organization or congregation. If you determine that a legacy society is not a fit in your context, I encourage you to consider the advice throughout this chapter and the case studies which follow for demonstrating thanks and building relationships over the long term with those who have committed to a planned gift. Arlene D. Schiff's case study explaining the Grinspoon Foundation's visionary program working with various regional Jewish Federations and Foundations to "Leave a Jewish Legacy" may be of particular interest. It highlights how the principles in this book can be successfully implemented.

Know the Basics

I have witnessed wonderfully evocative moments at legacy society gatherings: I have listened as individual members shared how their experiences in a congregation transformed their lives and made them worth living. I recall a completely unplanned series of testimonies made by five members of a society following one single planned affirmation. I was moved to tears listening to one woman's story on how her parish had truly become a part of her family as she raised her child as a single mother, with legacy society members and others helping change diapers and providing a variety of support in times of need. I have watched a proud member of the legacy circle explain the meaning and symbolism of the pin that had been chosen to represent his parish. Legacy societies enable the fullness of your planned giving ministry to loyal supporters through thanking, recognition, awareness raising, and providing opportunities for individuals to explain the depth of their commitment, as if they were showing pictures of a first grandchild. These groups can be transformational, both for your congregation/organization and for the people who become a part of them. They are much more than a tool; they can be a true blessing.

Past Attempts and Future Focus

A caution as you get started: discover if your congregation/organization ever had a legacy society in the past. Surprisingly, past attempts may have occurred but not been maintained at many mainline Protestant and Jewish congregations. A neglected legacy society can be a problem for current leaders, as those members who had previously made commitments will feel that they were forgotten or ignored. If this is your situation, hopefully records were kept of the previous effort and materials developed that could be reused and updated, making your efforts at resurgence easier. Being honest about the past and focusing on rebuilding trust throughout your renewed efforts can enable a stronger resurgence. Working with administrators or those keeping records, seek to gather any data and materials they may have, even reaching out to previous volunteers who may have knowledge of whom to contact or where older records may be stored. Don't dismiss the past and start again without acknowledgement of previous attempts: that may injure relationships further with those who were a part of an earlier effort.

How to discover if legacy societies had existed? You can ask leaders who have been active for many years of their memory or knowledge of past attempts and records of members. If you are able to determine a core of previous members, you may consider sharing a common list of those identified with a request for them to recall any additional missing people. Clergy or other leaders should be given the same opportunity to identify those missing from such a list, but with turnover in leadership roles, they may not be a source of useful information. If you are at a congregation where the classic "church secretary" (or similar role in your tradition) has been present for many years, you may be able to rediscover that history. This research is crucial to avoid potentially offending those who previously raised your charity to the level of family.

An Inclusive Opportunity

A legacy society should be the most inclusive group at the congregation, as most people can make one of the many types of planned gifts, and thus confer membership. To enhance inclusivity, I recommend any planned gift should qualify for membership in the legacy society, including contingent gifts. People will revise their plans in the future and better to be featured in the documents being revised. All ages should be welcomed to join, but please note that normally it will be an older group.

Demonstrating an economically diverse membership in your legacy society will also mitigate concerns that it is only for the rich or successful, and honestly may well shame, in the most positive way possible, those wealthier members to commit to a gift. Do not be surprised if you discover the well-known-wealthiest members of the congregation leave smaller gifts than those "average folks." The wealthy often give significantly in life, and those gifts are vital. However, it will be those average folks who feared outliving their assets or that simply wish to keep their substantial savings private who feel that they can finally release a substantial gift at death.

As an added benefit, it is also the experience of many development professionals that as individuals deepen their relationship with a congregation or organization by finalizing a planned gift, there is a greater connection and an increase in annual financial commitments.[1]

Even though a legacy society is an ideal way to thank and celebrate those who have made any type of planned gift, I have argued with many an Episcopal parish when they did not wish to create a legacy society, as they felt it would be perceived as elitist. Sadly, the parishes which expressed this concern about elitism often came from social contexts that appeared much more class conscious than the average congregation. When I privately reviewed the elitist issue more deeply with various leaders, I found that there were normally two things at play in those resistant congregations. First, I found that the main resistance often came from the wealthier members, many of whom may have not wanted to make a gift since they did not feel that the congregation could handle their significant donation, or they demonstrated great distrust of current leadership. (See chapter 2.) Another barrier came from a misperception that proof of finalizing a gift would be required and would reveal the dollar amount of the future gift. As you may already have anticipated, I recommend that dollar amounts should never be requested. Since you are not asking for people to tell you the dollar amount of their gift (but eventually inquiring on type), anyone at your congregation or organization can commit to making one.

I recommend that congregations/organizations never ask for a dollar amount for two reasons. One, asking for the dollar amount will again demonstrate a concentration on the money and not focus on the celebration and thanking of supporters for their ultimate gift. That psychological switch in the minds of supporters of more average means is a substantial barrier to overcome. Second, from a practical perspective, asking for a dollar amount will also encourage supporters naturally to lowball their ultimate bequest to you. In most cases, donors will choose a dollar amount that they would certainly be able to achieve regardless of what may happen in the future. As previously reviewed, percentage and remainder allocations are often larger gifts than specific dollar amounts.

---

1. "Planned Gifts Increase Annual Gifts, Study Finds," *The Pentera Blog*, accessed September 18, 2021, *https://pentera.com/blog/planned-gifts-increase-annual-gifts*.

To demonstrate this principle, a few years ago a large social service organization was seeking my feedback. They were surprised that several of their most significant donors with great capacity responded with very low dollar amounts for anticipated estate gifts when they were asked to confirm their planned gift amount. I shared my experiences and perspective with them and the risk of lowballing planned gifts. They have now changed their practice and no longer seek that information.

Documentation of Gifts

Avoiding a requirement for proof, such as a copy of a will, is also advisable. Asking for a copy of a will or trust document is futile, as supporters can always rewrite theirs wills and trust allocations. Though some secular organizations (especially universities) may require these documents as a matter of policy, for congregations especially, asking for proof sets up a more transactional relationship. Such a "give and get" exchange is not what most people are seeking with their community of faith. Based on your context, documents to affirm intent may be most effective. (See the Schiff's case study that follows and the online resources.)

There are a couple of exceptions, though, to this general caution of not asking for proof: gifts of life insurance, or residual values of designated accounts like IRAs and 401(k)s. (See chapter 4 on gift types.) Though you should never ask the expected dollar amount of the future gift, it is beneficial to discover what types of gifts people have set up to discover if insurance or retirement accounts are the intended vehicles. Inquiries could be done a year or so after a planned giving effort has begun or following the inaugural event of a legacy society.

To uncover this information, you could use a version of the survey of gifts in the online resources asking the type of gift that people have chosen to make. This is for a few important purposes. First, as referenced in chapter 4, if someone has noted that the charity was made a beneficiary of life insurance or a designated account like a 401(k), you will want to gently ask for a copy of the beneficiary confirmation document that identifies the charity in this way so that in the future, it may be more easily pursued. For designated accounts, it will simply expedite future efforts to claim the assets. Few investment vendors are incented to act quickly on liquidating assets to beneficiaries who are not keeping those assets with them, so better to contact them early. With life insurance, though some may, there are no strict requirements for insurance companies to contact beneficiaries; beneficiaries must contact the life insurance provider to collect proceeds.[2] When you send out the survey of gifts, this may be an opportunity to ask for future estate contacts as well. This information will be useful after the beloved supporter dies. Confidentially retaining this information in databases, as well as other donor information previously noted for its importance to their family, will make future follow-up that much easier.

Naming Conventions

Creating a name for your legacy society may be as easy as simply calling it the *<insert congregation/organization name> Legacy Society* or you may wish to be more creative. (I normally recommend simplicity.) Most charities should keep things straightforward and not spend an inordinate amount of time determining an alternative name. Unless, of course, your congregation/organization really likes to have fun with surveys and wants people to vote and stir up initial interest (which might be an interesting idea).

There are some cautions regarding the name. Much like how municipalities try to avoid naming a bridge or stadium for a living politician, I strongly recommend you avoid using a person's name for a legacy society. The exception might be a name of a beloved and uncontroversial founder or similar person in the history of a long-standing institution that clearly connects with the ongoing ministry of the congregation/organization.

However, another caution about avoiding the lure of exclusivity. I was working with an organization following someone else's direct work forming their legacy society. I discovered that the choice was made to name their legacy society after a living individual who was known as one of the wealthiest members of the community. They mistakenly believed that the visibility of his family's name would inspire other wealthy families to desire to be a part of the legacy society. Unfortunately, materials had already been developed and promotion done by the time I became involved. To my knowledge, few people ever joined the group, as most perceived that the organization was intended for the wealthy and even resurgent efforts struggled for much the same reason. My suggested rebranding of the legacy society was tried and eventually a new more generic name was attempted as a relaunch.

---

2. Investopedia Team, "How Does Life Insurance Work?," *Investopedia*, January 24, 2021, *https://www.investopedia.com/articles/personal-finance/121914/life-insurance-policies-how-payouts-work.asp*.

How to Get Started?

As I have now told hundreds of Episcopal parishes and various organizations, legacy societies fulfill the basic needs of thanking your most committed donors, but also regularly raise awareness about planned giving opportunities and create a naturally receptive audience to learn even more about additional planned gifts. Legacy societies also provide a tremendous "human resource" of new potential leaders in your planned giving efforts and committed individuals who may be willing to make formal testimony in writing, speeches, videos, and other means. The key to taking the most advantage of all these opportunities is maintaining a commitment to thanking and celebrating the members of this group. At a minimum, plan at least one official thank-you event each year (see ideas later in this chapter for special legacy society events to try beyond the official annual "thanking" event).

It is important to remember that your planned giving efforts are intended to be long term and communication cannot come across as pushy or aggressive. However, it is important to discover who of your constituents has already made this commitment. (Chapter 5 offers some insights on raising awareness and the importance of asking if people have already completed a gift.) Anyone who has confirmed any planned gift should be invited to join your legacy society. After the necessary research to uncover any previous iteration of a legacy society, the next step will be to plan an inaugural (or resurgent, if you previously had a legacy effort) event to thank and celebrate those who have made this commitment. Give your team about a year for this work.

This span of time may seem overly long for those anxious to implement a new planned giving effort. However, it is crucial not to rush the process so that supporters perceive they have enough time to consider the best gifts for themselves, to notify family, and to work with professional advisors. Rushing the initial celebration event is an aggressive move that will make people feel pressured. And the push may prompt individuals only to state that they have done a planned gift, so that they can be included in the expedited event, though they have not yet actually completed their plans. Although a bit scary for planned giving leaders, accepting an affirmation that an estate allocation was finalized is a best practice, so don't rush your process!

Initial or Resurgent Legacy Society Events

Advance scheduling of your inaugural thanking event is meant to motivate the finalization of gifts. As a part of the gentle kick-start, you want to encourage as many supporters as possible to finalize their plans prior to the event so that they may become "founding members" of the society. In future years, leaders should not continue to differentiate founding members from others, but that initial incentive is simply to get your efforts moving with as large a group as possible at the beginning. Founding members will be filled with pride to tell others that they were there at the beginning; you won't have to.[3]

When considering the best future date for the first inaugural (or even for a resurgent) event, consider first if there is a special anniversary coming up in the next year or two. There may be the one hundredth anniversary of the founding of your organization or the seventy-fifth anniversary of the building of your main worship space or some other cause to celebrate. That event should be celebrated anyway, but if such commemoration helps people reflect on the past, treasure the present, and look forward to the future, it may be an ideal event to pair with the first legacy society event. Given what inspires people to want to participate in your future mission through a planned gift, this will make your inaugural event and raising awareness about planned giving all that much easier. To be clear, the following suggestions are most effective for congregations that gather in person and for local religious organizations that have constituents who can easily caucus. For more dispersed or national organizations, take advantage of online opportunities or gatherings where you have local concentrations of supporters.

If you don't have an anniversary or celebration coming up, simply pick a date about a year or more out. Then, plan backwards, select a few events over the course of that year for raising awareness about planned gifts or end of life issues. Closer to the actual date of the thanking event, and in conjunction with program planning for the upcoming year, pick the date for the following legacy society event. Use this year-in-advance-planning annually. Having a specific date set in the upcoming year's program calendar will help keep leaders accountable for doing something annually. This annual planning keeps leadership aware of maintaining these crucial relationships and

---

3. Thanking my predecessors at ECF for the concept of "Founding Members" of a legacy society.

creates a natural and ongoing process for raising awareness of planned gift among supporters. In announcing and planning for the upcoming legacy society event in each year, making a planned gift will need to be explained, continually raising awareness in a gentle way. Leadership accountability and relationship building is assured by scheduling these events well in advance, year after year.

Thoughts on Legacy Society Events

I am often asked if these events should be "fancy." For organizations, this really depends on a variety of factors from the type of work the institution does, your constituents, and whether or not there is a national or large constituency. For congregations and locally based charities, my answer is normally that they should be "culturally appropriate." The inaugural event should lean toward whatever would be considered "nicer" or more formal for most constituents. Depending on the local or congregational culture, sit-down dinners, pot-luck suppers, or even a lunch buffet may be appropriate. Future thanking events can be simpler but should remain pleasant and retain the clear opportunity for members to feel thanked and honored. Themes and programs can alter from year to year, but they should always afford opportunities for individuals to share stories about personal experiences in the congregation or organization and give people a platform to share what moved them to make this gift. Don't forget to video-record these testimonials for future playback or posting on websites.

Avoid holding legacy events at the homes of the wealthy or at country clubs. You want to make it clear that everyone is invited to make a planned gift and fight against that common misunderstanding that these sorts of gifts are only for the obviously wealthy. I would also warn against overly lavish events: donors want to trust that their gift will be well used and not spent frivolously. I am aware of congregations that hosted events at exclusive clubs or homes. Within a few years, the elitist perceptions of planned giving grew, and those regular congregants (who may be the more significant donors at life's end) were dissuaded from becoming a part of the society. If your congregation/organization made that mistake in the past, you can recover by toning down your next event in more modest surroundings and making sure that any featured speakers, or promoters for attending the next event, are the most average folks you can find among your constituents.

Will You Wear My Pin?

I am a strong advocate of pins or some other subtle emblem representing the legacy society to be worn by members. Such things are not to segregate and create elitism, but, when the pin is noticed, to allow individuals to be prompted to give their own extemporaneous, verbal testimony to others for why they personally chose to make a planned gift. Once you have your legacy society well underway, you can encourage members to wear their pin at various occasions throughout the program year and allow for those natural conversations to arise. Those who don't like pins, because people don't wear clothing that is suited (no pun intended) for that, name tags with preprinted legacy society symbols or with the attached pins might work well. Or perhaps there is another creative idea to consider? It simply needs to be visible. According to Arlene D. Schiff at the Grinspoon Foundation, they encourage organizations to include a ribbon with a name tag or print directly on the name tag the phrase "Ask me about my legacy" as a way to get conversations started. I always love the times I have been in the Episcopal Diocese of Hawaii for their legacy events; they featured many different types of thematic leis. Devices like these can create pride (in the very best sense of the word) in one's commitment to a congregation/organization's mission, highlighting that a supporter is an intentional part of its future. Your creative ideas will enable this.

Legacy Society for Estate Gifts Only?

Based on local context and culture, it is certainly possible to have a successful legacy society and include both those who make gifts during life and through their estate plans at death. The important steps are deciding and clarifying parameters at the onset, and then continuing to thank members annually.

I had the privilege of speaking with two synagogues that went through the Grinspoon Foundation program for their regional Jewish Federations: Temple Shaarei Shalom in Boynton Beach, Florida, and Temple Sinai in Pittsburgh, Pennsylvania. Both congregations recognized members who finalized planned gifts, and both invited those same individuals to become members of their respective legacy societies. However, while Temple Sinai's Legacy Circle only invited members who had completed a planned gift from their estate plans, Temple Shaarei Shalom also invited current givers to their endowment funds (for gifts of $1,000 or more to existing funds or $10,000 or more for a named endowment) to become a part of their legacy society as well. Although I normally recommend celebrating and thanking people for any current gifts separately from the legacy society, for Temple Shaarei Shalom that inclusion worked well and benefited their planned giving efforts. Since gifts to endowment funds continue to fund ministries for years to come, making those donors a part of a legacy society makes sense for many congregations and organizations.

My reasoning for keeping the legacy society membership only for gifts made at death is that it enables clearer messaging to those making those future gifts and avoids confusion with current gifts. For many communities of faith, there may be various cultural contexts that necessitate the inclusion of various "giving-while-living" donors into the legacy society. This is a decision leaders should make early in legacy society planning, so that the parameters for joining the society are clear. If you accept those who make current significant gifts for legacy society membership, I recommend cultivating a gentle process of encouraging other "at death" planned gifts from those current donors as well. That way most of the legacy society members will feel more in common with each other and it will simplify communication to this group in the long run.

It is possible that in combining current and future estate gifts, leaders can plant the seeds of confusion that what the congregation/organization actually wants are large current gifts. The either-or option can cause that psychological switch to be flipped in some people's minds that planned giving is really for the more well-to-do. However, context and culture rule: if a supporter indicates that they are making a significant gift to the charity out of assets now, in place of a gift after death, those instances can be judged on a case-by-case basis or simply accepted as a part of the legacy process.

To Plaque or Not to Plaque

Cultural tradition and context will determine public displays, such as plaques, books of remembrance, giving trees with engraved leaves, and similar tools. I encourage leaders to reflect carefully, get feedback from actual planned givers on this before deciding, and then commit to a decision. Making wall displays has often been a staple device in capital and major gift campaigns as current recognition for those donors. I think that is just fine for those efforts, if the donors wish to be recognized.

I have seen several planned giving donor walls that combine both future donors and current donors to the endowment or some other special project. As previously noted, mixing present and future gifts can cause confusion and may promote that sense that what the congregation is more interested in is receiving large current gifts. Public displays may actively discourage members to choose not to make a planned gift, as they fear their future gift may not be substantial enough, since they fear their estate at death may be too small.

For a variety of reasons, some congregations are dedicated to public displays to recognize donors since it fits culturally. If feasible, a charity could create separate displays or plaques for living donors. Such types of recognition may be inherently beneficial in your context for cultural/faith-based reasons. Some congregations with successful programs, such as Temple Shaarei Shalom in Boynton Beach, Florida, have effectively differentiated donors on additional plaques for being both a legacy as well as being an endowment donor. That congregation and others are featured as examples in our resources, for effectively using their websites to highlight current endowment gifts and designated funds from various families. More on this in chapter 8.

Dr. Manzoor Tariq of the Islamic Foundation of Greater St. Louis (Missouri) told me, "Though making charitable gifts directly to benefit an individual should always remain private and confidential, plaques and other public displays are tremendously beneficial, as they can encourage giving by others in the local community." As a leader, you will know what works best in your context. I generally discourage plaques for living planned giving donors, and only promote placing a name on a plaque after someone has died and delivered a planned gift to the congregation/organization. My concern has been that recognition wall displays for living legacy society members, in a more subtle way, may promote a potential guilt-focused motivation. What will work best in your situation will depend on culture and context and if such displays inspire new gifts. There is clearly no single solution or perfect pattern.

For religious institutions who may want to have a recognition wall at the main office or other facility, that is a more complex choice. (Stacy Sulman's case study mentions their use.) There may be religious orders who have memorial gardens and other spaces that may work well for such displays to inspire visitors to consider and realize, "Oh yes, I can make a planned gift too." Since few supporters may visit some headquarter locations, in place of a public display, another great option would be a published or online listing which can easily be updated and to which individual member may affirm to be included. Such a list could be used at induction events or in a newsletter or mailing. Culture and context ultimately will determine this. The main consideration remains that your efforts are able to inspire new planned gifts.

Take the Next Steps Forward

Legacy societies take time to form and require ongoing discipline to ensure that a charity continues to build trust and relationships with donors over the long term. Not every event will be as evocative as initial events, but at least one prescheduled thanking event annually should be on your calendar. Maintaining that spot on the upcoming program year calendar will demonstrate that you are encouraging relationships. For organizations that have a national or international constituency, build on the new comfort with using simple video conferencing technology and conduct annual online events if you are not able to have a local in-person event. (See the afterword.)

What If a Legacy Society Won't Work for Your Context?

Although I believe that the creation and maintenance of a legacy society is the ideal for thanking, raising awareness, and ongoing planned giving continuity efforts, it may not fit for every context. In addition, culture, tradition, or faith-based issues may make a society inappropriate. There is a commitment of time and energy that must be expended (even just for an annual thanking event) for a legacy society to function well. If the creation of a society does not work for your context, I encourage you to be creative and seek to incorporate the thanking and awareness raising aspects of a society into the programming of your congregation or organization. As you read this chapter and the following case studies, consider what will work best in your context. If not a classic legacy society, then how can the best of the legacy society model be conducted without actually creating one?

Additionally, many newer congregations may struggle with setting up a legacy society and this may also be an issue for some growing faith traditions in the United States and Canada, even with ongoing "congregationalizing" taking place.

Additional Events and Ideas

It would be wonderful if a charity can have additional events for legacy society members (or similar thanking opportunities). They do not need to be lavish or expensive. Normally updating members on the ministries or mission of the congregation/organization is more than enough. Remember, these are your most dedicated and engaged supporters. However, events like this are normally done most easily in congregational or locally based religious organizations.

Congregations will have multiple opportunities. Events could follow services or at a convenient time during the week. Some ideas for congregations would be a reception to update the legacy society on a building project or new ministry to the local community. Other options might be a tour of an updated facility for Sunday school or, if music is a big part of a congregation's worship, attending a final rehearsal for a recently commissioned or new-to-the-congregation piece of music. (Years ago, at my Episcopal parish in New Jersey our choir did just that. During Covid, I was excited to learn that Temple Sinai in Pittsburgh featured congregation members, who are also in the Pittsburgh Orchestra, playing for an online legacy society event.) Or perhaps the local historian of the congregation might give a brief presentation on the congregation or its context in the community. You may also consider making any presentation a part of a simple social gathering. Be creative but remember what is important and/or culturally appropriate for your community of faith. Reflect on how leaders could offer prayers and thanksgivings for legacy society members at various designated services or appointed times to celebrate their commitments and the memories of their deceased loved ones.

Locally based religious organizations might consider inviting legacy society members to hear updates on a new initiative or volunteer opportunities. Nowadays such activities to highlight the work of the organization could easily be done online. Nationally/internationally based charities might also consider gathering supporters in specific urban centers when already conducting local interest raising events too. Combining existing events with your legacy society members may inspire other attendees to join by finalizing a planned gift.

Evaluate Your Efforts from Time to Time

Though there is no central tracking of faith communities or religious organizations for the financial benefits of maintaining legacy societies, there have been studies by the Lilly Family School of Philanthropy at Indiana University. In a recent case study highlighted by Pentera comparing estate gifts made by legacy society members versus nonmembers, the average estate gift of a legacy society was $247,703 (median estate gift $47,598) versus a nonmember legacy gift of $122,550 (median estate gift $12,546). The difference between legacy society members and nonmembers here is staggering.[4]

In future years, review what worked well and what did not with your senior and planned giving leaders. Your context may indicate trying different options. As previously noted, leaders also need to assess how they maintain their endeavors. Legacy societies are a serious commitment but well worth the effort over the long term. The level of appreciation demonstrated, and relationships built can be tremendous and will help maintain the commitments made in wills and other estate planning even through challenging times. Remember, once the society is established, you will also have a new focused source of feedback, not to mention from those who have not yet joined.

Summary of Main Points

- Legacy societies provide "all of what's necessary" for planned giving, processes for recognition, easy avenues for follow up and scheduling, and a natural audience for learning about other gifts; legacy societies also keep planned giving in everyone's mind every time they are mentioned.

- Members of your legacy society will be your best advocates to other constituents, providing unscripted opportunities to endorse planned giving, but will also create opportunities for ongoing visibility and testimonials at heartwarming public events. Don't neglect to record these in video and through written articles.

- Do not rush your initial (or resurgent) legacy society event. Provide enough time for individuals actually to complete their plans and not feel pressured.

4. Indiana University/Lilly Family School of Philanthropy, "The Planned Giving Study," *Pentera*, September 2016, *https://pentera.com/pdf/whitepapers/Pentera_Whitepaper-The_Planned_Giving_Study.pdf.*

- If legacy societies won't work for your context, focus on thanking and relationship-enhancing opportunities that demonstrate your context and culture.
- Your current planned givers will be a tremendous human resource for raising awareness to others. Make use of old and new technologies to capture testimonials of why individuals made their choice of a planned gift. (See afterword on post-Covid developments.)
- Be mindful when allowing current givers to join legacy societies. Seek to inspire new giving and not to flip that psychological switch to dissuade "average folks" from realizing they can do it too; don't make it about money or creating an elite group but about thanking and celebrating.

CASE STUDY

Reflections on Legacy Planning in Hawaii

Peter C. Pereira

Introduction

In 1991 I started my career as the treasurer and chief financial officer for the Episcopal Diocese in Hawaii. When I started in the diocese, our investment portfolio was $10 million and today it is worth over $46 million, with an operating budget of approximately $2.5 million with 30 percent of the income derived from our endowment fund income.[1] Much of the endowment growth, which brings greater security for our future ministry in the Islands, has come from our planned giving efforts and stewardship of the endowment portfolio with the help of the various committees and with the diligent backing of our bishops over the past thirty years, including our current Bishop Robert Fitzpatrick, who has been very supportive.

During the 1990s, I was reading in CPA journals about the enormous transfer of wealth that was going to take place in the coming years as the Greatest/Silent Generations and Baby Boomers pass on. I realized that the church was not in a position to take advantage of the opportunity, as no one in the diocese was assigned to do planned giving. I decided to learn as much as I could and, in a limited capacity, began helping our churches with others in the diocese in these efforts.

I quickly found that I greatly enjoyed the field of planned giving. What was especially attractive was meeting people throughout the diocese and getting to know their family stories and history. It helped give me insight into why people volunteer and give time to their church. I learned that relationships are key to planned giving. Donors become lifelong friends as they grew more comfortable with sharing their financial situation. In addition, as many of these relationships grew, these same people became more willing to serve

---

1. Episcopal Church in Hawaii Annual Audit Report. Accessed April 9, 2022. *https://www.episcopal-hawaii.org/uploads/2/5/4/8/25486559/tech_audit_report_2020_final.pdf.*

on various committees and commissions within the diocese when I would ask them. Their volunteer service continues to benefit our diocese to this day in addition to their financial commitments.

In fact, the more I became involved with planned giving, I noticed increases in my own personal giving. I went from being a person who put a couple of dollars in the offering plate on Sunday to someone who moved toward the giving of a tithe (10 percent) and my wife and I have even included the diocese in our will. I was also able to learn about the various planned giving instruments and the changing tax laws. In my experience, people need to first be inclined to give, but when you can share with them about the creative ways they could potentially give, and receive various benefits, they would get excited about the potential legacy they could leave.

Extension of Faith

I like to challenge people to think of their finances as a matter of faith. Yes, we work hard in our day-to-day lives to support our families and accumulate some resources for the future, but God is ultimately the one that provides for our needs. We are merely stewards of what God has given us. Our giving back to God reflects our faith in the one who provides it. When people see that what they have is a result of God's faithfulness to them, they can in turn give it back to God.

It is difficult for someone to give a planned gift to the church if they do not see the issue as a spiritual matter. Jesus encourages us in St. Matthew's gospel to build up for ourselves treasure in heaven, and not treasures on earth. "For where your treasure is, there your heart will be also" (Matt. 6:21). Once people can grasp that financial matters are spiritual matters, they are far more open to committing to a planned gift. Once people cross over this threshold, it is much easier to discuss planned giving options.

As is true for most spiritual matters, people are at different levels of understanding and commitment. Planned giving is a marathon and not a sprint. It may take some people years, even decades, to get to the point of even being open to discussing options. When they do reach that point, it is much easier to discuss what they could do in response to God's faithfulness in their lives. The key for someone involved in religious planned giving is to be patient and let God work in the peoples' lives. My experiences in Hawaii may be similar or very different to your context, but I hope that you find my insights helpful.

Tithe in Death

Hawaii has some special challenges when it comes to doing planned giving. The most notable is the economy. Hawaii has one of the highest costs of living in the United States. With the median price of a single-family home in O'ahu over \$900,000[2] and the added expense of shipping everything from gasoline to toilet paper into the state leaves very little room for discretionary spending. On top of that, many families in Hawaii choose to pay for private education for their children. Hawaii has the highest private school enrollment in the country, with over 20 percent of Hawaiian students attending a private school. Tuition at these schools can reach up to \$20,000 per child per year.

Although the Bible talks about giving a tithe of 10 percent of one's income to the church, many people in Hawaii have a very difficult time achieving this goal or even coming close. The financial pressures of living and raising a family in the islands makes it very difficult for many to even think about giving anything close to an annual tithe in their lifetime. However, for those who own a home, wealth has often accumulated as the price of housing continually increases. They just do not have the liquid assets to give significantly while they are living.

Also, people feel that pledging or including the church in their will is a promise they have to keep. They are not comfortable putting it in writing because of their families' future economic uncertainties. I would frequently hear the excuses when beginning to have conversations with people about planned giving. One of my responses would be, "I know you are unable to tithe right now, but what about giving a tithe when you die?" I would ask them to simply consider giving 10 percent of their estate when they die. This is a simple starting point for many people, and I have been pleasantly surprised at how people have responded that this might be possible. As they think about leaving just 10 percent to the church, they quickly realize how doable this is and make a commitment to updating their will accordingly.

I have also noticed two benefits from this approach of asking for a tithe in death. The first benefit I have noticed is that some people over time increase the percentage amount of their gift beyond the initial 10 percent

---

2. "Here's Where You Can Often Buy Single-Family Homes on O'ahu for Under \$1 Million," accessed April 9, 2022. *https://www.hawaiibusiness.com/buy-single-family-homes-under-1-million-oahu-hawaii-real-estate/*.

ask. The second benefit I have noticed is that many of them increase their current giving to the church. In my experience, once donors commit to leaving a gift in their will to the congregation, their heart is fully behind supporting the ministry.

Church as Family

The importance of *Ohana* ("family" in Hawaiian) is a strong concept throughout the Asian and Pacific Islander population of the state. Hawaii is a true melting pot, with nearly 75 percent of the population being Asian, Hawaiian, Pacific Islander, or mixed race. There are strong ethnic cultural ties to taking care of family first and many feel an obligation to provide for children and grandchildren. Many in Hawaii could not afford a home or private school tuition if it were not for the financial help of parents and grandparents. Many feel it is their obligation to ensure that their children and grandchildren are left financially secure. This commitment to family can be a challenge when discussing planned giving with church members.

Building on that commitment, I first try to help people to see that the church is also a part of their family, their spiritual *Ohana*. I encourage them to think of the people with which they worship, and the community created there is just as important as blood relatives. As people consider this concept, some people come to realize that their church relationships are as strong, if not stronger, than those with actual family members. They start to see their church in a different light and open their hearts and minds to financially supporting their church like a family member.

I have also challenged people with the notion that if you really care about your family and their spiritual well-being, then you need to help ensure that the church will be here for your children, grandchildren, and generations beyond. As is often the case these days, most churches today are barely sustained by their pledge commitments and collection plate offering. There are no funds for capital repairs, improvements, or expansion. The development of endowments and planned giving gifts can go a long way to help put churches on a solid financial footing as it looks to the future. It has been exciting to see the light go up in people's eyes as they realize an important way for them to take care of their family when they are gone is to leave a planned giving gift to ensure that the church will be around to take care of their families' spiritual needs for generations to come.

Power in Numbers

In order to build momentum for planned giving in the diocese and its congregations, I felt it was necessary to create a legacy giving society. In 2010 we created the *Ho'ike Ulu* (which means growing/spreading witness in Hawaiian) Legacy Society for people in the diocese of Hawaii who have made a commitment to leave a planned gift to their church or to the diocese in their will or estate. Having a legacy society gave us the opportunity to bring the members together to acknowledge and thank them while they are living for their commitment to the work of the church in the islands. We have held many different types of receptions and special events over the years for legacy members.

In planned giving, recognition is vitally important. Private recognition is a must, but many Christians are hesitant to have their gifts made public. Also, for many people of Asian descent, financial matters are deeply personal and, several cultures dictate, should never be made public. This was one of my biggest challenges with getting the *Ho'ike Ulu* Legacy Society off the ground and moving forward, but found it was still possible to overcome these cultural barriers.

One of the first questions I ask someone who commits to providing a gift in their will and joins the legacy society is "may I publish your name as a society member?" For most people in Hawaii there is a strong reluctance to do so. I share with them that it will be an encouragement to others in the legacy society to know that they are not alone in seeking the long-term welfare of their church or the diocese. I also share with them that it could be the encouragement needed for someone considering making a planned gift. "Hey Joe, Sam just became a member of the legacy society. Would you like to join as well?" I might tell someone. It gets them thinking, "Sam did that? I know Sam. I know I can do the same thing. Maybe I should join too."

Due to the cultural aspects, not everyone has allowed the diocese to publish their name as a member of the legacy society, but I am happy to say that many have. After many years of faithful effort, I am convinced that this is an important element to build momentum for planned giving in any community of faith. People like to be a part of something bigger than themselves and a legacy society can help provide that for them.

It can be a challenge to get a legacy society up and running. The one element that I believe to be necessary for success is to have clear buy-in at the highest levels of leadership. In a denomination like ours, the bishop at the diocese level (or other presiding authority in a judicatory) needs to support the efforts and, ideally, be one of the first members of the legacy society as well as any other judicatory administrators, if possible. At the congregational level, long-term clergy, main lay leaders, treasurers, and other key volunteers should all be encouraged to become members. Leadership participation and support makes it so much easier when inviting someone to consider a planned gift, especially if they are actual members of the legacy society.

For those undertaking leadership roles in planned giving, I encourage you to learn from this book and to focus on what will bring you joy in this important work. Personally, I like meeting with people, learning their story, and asking them to be an important part of God's work in the community by committing to provide a planned gift when they pass on. I also realize that not everyone is like me and that most people do not like asking people for money. Yes, there are challenges to doing planned giving in a community like Hawaii, and you will have your own unique challenges. I believe what has made a difference for me is that I am not asking for something that will benefit me, but instead I am asking people to be involved in advancing God's kingdom here on earth for generations to come. That excites me and I hope it will excite you as well.

CASE STUDY

LIFE & LEGACY®

Arlene D. Schiff

"Providing Jewish communities with proven tools and training to help them secure their long-term financial goals is absolutely vital. Through the LIFE & LEGACY program, I am hopeful that we will be able to help sustain vibrant communities that allow future generations to enjoy our rich Jewish culture and heritage."

–Harold Grinspoon, Founder, Harold Grinspoon Foundation

Background

Established in 1991 by real estate entrepreneur Harold Grinspoon and, his wife, Diane Troderman, The Harold Grinspoon Foundation (HGF) funds creative programs to engage the Jewish community by meeting people where they are at key life moments and by providing access to the best of Jewish culture and tradition, while using philanthropy to encourage others to invest in the Jewish community.

LIFE & LEGACY® has its roots in San Diego, California, where Gail Littman (of blessed memory) and Marjory Kaplan, then CEO of the San Diego Jewish Community Foundation, launched the Endowment Leadership Institute (ELI) in 2004. Word of their success in motivating Jewish organizations to secure legacy commitments from their most loyal donors reached Harold Grinspoon, a philanthropist who is committed to preserving Jewish life.

In 2008, Harold invited Gail to launch a similar initiative in western Massachusetts, where he resides. Following its success along with two other similar initiatives, Harold decided to invest in a national program to motivate Jewish organizations to build their endowments by securing legacy commitments.

The first cohort of LIFE & LEGACY communities was accepted in the fall of 2012. Today seventy-two communities across North America (with more than 750 participating Jewish organizations) have partnered with HGF to integrate legacy giving into their philanthropic culture.

What is LIFE & LEGACY?

LIFE & LEGACY provides training, support, and monetary incentives to Jewish organizations who commit to securing legacy commitments to build their endowment. In the eight years since its launch, participating organizations in the United States and Canada have secured more than $1.2 billion in legacy commitments of which more than $130 million has already been placed in organization endowments. These endowments are distributing money each year to support operating budgets.

From large cities like Chicago, Illinois, to smaller ones like Chattanooga, Tennessee, more than 18,000 individuals have answered the call, making nearly 30,000 legacy commitments to date. Loyal donors are honoring values instilled by parents and grandparents, commemorating loved ones, and perpetuating Jewish values of generosity and *tzedakah* (righteousness.)

The success of LIFE & LEGACY is the result of a four-year structured curriculum. Our methodology is simple: we make endowment building an organizational priority by providing training workshops, holding organizational leaders accountable to reach specific goals in a specific time, and we reward them for doing the work. The program focuses on changing both organizational and community culture so legacy giving becomes a social norm. The goal is to assist organizations in developing a sustainable endowment building process that provides them with a steady stream of funding to support their operations in perpetuity.

LIFE & LEGACY does much more than support and encourage legacy giving. It is a community-building enterprise that emphasizes collaboration. The community-wide initiative brings together organizations that previously saw each other as competitors. They become trusted partners who cooperate, share resources, learn from, support, and celebrate one another. As a result, we create a stronger and more united Jewish community.

How It Works

To begin, a Jewish Federation or Jewish Community Foundation (JCF) (look in our appendix and this book's online resources for assistance in finding one) makes a commitment to help local Jewish organizations (synagogues, day schools, community centers, social services, etc.) within its catchment area build endowments through after-lifetime giving. Once accepted to be a LIFE & LEGACY partner, HGF assigns one of its three legacy community consultants to work with the community.

HGF commits to pay one-third of the Federation/JCF LIFE & LEGACY budget for each year of the four years, up to a maximum of $100,000 a year. Most of these funds are used to incentivize organizations to reach legacy commitment goals, but depending on the community budget, funds can also be used for staff salaries, marketing, and other program expenses. In most of the communities, the annual cost of the program is between $200,000 and $300,000. The Federation/JCF provides the remaining two-thirds of the annual budget either through their annual fundraising, proceeds from an endowment, or funding provided by individual donors. Communities submit a proposed budget at the beginning of each year. HGF makes a payment to the community at the conclusion of each year based on their actual expenses.

Each community is required to hire a legacy coordinator to administer the community-wide effort. The legacy coordinator (who works a minimum of three days a weeks) is responsible for administration of the program, planning and executing all training sessions, events and meetings, coordination of consultant visits, community marketing efforts, and supporting participating organizations to achieve their goals. They are the person on the ground, day in and day out, mentoring organizations throughout the process, helping them integrate legacy giving into their organizational culture in a sustainable way. The legacy coordinator is instrumental to the initiatives, success, as their main priority is to ensure that organizations maintain their commitment to the initiative and stay on track.

HGF's legacy community consultant leads all the training workshops (twelve or more over the four years), coaches and mentors the community's legacy coordinator, and meets with individual organizational legacy teams as needed to ensure each community implements a successful initiative. Prior to the Covid-19 pandemic, all workshops and team meeting were held in person. During the pandemic, legacy community consultants offered workshops and team meetings via a virtual format to keep organizations moving through the four-year process.

Upon acceptance, the Federation/JCF invites all the Jewish organizations in the community to attend a presentation titled "Why Legacy? Why Now?" The legacy community consultant shares why HGF started the program, busts myths about legacy giving, makes the case as to why organizations should participate in the initiative, and outlines program requirements. The Federation/JCF distributes an application and gives interested organizations two weeks to a month to complete. The application process can be as competitive or noncompetitive as necessary, depending on the number of Jewish organizations in the community and the amount of funding available for the initiative. The Federation/JCF establishes a lay committee to review the applications and selects ten to fifteen to partner with. Each organization forms a legacy team consisting of four to six professionals and lay leaders who commit to the concept of legacy giving and are willing to ask others to join them in leaving a legacy.

Incentive Grants

Incentive grants are a key component of LIFE & LEGACY's success. During the four-year curriculum, organizations are rewarded with cash for reaching annual legacy giving goals. We require that the incentive grants to local organizations be a minimum of $5,000 each year. We also encourage communities to offer a tiered incentive grant. This helps ensure organizations remain motivated once they reach the minimum incentive goals, as once their initiative gains momentum we want them to keep going.

Initially, the incentives are key to motivating organizations to do the work necessary to meet stated goals. As legacy teams experience success, they become internally motivated and begin applying the lessons learned through LIFE & LEGACY to their organization overall and its other development efforts.

The incentives also motivate donors to act on making a legacy commitment in a timely way, rather than putting it off as something they can do in the future, in much the same way a matching grant motivates donors to make a cash gift today.

Each organization is provided with a community tracking database (Excel formatted spreadsheet) that they use to track their legacy conversations, commitments, realized gifts, marketing, and stewardship efforts. This database is submitted to HGF on a quarterly basis so the legacy community consultants can monitor both individual organizational progress as well as the community's success overall. At the end of each year, this database is used to confirm that each organization has met the required goals and is eligible for the incentive grant.

Legacy Commitment Forms

Securing a legacy gift is a multistep process. LIFE & LEGACY uses a Letter of Intent (LOI) form to secure a donor's commitment to leave a legacy. This one form provides donors with the opportunity to declare their intent to support one or more organizations with either a current cash endowment gift or an after-lifetime commitment. The donor can disclose that they have already included organizations in their estate plan or make a commitment to do so within a time frame that works for them, of a year or less. All participating organizations use the same LOI. (You may download a version of this document through this book's website resources.) Once an organization receives a signed LOI, they begin stewarding the donor and continue to do so until the gift comes to fruition. Stewardship is a critical component of moving a donor to legally formalize their commitment and to ensuring that the commitment stays intact over the course of a donor's lifetime.

While the first two years of LIFE & LEGACY focuses on securing LOI's, it is important that legacy team members understand from the very beginning that legally formalizing a legacy commitment is an integral part of ensuring a gift comes to fruition. We have found that quality conversations during the initial stages lead to a greater likelihood that a donor will take the steps necessary to formalize their commitment in a timely way.

Once the donor's declared time frame on the Letter of Intent has passed, a legacy team member reaches back out to them to see if they have legally put their commitment in place and if not, offers to help them do so. Once the commitment is legally in place, the donor is asked to sign a Legacy Gift Confirmation (LGC) form stating so. (You may download a version of this document from this book's website.) While the donor's gift remains revocable throughout their lifetime, experience has shown that if a donor is stewarded appropriately, most legacy commitments remain in place.

If a donor does not disclose the value of their gift, organizations use an estimate. Based on our research, the national average for legacy gifts is in the $32,000–$72,000 range. We decided to be very conservative and most of our community partners use $25,000 as a placeholder. Actual gifts range from $1,000 to $10 million, with $52,000 currently being the value of the average legacy gifts received to date.

Stewardship

Keeping donors connected and showing our appreciation and gratitude over the course of their lifetime is the right thing to do and is key to keeping legacy commitments intact. Effective stewardship is stressed throughout the LIFE & LEGACY curriculum with the intent that organizations begin to integrate strong stewardship practices into their organizational culture and calendar from the very beginning.

A personalized handwritten thank-you note has been noted by donors as the one thing an organization can do to make them indefinitely loyal and so all legacy teams are encouraged to put in place a process where donors receive thank-you notes within forty-eight hours of having signed a LOI or LGC. (Please note this as a best practice noted in earlier chapters.) This thank-you note is followed up a few days later with a thank-you phone call from either the CEO or board president. These efforts lay the foundation for a series of stewardship activities throughout the year that express the organization's appreciation and gratitude for the donor's legacy commitment and keep them connected and feeling like they made a good investment. Other stewardship activities include sending holiday cards, listing donors' names, sharing donor testimonials, gathering legacy donors at least once a year as a group, and honoring legacy donors among each organization's "community."

LIFE & LEGACY requires each Federation/JCF to host an annual legacy celebration each year of the four-year curriculum. The purpose of this annual celebration is to bring together donors who have made a legacy commitment to one or more organizations to celebrate all those who have stepped forward to ensure the continued strength and vibrancy of the Jewish community.

Each community celebrates differently. Options range from a cocktail party with a few remarks and distribution of actual or representative incentive grant checks to sit-down dinners with paid speakers. Some organizations hold a standalone event; others integrate into an annual meeting or other gathering. Some organizations chose to have the same type of celebration all four years, others change it up. During the pandemic, many communities held their celebration virtually—using technology to ensure that legacy donors felt appreciated and stayed connected despite physical distancing.

The Curriculum

The first year builds the foundation for a sustainable legacy initiative. Legacy team members receive training and guidance on writing and implementing a legacy plan (like a strategic plan but focused on their legacy initiative), having legacy conversations, marketing their legacy initiative, and effectively stewarding donors. Incentive grants are awarded to each organization who attends the required trainings, prepares and implements a legacy plan, and secures a minimum of eighteen legacy commitments, with a stretch goal of twenty-five. Legacy coordinators use each organization's legacy plan to help them stay on track, in addition to sharing best practices with all the legacy teams, celebrating individual organizational successes and community benchmarks, helping teams brainstorm around challenges, and holding them accountable for achieving goals.

Year 2 builds on what was established in year 1. Organizations continue to implement their legacy plan, meeting with donors to secure another minimum eighteen legacy commitments with a stretch goal of twenty-five. They receive training on how to move donors who have made a legacy commitment to legally put that commitment in place, how to integrate legacy giving into all their fundraising efforts, and how to be more donor centric. Additional emphasis is placed on creating a legacy society, listing donor names, and publishing donor testimonials, as these efforts not only honor legacy donors but encourage others to join them.

Year 3 is focused on moving donors to legally put in place their legacy commitment. Each organization is incentivized to formalize a minimum of 50 percent of the legacy commitments secured in years 1 and 2 while further integrating legacy giving into their organizational culture by continuing to secure new commitments (generally four to six), market the concept of legacy giving, and implement a defined stewardship plan that can be sustained in perpetuity.

Year 4 builds on the efforts of the past three years and focuses on ensuring the sustainability of each organization's legacy initiative. Organizations are provided training and a sustainability workbook to assist them in thinking through the necessary steps to fully integrate legacy giving into their organizational culture. Each organization is incentivized to formalize a minimum of 75 percent of the commitments secured in years 1 and 2, secure new commitments (4–6), and implement their stewardship plan. At this point, legacy giving is becoming a social norm at both the individual, organizational, and community level.

Developing a Culture of Philanthropy

One of the long-term goals of LIFE & LEGACY is to change the culture of philanthropy in Jewish organizations. This culture shift occurs when organizations embrace fundraising as relationship based (as opposed to transactional), integrate development efforts and stewardship throughout the organization, treat the donor as a partner and investor, and offer donors various ways to make a difference in the organization.

A key role of the legacy coordinator is to help organizations take responsibility for their legacy initiative from the beginning and integrate it over time into the ongoing work of the organizations. If legacy teams do not take responsibility for making systemic changes in their organization, then this legacy effort is simply another "program," sure to lose steam when community support ends.

Conclusion

Endowments are no longer a luxury; they are a vital part of every nonprofit's financial stability plan. With the $59 trillion transfer of wealth[1] currently taking place, now is the perfect time to launch a legacy initiative. Donors who have supported your organization during their lifetime, when given the opportunity to continue to have an impact and ensure your financial future, will want to participate. Legacy giving is a perfect way to do so because it allows everyone to be a philanthropist, to leave a meaningful after-lifetime gift without impacting their current financial situation. While you may not be able to implement an initiative modeled after LIFE & LEGACY, what I hope you have taken away is that with some planning, a group of committed individuals who are willing to have conversations with your most loyal donors, setting goals and holding yourself accountable, your organization can take the necessary steps to secure its financial future. Based on the tremendous success of LIFE & LEGACY we know that a long-term legacy giving initiative can absolutely work for you. Stop thinking about it—just do it!

---

1. John J. Havens and Paul G. Schervish, *A Golden Age of Philanthropy Still Beckons: National Wealth Transfer and Potential for Philanthropy Technical Report* (Boston: Center on Wealth and Philanthropy, Boston College, released May 28, 2014), *https://www.bc.edu/content/dam/files/research_sites/cwp/pdf/A%20 Golden%20Age%20of%20Philanthropy%20Still%20Bekons.pdf*.

CHAPTER 8

Memorial Funds

Know Thyself

If you have read this far, you likely have a healthy and faith-filled view of your own ultimacy and of those whom you love. Facing your own issues around death and how you wish to be remembered are important internal conversations to have and could be enabled through some of the resources on end-of-life planning in this book's online resources. How would you like to be remembered? Do you have others in your family whose plans are very different from your own? Do you wish to memorialize in some special way someone you have loved, such as through a creation of a fund to sponsor ministries which were important to that person? If you created a designated fund while you were living, to be further funded at death, what would its purpose be?

In your personal plans, do you wish to be buried, cremated, interned, and do you have a preplanned and particular resting place? Obviously, your faith tradition and personal belief systems will guide many of these decisions, as will access to family graves and other options. How would you like to be remembered? Are there loved ones you would like to commemorate? And are there special funds you wish to create for maintaining where yours and your family's remains will be? Or is endowing your pledge of annual support a good choice for you?

Know Your Constituents

Do your constituents share any of your preferences? Unless you are all coming from a very similar cultural context, possibly, but even then, maybe not. Each person will have their own goals and desires regarding remembrance and recognition. As an informed leader, you will need to ask constituents how they wish to be remembered, as it may be very particular.

Although a legacy society thanks, recognizes, and raises awareness about planned giving to all constituents, there will never be any program or process that satisfies everyone equally. Individuals may have specific needs that are not fully satisfied through group events or personal recognition while living. There are some who wish for their family or themselves individually to be remembered on a building or named endowment, but there are many more who hope to enshrine a memory of a loved one who was gone too soon. Charities may have many opportunities to help a supporter fulfill this need to commemorate a beloved person in this way, especially through the creation of memorial funds.

Know the Basics

There are many aspects to honoring loved ones too diverse to detail for the many religious traditions who are reading this book. These general thoughts on memorialization and procedures for creating funds from current and planned gifts apply for both organizations and communities of faith. As an added benefit, these funds can easily be created during lifetime and then receive subsequent (and often substantial) additions through planned gifts.

Opportunities from Creating Memorial Funds

As planned giving leaders, it will be important to make confidential notes about some of these unique situations and to be mindful of opportunities for individuals to make these very special gifts. Retaining these possibilities in the secure records of your databases confidentially will be vital. Having endowment/designated fund and gift acceptance policies in place on how to create named funds and/or those for specific purposes will help make any conversations with potential donors easier and more productive. Of course, there are dangers in accepting restricted gifts of this kind, but they can also be wonderful opportunities for family legacies and the opportunities to have special funding for new or developing ministries, as long as they comply with your mission and the policies you have in place. Clarity about gift acceptance and designated fund procedures is important, as is having conversations with donors in advance of making a gift.

Funds are often set up by families to memorialize teenagers who died suddenly and tragically, and annual draws from these funds are used for a variety of ministries like youth education or other beneficial causes. There have also been scholarships awarded to high school seniors in memory of a beloved child who never made it that far. What is special for many of these memorial funds is that multiple family members and friends may continue to make gifts to the fund over a significant period of time, including planned gifts.

In my own family, after one of my beloved sisters died following a long illness, her husband and several members of our family made gifts to fund an endowment at her medical school to give scholarship funds to women who like my sister came from economically disadvantaged backgrounds and were also pursuing her specialized medical practice of holistic care for families. That family endowment fund has continued to grow from new gifts in the many years following her death and will be the destination of many planned gifts from my family. The motivation to continue a legacy of someone's kindness and grace is deeply moving for those who remember the named loved one. Giving to such funds are a cathartic way to allow for the deceased to continue their impact.

The desire to memorialize through giving is also noted in Dr. Lucinda Mosher's introduction and throughout this book. Gifts like this have been called "tribute bequests" and are highlighted in the work of Dr. Russell James from Texas Tech. His research from a 2014 survey showed that one of four donors increased their bequest if it honored a loved one.[1] As elaborated in the multiauthor United Church of Canada and Fr. Charles Cloughen case studies following this chapter, one's gifts can be both a memorial and a true testament to deeply held convictions. Such gifts continue blessed memories and enhance the ongoing story in a congregation or religious organization. Such honoring and memorializing are encouraged in a variety of faith traditions.

For some contexts, creating a variety of funds for memorials, families, and dedicated causes can be very effective for increasing generosity. Please review the many endowments and other dedicated funds created at Temple Shaarei Shalom in Boynton Beach, Florida, and the Islamic Foundation of Greater St. Louis (MO) noted in our online resources. Many of these funds would be well suited for receiving additional gifts from other donors as well as for future planned gifts.

---

1. Russell N. James, "Inside the Mind of a Planned Giving Donor," *World Documents*, accessed August 22, 2021, *https://vdocuments.net/inside-the-mind-of-the-planned-giving-donor-with-russell-james.html*; and Russell N. James, "An Emotional Connection," *Remember a Charity*, accessed August 22, 2021, *https://www.rememberacharity.org.uk/stories/an-emotional-connection/*.

Considerations for Memorial Funds

The concept of "pooling funds" is quite common, whether it is a family doing so to commemorate and continue the legacy of a loved one or a collaboration between likeminded individuals in a community of faith or constituents giving to an organization. For example, see M. Yaqub Mirza's case study noting "pooling" of gifts for a purpose as well as Yvonne Lembo's mention of a centralized "memorials" fund for a Lutheran congregation. Such funds can be used for undesignated gifts often accumulated over time to benefit a congregation when a decedent's request is "in lieu of flowers, please make a gift to X." Those types of memorials can benefit a congregation with gifts that can be used for any purpose. Encouraging giving to such funds may be a good choice for your charity. Those congregations with a cemetery, columbarium, or other means of physically housing the remains of deceased loved ones offer opportunities for creating a variety of memorial funds both for perpetual care and for opportunities to make gifts providing for the future burial of the poor; such charitable possibilities are tremendously important in the Muslim tradition.

Reporting to Family and Friends

As leaders, be diligent if your congregation creates memorial funds. As previously noted regarding maintaining trust and accountability, continue to be mindful of family members who may consider making additional lifetime donations leading to planned gifts. An annual reporting should be given to family members who request it to demonstrate that the fund is making grants for the purposes intended. Family members speak to each other and will carefully observe, especially at the congregational level, that funds are properly managed and disbursed. If there is a perception that funds are not being handled as originally specified, the other family planned gift allocations will quickly be changed or current donations to build up the fund may not be made.

Often organizations and congregations will invest most of their endowment funds together in a single account with an investment advisor for better fees and wider access to diverse investment options. Individual funds like the memorial funds discussed will need to be tracked separately for reporting and distributions; this activity is often called subaccounting. The ability to subaccount can be a tremendous opportunity for your congregation/

organization, as charities can share those reports with family and friends of the founders of the funds. This not only expands a sense of transparency and accountability, but it also demonstrates a professionalism not always witnessed in religious organizations or congregations.

Subaccounting and other types of fund reporting can encourage additional future donations from those who would support the fund's purpose. Many family members and friends could be inspired to add to the fund since they are made aware of its status and impact through regular reporting. Additionally, the ability to subaccount may encourage more supporters to create new memorial or other funds while they are living and continue to add to it later in life and through a substantial planned gift. This is often how universities fund new "chairs" or professorships as referenced in this book that will beneficially serve growing faith traditions in the United States and Canada.

Endowing a Pledge

Pledging may be a foreign concept for many faith traditions, though it has been the common way for raising annual funds and planning next year's budget for numerous mainline Protestant churches in the United States and Canada for decades. Basically, as a part of one's individual stewardship commitment of time, talent, and "treasure," members of a congregation would voluntarily confirm the expected amount of annual giving one's family would make toward the upcoming year's budget. Although I and many others involved in these efforts in churches would typically recommend that a congregation should be raising awareness of stewardship of resources throughout the year, many congregations focus their efforts of fundraising for pledges in the fall every year to get a sense of budgeting for the next year.

As reviewed in Yvonne Lembo's case study, some committed members of a congregation or organization who have been contributing consistently for many years may wish to consider making a significant gift at death so that their gift could be invested as part of the existing unrestricted endowment to provide an appropriately prudent draw to match the financial support they had been contributing during their lifetime, accounting for future inflation of course. This could be a wonderful opportunity for someone wishing to continue a legacy of support for generations to come. And, although not the right choice for everyone, this may be a good option that may have never been considered until it was raised as a possibility.

Take the Next Steps Forward

For all religious organizations and congregations, building into your fundraising efforts ways to memorialize loved ones through current and planned gifts can create bonds with donors that are very strong. Creating opportunities for general operating needs, scholarship funds, ministry engagements, and other occasions can be a wonderful way to create a current fund to which many individuals can contribute and enable even more significant giving at death.

Clearly planning and conforming these special memorial funds to the overall endowment or fundraising effort are important. Leaders will need to accept any restrictions attached to funds with great caution. Not every gift must be accepted, especially if it would burden future boards with restricted assets that could not easily be used. Balancing donor goals with the missional goals of a congregation or religious organization can be a challenge in these cases, especially when involving a significant donor.

Evaluate Your Efforts from Time to Time

If you have made the choice to encourage memorial funds and have documentation in place to guide both donors and leaders, planned giving and other leaders should plan to meet at least on an annual basis to determine if adjustments to policy are needed to better manage the assets for investment and reporting. Various questions may be considered. Are family members or friends making additional gifts? Are individuals being approached to add gifts on special memorial days, birthdays, or dates of death? This may continue a connection even after various family members have moved and changed their affiliation with the organization or congregation.

For congregations which have cemeteries or a columbarium, a similar annual review with the financial leaders of the parish will be valuable. Should additional space be opened in the cemetery or new niches created in the columbarium? Is it possible for the administrator to send a note annually to commemorate a family member who is buried or interred there? That could both enhance the relationship and may open a new opportunity for a memorial gift. And are there opportunities to make gifts to bury the poor who could otherwise not afford that? This would be a tremendous opportunity to be generous for many from a variety of faith traditions.

Summary of Main Points

- People are motivated to memorialize loved ones, and this is a deeply personal action. Be very cautious on naming practices for funds (not to mention buildings and rooms, such as if a name could ever be changed for a dedicated space). Family memory and emotions are very deep and sudden changes without explanation can be quite hurtful to remaining family members.

- Family-based or designated funds can encourage further "giving while living" as well as additions through ultimate gifts.

- Cemeteries, a columbarium, and other burial locations can be both challenges and opportunities. Make sure that policies are public and clear. Keep careful records and if gifts are given for perpetual care, track well and check with all state/provincial regulations.

CASE STUDY

Context for Planned Giving and an Opportunity for Testimony

Sarah Charters, Jane Harding, and Roger Janes

The United Church of Canada is the largest Protestant denomination in the country, created in 1925 when Methodists, two-thirds of the Presbyterian congregations, the Congregational Union of Ontario and Quebec, and the Association of Local Union Churches joined together. In 1968, the Canada Conference of the Evangelical United Brethren Church became part of The United Church of Canada. More recently, the United Church has joined in "full communion" with some of its ecumenical partners, such as the United Church of Christ (USA) and the Christian Church (Disciples of Christ) in the United States and Canada, meaning that clergy can move between the denominations and that we recognize each other's sacraments.[1]

Throughout the history of The United Church of Canada, giving to and through the denomination has been a part of our culture. At the time of church union in 1925, the assets of the merging denominations came together to support the work of the new church. A significant amount of those assets were the results of bequests from members whose generosity continued after they passed on. Since 1925, members have faithfully planned gifts to ensure the ministries they love can carry on. In fact, in 2013 when a review was done of all the endowments and long-term trusts that people had so generously gifted over the decades, archival documents from pre-union and the early 1930s through the 1990s were unearthed, examined, and some very carefully preserved, as they were old enough to crumble at a touch. One bequest was particularly striking. It was from the estate of a woman who died in the late 1920s. Her bequest was to be invested and $400 was to be granted each year to help those financially struggling in Hamilton, Ontario. The intent was for the monies to

---

1. "History of The United Church of Canada," *The United Church of Canada*, accessed July 18, 2021, *https://united-church.ca/community-faith/welcome-united-church-canada/history-united-church-canada.*

be spent down over time. What happened in fact, though, was that the investment did very well, and the fund still exists, although it now grants much more than $400 a year. Its purpose remains the same and nearly one hundred years later, the faith-filled generosity of one woman has touched the lives of thousands of people.

Planned Giving

Clearly, legacy, or planned giving, has long had a significant place in the life of the church. Over the last twenty-five to thirty years, we have tried many different ways of supporting this type of generosity in our midst. Between fifteen and thirty years ago, the denomination had regionally or locally deployed staff whose sole focus was to encourage individuals to make planned gifts—bequests, gifts of life insurance, annuities, charitable remainder trusts, etc. The staff would travel around giving workshops at congregations, gaining referrals and requests for follow up. They would meet with the individuals identified through those workshops and encourage and solicit gifts. Starting in the early 2000s, resource deployment in the church began to shift and fewer staff were employed in these gift-planning roles. By 2010, the deployed staff that remained began to focus not just on planned giving, but on helping congregations with their own revenue generation as well as encouraging giving to the denomination's work through the Mission & Service Fund. The shift coincided with the change in resourcing and with a change in church culture. It became harder for the gift planning staff to schedule workshops with congregations, and the number of referrals from those workshops dwindled.

The reason for the change at the local level is tied to the changing demographics in Canada and North America in general. As the people of the Greatest Generation pass away, the generations that follow are less inclined to give in the same patterns and with the same sense of duty of giving. That is not to say they are not generous; it just happens in a different way and requires different approaches than in the past.

One of our biggest areas of work in planned giving currently is to equip congregations to ask for, receive, and manage planned gifts. The focus of our deployed staff now is not to meet one on one with people interested in making gifts—we have a separate process for that. The focus now is to ensure that congregations have the education, confidence, and knowledge to be able to run and maintain their own planned giving programs.

To illustrate how we work in congregations, we offer two examples. The first is a first-person account from one of our deployed staff, now retired, about working with a congregation on a particular gift. The second account is from another of our deployed staff who helped a congregation set up a planned giving program. As you reflect on how to encourage planned giving in your congregation or religious organization, consider how you might do something similar, even with volunteers.

Example 1: Jane Harding Works with a Congregation to Set Up a Planned Gift

It was a beautiful day in the Okanagan. This central part of British Columbia is known for its warm summers and mild winters. Those that seek year-round recreation flock here to take advantage of skiing, snowshoeing, skating, swimming, fishing, hiking, and eating farm to table treats. It is also home to some of the most generous people on the planet.

It was in this context on a beautiful day that I met a donor who was not only a kind person with such a positive outlook on life, but a woman who deeply cared about her community and her church and its mission and ministry.

I was working as a stewardship and gifts officer for the United Church of Canada at the time. One of my favorite aspects of my work was the opportunity to meet with donors and share their dreams and plans for the church using their wills and estate planning. There are many creative ways to use your estate to create a gift/donation that will have lasting impact on the people you leave behind.

My inspirational donor was very clear with me. She had a debilitating disease that would claim her life within about three years. She didn't want to "dilly-dally" around. She didn't have time for that. During our first encounter, she was quite well and needed little help to meet me at the coffee shop to get to know one another. She shared her interesting memories and her thoughts on the world. She felt strongly that people should help each other as much as possible. Of course, I agreed. We explored various ways she could leave a substantial gift to her congregation in her will for ongoing mission work.

Over the course of our next visits, she became clearer about what she wanted to accomplish with her bequest. She also had some very dear friends that she wanted to leave bequests.

Finally, she decided to leave her home to the church. She did not believe in strings attached to the gift except that the house was to be sold after everyone received their bequests and gifts from it. She did not want the house to be cleaned up and rented out with a stream of income to the church. She said that would make the church landlords and she didn't feel that God was calling the church to be that. She wanted to leave a lump sum of funds to the congregation that would inspire them to accomplish great things and help as many people as possible. What vision.

In February of 2020, she died. I had the opportunity to see her in her last week and she had so much clarity and so much joy about her gift to the church, her beloved home. She was at peace with her decisions. She had some wonderful, rich friendships through the church, and she chose a dear and willing friend to be her executrix. It was her job to go through the house, make sure everyone on her list received the personal item she wanted to give them, and then bestow the financial gifts. It's not an easy task to serve as executrix and I was happy to help her jump through the hoops.

Then it was up to the team to clean the house and put it on the market. The house sold quickly and after all the expenses were covered, the congregation received approximately CAD$500,000.

The congregation formed a "vision" team to look at the best way to honor the donor and to also help as many people as possible. They kept about $100,000 in an accessible bank account, so they could be responsive to community needs in the first year. They already supported many ministries and did hands-on mission work with homeless people in the neighborhood. There is always so much need. I applaud their decision to take a little time to make good and informed decisions.

With the assistance of the United Church of Canada Foundation, the balance of the funds is now invested. They will use the first five or so years to see what sort of earnings they will make and will then create an endowment to be named after the donor.

The board of the church remains committed to criteria specified by the donor to use the funds to help as many people in need as possible. Through her generosity and care for those in need, the donor became an amazing role model of kindness and discipleship to the other members of her congregation. She blessed future generations that she will never meet just by being her generous, forward-thinking self. That's about as faithful as it gets.

Example 2: Roger Janes Helps a Congregation Set Up a Planned Giving Program

When working with a congregation as field staff on any stewardship "best practice," I always try to employ three essential tasks—inspire, invite, and thank. Here is how I do this with planned gifts.

Inspire

It starts with a relationship. A pastoral charge in New Brunswick approached me in late 2016 to make a stewardship visit because they wanted to increase generosity and grow giving. Every presentation and workshop I do includes a conversation around planned gifts. This one was no different. Their next question was a very common one, "Can you come back and tell us more about planned giving?" It is my experience that once congregation leaders become aware of the power and potential of planned gifts, they want to know more, and they want their other congregants to know more. So, I went back to the church a second time and met with leaders and other interested folks. We discussed the different types of planned gifts. I shared our denominational resource for setting up a planned gift program and several sample materials they could adapt and use to educate and motivate their members. Many of the tools focused on how individuals can use their estate and accumulated resources to make an incredible impact on a ministry they love. There were also personal testimonies from past donors whose ability to offer these gifts touched their own lives profoundly. I find that many generous church donors have not been prompted by their church to prayerfully consider making a planned gift. Informing and inspiring, then, is very important, and often enough for some people to decide to make such a gift. However, not everyone will be motivated to act, so we do need to make a personal ask.

Invite

The congregation now had the tools and the motivation to set up their own planned giving program. The key now was to keep the momentum going and encourage them to think about next steps. They didn't need much support at this stage, but many congregations do; most need to start with selecting a small team and then quickly creating a time-bound plan about how they will inform and ask for planned gifts. The strategy should be broken down into small, concrete steps. My role changes at this point to that of resource person and cheerleader. Follow-up is key. I troubleshoot and further encourage if needed. In this congregation's experience, they promptly set up a small team, appointed a knowledgeable just-retired financial planner as the chair, and got busy. This reminds me of a crucial tip for congregational leaders—do not leave this committee's selection to a sign-up sheet; making personal invitations to appropriate leaders is a key to success. When in the invite stage, I remind leaders that when they are encouraging planned gifts, the relationship is what matters. The more personal the invite, the greater the positive response. I offer to meet personally with any person that has any questions or who would like to explore making a gift.

Thank

Planned gifts come from a place of gratitude for the giver, and thankfulness on the part of the receiving congregation or ministry is critical to future success. Not every donor may expect to be thanked, but every donor wants to know that their gift made a difference. Making gestures of thanksgiving for planned gifts, including incorporating these into a service of worship, tells everyone, not just the donor or the donor's family, that their gift is meaningful and appreciated, and it offers us an opportunity to teach others about planned giving! It is no coincidence that congregations who receive planned gifts with publicly expressed gratitude receive more gifts than those who do not. The congregation has already received two gifts since they started their planned giving program four years ago.

Learning and Conclusions

What we have learned through the years working with individuals and congregations is that it is vitally important to plan carefully and to communicate clearly. When working with individuals, fostering and nurturing genuine, honest, and open conversations between the prospective donor and their intended beneficiary means that we have clarity when the bequest arrives. There is no wondering whether the donor meant this program or that aspect of ministry. There are no surprises in terms of the scope of the gift or how to use it correctly. It can also lead to increased connection, not only between the donor and the congregation, but within the community of faith itself as the members discover the passions within their midst and focus on the meanings for their current and future ministry.

When working with congregations, clarity comes through creating the foundations for the planned giving program. It's the structures, the policies, the work groups or committees, the reporting, etc. that provide insight into where the community is called to share ministry, their future directions, and how to handle both expected and unexpected gifts with the utmost care and compassion for the intent of the donor.

As we do our work now, in the midst of demographics where the majority of regular church attenders are over sixty, if not seventy years of age,[2] we recognize the short window of time we have to enable members and friends to create meaningful and meaning-filled gifts for the ministries that are closest to their hearts. We will continue to focus on offering opportunities and seeking out individuals and communities of faith ready and prepared to do this wonderful work. We thank God for the many generous people who are now part of the Communion of Saints, and for those that are still with us, who have carefully arranged their plans, and for those who wish to do so.

In conclusion, successful planned giving efforts combine the emotional commitment of your members as well as an understanding of the best process for encouraging people to make these special gifts. All religious nonprofits and congregations can learn from these examples that it is your member's devotion to the transformational mission of your organization which will move their hearts to make these gifts.

---

2. Private survey, "2011 United Church of Canada Identity Survey" by Jane Armstrong Research Associates.

CASE STUDY

Planning Your Estate: What Does It Mean to Give a Percentage? What Does It Mean to Give from Your Heart?

Charles E. Cloughen Jr.

I spent the first four years in ministry as an assistant at an affluent congregation in Providence, Rhode Island. At the request of their well-respected rector, I attended all meetings of their parish governing board. During that time, I heard we had an endowment from which we took some funds each year to balance the budget. That was all I knew about endowments.

In 1973, I was called to be rector of St. Matthew's Church, Jamestown, Rhode Island, a pastoral-sized church on an island in Narraganset Bay. I served there for nine years. When I arrived, I knew nothing about planned giving. That subject had not been covered during my three years of study at seminary.

I used home visitations to get to know my congregation. I remember calling on a longtime parishioner who lived off the main road on the island (back then you made visitations by just stopping by during the day). When I stopped by one day, I found him at home. His house was modest, with green shingles. An old Mercedes Benz sat in the driveway. Wearing work clothes, he invited me into his living room for tea where I sat in a well-worn chair. Our conversation covered a number of topics. He told me that he had never married, but he had a cousin on the island with whom he shared a weekly dinner at her home. He admitted that he was not an every-Sunday churchgoer, but he financially pledged because he cared about his church. I heard from others in this small community about his frugality. He also owned a family farm that raised cattle.

In 1979, he died peaceably of old age. I officiated at his funeral in the church and at his burial on the island. In a few months we received notice that he remembered St. Matthew's in his will for $5,000. He also bequeathed $5,000 to our island's library where he liked to visit. In addition, he made specific bequests to his favorite cousin with whom he dined, to a deceased cousin who had dug clams for a living, and to two lady friends. His 248-acre family farm went to a local land preservation society. The rest of his estate went to two prominent New England institutions and the local hospital.

The shock for me and the community was that these three final beneficiaries received checks for about $3,000,000 each. It was clear to me after reading the will that it was an old will and his estate had grown significantly since he had made his original plans. His cousin had been dead many years. His frugal lifestyle meant that the dividends were reinvested, increasing the value of the estate exponentially.

I served St. Matthew's as a pastor to the entire island. I was one of the unofficial chaplains to the police department and fire department. When someone standing on the bridge connecting Jamestown Island to the mainland or Newport, either the Roman Catholic priest or I would be called to talk the person back from the edge.

My work with the fire department bore fruit in a surprising way. Behind St. Matthew's, in a small house lived "Windy," a retired veteran and a member of our volunteer fire department's fire police. When the fire alarm rang, Windy would race to the fire and set up a perimeter to keep members of the public safely back from the situation so the firefighters could do their work safely. Windy had this nickname because he loved to talk. One never had a short conversation with Windy. He was independent and respected on the island.

One day in the winter of 1979 he caught me outside as I was entering the church office and asked if he could speak to me. I invited him into my office, and I have never forgotten the conversation. Windy shared he had been diagnosed with advanced cancer and had a short time to live. He had no close relatives, only two distant cousins. He said he had witnessed my ministry and asked me to help him plan for what lay ahead. I agreed to help. I checked with an attorney in my congregation who then advised Windy to set up a power of attorney. As Windy worked on his will, he shared with me what our church meant to the community. He told me wanted to leave his small home and savings account to the church. Since he was not a member of St. Matthew's, I was shocked! He drew up his will with an attorney's help and named that attorney the executor of his estate.

I ministered to him when he had to enter a nursing home, and he died peaceably a few months later. He had a simple funeral at St. Matthew's, and I scattered his ashes off the rocks of Beavertail. When his estate was settled, Windy left St. Matthew's some $40,000 for the ministry of the church, specifically to care for the residents of Jamestown, the community that Windy loved.

These two experiences changed my perspective about bequests. In most cases, the individuals or charities who receive bequests from an estate will be best served if the bequests are stated as percentages rather than dollar amounts. Out of an almost $10,000,000 estate, the church to which the owner of the family farm—and other valuable assets—belonged and about which he deeply cared received very little. If he has designated just 1 percent of his estate to the church, St. Matthew's would have received $100,000. He had made his will when his estate was significantly worth less: probably less than $1,000,000 in value versus the final $10,000,000 value of his estate. On the other hand, "Windy," one of the most financially limited residents on the island, gave all he had to the church and left the largest bequest the church had received to that date.

I left St. Matthew's as rector in 1982. When I checked in with them recently, I learned that their endowment funds now total over $1,000,000, having grown substantially invested with the Diocese of Rhode Island Investment Trust. The church also has a trust of over $100,000 whose income is used for outreach.

Since my experience at St. Matthew's, when I make a presentation about estate planning as a planned giving consultant, I always stress the importance of designating percentages rather than dollar amounts for beneficiaries. I also note that it is not always the wealthy who are most generous, but also ordinary folks who simply love their church.

When I do a presentation, I begin with the statement "For all of you present, there is a 100 percent mortality rate." We all will one day die; I then ask, "Do you have a will?" This is a trick question. Either you have your own will/estate plan or the state in which you reside has one for you. When they hear how the state will divide up their assets, few people like what they hear. And nothing will go to the church or to a charity. I also ask whether their grown children or heirs will need their entire estate. In most cases the answer is "no." Often, they realize they would like to include bequests to their church and one or more charities. When they do this, they are raising the church to the level of one of their family.

When I preach on stewardship my sermon title is "No gift is too large." I ask the congregation, "What is the largest financial gift in the Gospels?"

There is usually some hesitation but with some coaching finally a parishioner will murmur "The Widow's Mite," found in Mark 12:41–46. She gave all she had. I then ask what the second largest gift is? Usually there is some confusion, and I remind them about Zacchaeus, found in Luke 19:1–10. Zacchaeus, a despised tax collector and a short man, wanted to see Jesus, so he climbs a tree. Jesus notices him in the tree and says, "Zacchaeus, hurry up and come down; for I must stay at your house today." Zacchaeus welcomes him and says, "Look, half of my possessions, Lord, I will give to the poor; and if I have defrauded anyone of anything I will pay back four times as much." What a generous gift. How large or generous a gift is depends on your financial resources and obligations.

When I consider a person's generosity, I always consider it as a percentage of the person's resources. What you will leave in your bequests should depend on your net worth. Most of us with a few hours of work could figure out what we are worth today. But what will it be after our husband or wife dies? Will our home be worth 20 percent more than it is now? Or 20 percent less? Will the stock market be 10,000 points higher or 10,000 points lower? Have you or your spouse spent five years in a nursing home, depleting your assets? We have no way of knowing what our estate will be worth when God calls us home. Using percentages makes it fair to all.

In my presentations I always talk about the "Three Testaments." The first, often called the Old Testament or Hebrew Scriptures, tells us about Creation, the Exodus, and the words of the Hebrew prophets. The second, called the New Testament or Christian Bible, contains the story of the birth of Jesus, his life, his death, and resurrection. The Third Testament can be called your Last Will and Testament. When your family gathers to learn about the contents of your will, they will hear what you really cared about and who or what you are thankful for—your family (husband, wife, children), your close friends, your church, your college, and/or community organizations.

In my presentations, I always share my Third Testament—my will/ estate plans. I have two biological children and two stepchildren who all call me "Dad." Each will receive 20 percent of my estate. Then 20 percent of my estate will go to charity: 5 percent will go to Hobart College in Geneva, New York, that has enabled me to live a life of consequence, 5 percent will go to Berkeley Divinity School at Yale that prepared me for a priesthood of over fifty years, 5 percent will go to the American Friends of the Episcopal Diocese of Jerusalem of which I am a past president, and finally 5 percent will go to the congregation I served for eighteen years, St. Thomas's, Towson, Maryland, now through a merger, St. Francis Episcopal Parish, Timonium-Lutherville. I also have a $10,000 gift annuity for the Cathedral of the Incarnation, Baltimore, Maryland, where I now attend.

As you can see, I have put into practice what I preach.

AFTERWORD

In Time of Covid-19

Margaret M. Holman and James W. Murphy

When Covid 19 first appeared on everyone's radar, few would have imagined the enormous impact it would have on the entire world and few people in fundraising completely understood how it would radically change 2020 and 2021, especially in how we would seek to engage our constituents and donors. This book is written as Covid continues to be clearly with us, even as vaccines, and now booster shots, are being widely distributed. There continues to be hope for some returns to normalcy in 2022. However, the lessons learned during this difficult time bring a variety of opportunities for reassessment and new engagements.

Margaret's Perspectives

We all thought the pandemic would be short-lived, over in a month or two. Planned gift officers (PGOs) tend to take the long-term view in most cases, so the thinking was that people would be back at work within a couple of weeks, or a couple of months at the longest. Many had just sent out planned gift marketing pieces that emphasized the common fears of planned gift donors: living too long, outliving their resources, or being unable to care for themselves. Not only did many of those publications not reach their prospects/donors in a timely fashion—the post office was unable to deliver most mail for weeks—but these mailings also emphasized what we know now to be the wrong message at the wrong time.

Planned gift marketing vendors were scrambling to construct new messaging and development officers were hesitant to send out any planned gift marketing as the days and weeks lengthened and the number of people ill and dying continued to grow. Staffs were working remotely, events were canceled, and we discovered that our oldest planned gift donors and prospects really didn't know anything about connecting virtually.

Everyone paused to take a breath. Then virtual groups of PGOs sprang up, trading stories and techniques. Our partners in the law profession began to report a huge uptick in calls and e-mails to establish or revise wills. National media began covering this phenomenon. About three or four months after the close down was declared, planned giving programs began connecting with their current legacy society donors. They were calling to check in, to see how people were faring and to offer support. Faith-based organizations began having weekly prayer meetings—but discovered that it took quite a bit of hand-holding to instruct people how to use conference calls. Once they were able to successfully engage donors, pastors became involved, hosting the calls and offering prayers and Bible readings to comfort and assure people that they were not forgotten.

The next step for many organizations was to survey their donors about their current circumstances and to take the time to segment their lists of prospects to be able to get the right message to the right person at the right time. Surveys were done electronically to those who had viable e-mail addresses. The response rates climbed because people were at home checking e-mail and looking for a way to remain connected to the outside world. Many organizations took the time to perform a file overlay (or database review comparing various records) to identify or update their planned gift prospect pool. They looked for those frequent, longtime, older donors who might have aged up into the planned gift prospect pool or slipped under the radar.

Armed with this knowledge, and sometimes with the assistance of planned gift marketing vendors, they developed new, more appropriate messages of hope and resiliency. Gradually newsletters were developed, direct mail campaigns returned, and prospects began to respond, especially now that they had already been to their attorney or were contemplating contacting their attorney to update or add to their wills. So now the right message was going to the right people at the right time—about the time of the exciting announcement of an available vaccine.

What about those events that PGOs had planned? Naturally, due to the ages of many planned gift donors and prospects and the fact that they were the most vulnerable to the virus, live events were sadly put aside. Instead, in addition to weekly calls or monthly prayer calls, PGOs began experimenting with virtual will seminars (not typically a success) or other gatherings. The key to success seemed to be waiting until the summer/fall of 2020 when older people were more familiar with the internet and how to use it for virtual meetings. The most successful planned gift events were not about planned giving, rather they were about the status of the organization and the people it served. (Please note the importance of demonstrating impact from earlier chapters.) Planned gift donors were anxious about the welfare of staff, if programs were able to continue, and wanted to be reassured that their past giving and future giving would support the mission. For some planned gift donors, this was their first exposure to the CEO or the program director. They liked it. It broadened out their understanding of the scope of the organization and they really felt as though they were part of the family. Nearly all of the organizations who tried this have plans to continue this into the future.

What also helped is that one organization sent printed invitations for these events along with a sheet describing how to log on to Zoom or Microsoft Teams or Google. These instruction sheets included pictures of the screens, making it easy for the participants to follow along.

What about closing planned gifts? Only one organization was successful in having several face-to-face meetings and then only after both the PGO and the donor had been fully vaccinated, and the weather cooperated to allow them to sit outside over a steaming cup of coffee. This inability to meet personally with donors had its obvious downsides, but the upside was that PGOs didn't have to fly to Chicago or Miami or Los Angeles. Once donors became comfortable with using virtual meeting platforms, it was easier to schedule a visit, complete with shared coffee or tea, and to have meetings simultaneously with other decision makers, such as the donor's spouse, family, and financial partners.

The outcome of these challenging times? Many relationships were deepened, more regular contact was made, more gifts were closed, and the message about how to leave a legacy was refined.

Jim's Perspectives

Similar to Margaret's experience, within a couple of months after Covid began to lock things down in March 2020, I was contacted by several Episcopal dioceses seeking to have online webinars, recorded both for donors to learn more about the different types of planned gifts, and also to help train leaders in how to set up and sustain a planned giving effort in their congregations. Several of these dioceses had been holding off taking action, even before the pandemic began. However, the shock of so many people contracting the virus so quickly and the ongoing reports of hospitals filling up rapidly appeared to have an effect. To me, it appeared much like those occasions when a close friend dies suddenly, and one's own mortality becomes so much more "real." Based on reports from the leaders with which I was working, judicatory (diocesan) leaders reported that many parishioners became more comfortable taking some actual steps to move forward with reviewing their end-of-life plans and considering possible planned gifts. Although some leaders may have found the increase in activity as morbid or "opportunist," others felt that their languishing efforts had suddenly become unstuck, and this was an opportunity to begin to move forward on efforts that they previously struggled to stimulate.

Whether it was the shock of the mortality-impacting aspects of Covid or the tremendous volatility in the markets, I and other denominational foundations noted an increased interest in creating Life Income Gifts. A BNYMellon Bank study in 2020 confirmed that an increase in planned gifts was actually taking place, especially for charitable gift annuities.[1] With the opportunity to create a mutual benefit gift like a CGA providing fixed and assured income, several donors who may have been considering such a gift began to investigate them from April through September, which is normally a slower time of the year for LIG creation.

In my experience and that of other religious fundraisers I spoke with in 2020, the necessity of having meetings through video and other technology seemed to finally break down the remaining, but long-standing, resistance to that technology. Many constituents grew not only comfortable with online video conferencing but would attempt to make use of it as a replacement moving forward. In fact, according to research done by well-known religious fundraising firm CCS, 61 percent of their survey respondents in 2020 held a virtual fundraising event and 56 percent of respondents held a virtual major gift solicitation.[2] I believe that the new comfort with using online technology for meeting and communicating also broke down resistance to taking chances in doing online events in general. I even worked with a cathedral that easily made the choice to replay a prerecorded ECF webinar on planned gifts for its Sunday adult forum instead of trying to put together a thinly attended, masked, and socially distanced in-person educational opportunity.

I believe the comfort with virtual events will only increase even after people return to regular in-person gatherings. As a leader, please know that

---

1. "2020 Annual Charitable Gift Report," *BNY Mellon Wealth Management*, accessed August 1, 2021, *https://www.bnymellonwealth.com/articles/strategy/annual-charitable-gift-report.jsp*.

2. CCS, *Snapshot of Today's Philanthropic Landscape 2021*, *CCS Fundraising*, accessed July 31, 2021, *https://go2.ccsfundraising.com/rs/559-ALP-184/images/CCS_Philanthropic_Landscape_2021.pdf?aliId=eyJpIjoid2ZQbDB1amxZR0FGc3lkeSIsInQiOiJTeWN4dG5lSXRSWkZOdmZuTWNabEp3PT0ifQ%253D%253D*.

this new comfort with video interaction may inspire other innovations. One of the curious developments I witnessed and which I think will be retained, was replacing the labor-intensive and space consuming "parish bazaar" (auctions to raise extra funds by gathering member donated furniture and other household items for sale on the church grounds). Several congregations I spoke with have told me that they had been doing annual in-person Bazaars for many years. The events raised needed funds for the congregation and often benefited their ministries to local communities. In 2020, participants could simply take pictures or videos of items to be donated, post them for review (live or recorded), and then individuals bid for them virtually and then arranged a convenient future pick up, all online. Several parish leaders, feeling suddenly unburdened by the technology, told me they may never do another live auction.

I also believe that this new obvious comfort with technology will be the final push for congregations to be willing to use a planned giving tool I have been encouraging for years: recording videos of individual testimonies of confirmed planned givers and of other storytelling. Capturing these highly personal and unique recordings provide a set of highly impactful resources that can be used and reused for years to come. In addition, they may well afford an opportunity to record a "living history" of a congregation from its members. (Having such recordings will also benefit any organization.) Due to the proliferation of cell phones and laptops with quality cameras, congregations and organizations can easily record and catalog such "testimonials" of their legacy society members and other planned giving donors for future use. In addition to creating a planned giving video library of affirmations for the future mission and ministry of the community of faith, it also creates a record of many of the wonderful members who have supported the institution for years. How heartening to have these living memories so accessible. What might your congregation/organization do to record its most loyal supporters and their stories for why they give and remain a part of your impactful story?

So far, I learned of only one Episcopal church that did a live legacy society event virtually. However, I confirmed at least two synagogues also conducted legacy society events during Covid and I hope that there were many more. Online events are a great consideration for the future even after most gatherings return to normal. However, the recording of evocative videos and the elimination of travel for meetings and events should only grow due to the convenience and cost savings. In fact, for many gatherings among religious leaders, I foresee an ongoing mixing of virtual and in-person content and events. For example, a major gathering of denominational foundation personnel in December 2021 was planned as a combination of in-person attendees video conferencing with other non-travelling attendees.

I cannot predict exactly what will happen with Covid by the time this book is distributed, but trusting in science, the diligence of our national leaders and the lessons of history, though online interactions will certainly increase, humans remain social creatures that crave interaction. From a religious perspective, faith development and the passing on of wisdom and tradition are best done in community. Though we may change some aspects, and perhaps be more mindful of wearing masks and sanitizing, we will gather again to pray, worship, commiserate, support each other, celebrate, and take action to do good works that improve the lives of others and our world.

Friends, always remember to focus on building trust and building relationships, no matter what! Be creative, try something new, and push the boundaries you may fear. Even if new attempts fail, few are complete disasters and most normally offer opportunities from which to learn. In addition, when incredible challenges like Covid force your congregation or organization to change your plan suddenly and radically, look for the benefits which may arise longer term, such as the opportunities presented from saving costs from limited travel or eliminating the time-consuming aspects of something, such as the burdens of reselling items at a church bazaar!

CONCLUSION

Bringing all of this together, there are so many ways of learning the basics of planned giving and figuring out what can motivate your supporters to finalize one or more gifts. I hope that the guidance, pointers, and insights we have shared will be helpful as you move forward with your efforts. I hope that the many case studies by leaders from various faith traditions have been helpful and inspiring to you as well.

Please contact me through my website www.murphyjw.com, to offer feedback on this book and its many resources, both printed and online. I hope that we can continue to improve on all of them overtime and keep them updated. If you feel that your faith tradition or denomination was not captured in this work, please let me know and please feel free to share resources that you think would be beneficial to congregations/organizations in your tradition.

I hope in a future endeavor that I and others can address the many ways which congregations and religious organizations of all kinds can thrive in the future. Even as situations change, and new challenges are presented, there are many practical steps leaders can take now to improve circumstances. I hope that all leaders will be open-minded enough to consider what other faith traditions or denominations are doing to help their faith tradition flourish. Since mainline Christian denominations are struggling the most at this time, I will encourage those leaders to seek the wisdom of many who are trying new organizational practices to bolster their position.

Because I have witnessed so many financial missteps among congregations, I will suggest the recently published books *Creating Financially Sustainable Congregations* by James L. Elrod Jr. (Church Publishing, Inc.) and *We Aren't Broke: Uncovering Hidden Resources for Mission and Ministry* by Mark Elsdon (Wm. B. Eerdmans) as great resources. Both focus on financial transparency and taking risks to refocus missional priorities in new ways. Elsdon even expounds a vision of recasting congregational assets, such as underutilized real estate into affordable housing, and other mission-based efforts to produce new income streams.

Building endowments, increasing alternative income opportunities, and enhancing donor support, especially through planned giving, will be key to the future of many congregations and religious organizations. Relying solely on annual member contributions is actually more of a recent development than you might think from the 1800s. Many faith traditions have been comfortable for centuries to expand their income streams by building endowments, *waqfs*, partnerships in developing housing and communities, rentals and leasing (including those recently for cell towers and parking), air rights, and other creative options. Though these practices need to grow, they are already quite common. According to the Lake Institute, 62 percent of congregations receive money from renting facilities and over a third or 34 percent have an endowment.[1] Be open to those possibilities as I hope you are now open and excited about building up opportunities for planned gifts and encouraging your faithful supporters to raise you to the level of family!

And finally, as has already been said in other places in this book, regardless of what the future holds, building trust through good fiduciary actions, by thanking our donors regularly and especially be actively listening to the needs of our supporters, will carry your congregation or organization through any number of expected or unknown challenges in the future. Through your deep faith in your congregation or favorite religious organization, as a volunteer or paid staff member, your own conviction and commitment can bring about exciting new opportunities!

May God's blessings always be upon you and those you care for and support.

---

1. David P. King, Christopher W. Munn, Brad R. Fulton, and Jamie L. Goodwin, *The National Study of Congregations' Economic Practices* (Indianapolis, IN: Lake Institute/Indiana University/Lilly School of Philanthropy, 2019), *https://www.nscep.org/wp-content/uploads/2019/09/Lake_NSCEP_09162019-F-LR.pdf.*

ACKNOWLEDGMENTS

I want to thank all of my fellow contributors to this book for their dedication, attention to detail, and their faith! Your varied wisdom and insights will be greatly appreciated far beyond your current faith traditions! My thanks to the great people of Church Publishing, especially Nancy Bryan for supporting and guiding me as I pulled this book together. Thank you, Donald Romanik, president, and all of my colleagues of the Episcopal Church Foundation for their support through the years. I thank my initial teachers in planned giving at NYU, Davida Isaacson and Margaret Holman, to whom I am also grateful for making contributions to this book. I also thank a number of friends and colleagues who pointed me in the right directions for extending my network of interfaith and ecumenical contacts, including the Episcopal Church's Margaret Rose; Episcopal Relief and Development's Rob Radtke and Esther Cohen; Anglican Church of Canada contacts Eileen Scully and Deborah Barretto; and many other friends and colleagues: Fakhir Ahmad, Drew Barkley, Meighan Corbett, Pat Daly, Ahmed ElHattab, Mohamed Elsanousi, Caryn Feldman, Seamus Finn, Leslie Fleisher, Steve Gross, Kimberly Jetton, Khalid Latif, Bashar Qasem, Jawaad Rahman, Zead Ramadan, Greg Rousos, David Saginaw, Nikky Singh, Manzoor Tariq, Erin Weber-Johnson, as well as Lucinda Mosher (who also contributed a wonderful introductory chapter to this book) and the amazing Robert Sharpe Jr. (now of blessed memory) for his wisdom and insights through the years. And a very special "thank you" to my former ECF colleague Amy Rome for your feedback and guidance on my earliest drafts.

Online Resources: www.murphyjw.com

ABOUT THE CONTRIBUTORS

(full biographies online at www.murphyjw.com)

Sarah Charters, CFRE, United Church of Canada Foundation, President & Director of Philanthropy, The United Church of Canada

The Rev. Charles E. Cloughen Jr., Author, Planned Giving Officer at the Cathedral of the Incarnation, Baltimore, Maryland, and Former Director of Planned Giving, Stewardship and Development for the Episcopal Diocese of Maryland

Jane Harding, Stewardship and Gifts Officer (Retired), United Church of Canada

Margaret M. Holman, President of Holman Consulting

Davida Isaacson, Former Director of Planned Giving and Endowments for WNET and Senior Philanthropic Advisor for The Seeing Eye, Inc., in Morristown, New Jersey

Roger Janes, Community of Faith Stewardship Support Staff, Eastern Canada, United Church of Canada

Anwar Khan, President of Islamic Relief USA

Yvonne Jones Lembo, Regional Gift Planner, ELCA Foundation

Karl Mattison, Vice President of Planned Giving Resources, Presbyterian Foundation

James W. Murphy, CFRE, Author and Managing Program Director, Episcopal Church Foundation

Dr. M. Yaqub Mirza, President/CEO, Sterling Management Group and Chair, Board of Trustees of the Amana Mutual Funds, and Trustee and Chair, Investment & Endowment Committee of Shenandoah University

Peter Misiaszek, CFRE, Director of Stewardship Development, Anglican Diocese of Toronto

Dr. Lucinda Allen Mosher, ThD, Faculty Associate in Chaplaincy and Interreligious Studies and Senior Scholar for Executive and Professional Education at Hartford International University for Religion and Peace (formerly Hartford Seminary)

Randall Nyce, Everence® (Mennonite Foundation) Stewardship Consultant

Amy Palmer, CFRE, Director of Development, Adrian Dominican Sisters, Adrian, Michigan

Peter C. Pereira, Treasurer and Chief Financial Officer of The Episcopal Church in Hawaii (Retired)

Arlene D. Schiff, National Director of the LIFE & LEGACY® program of the Harold Grinspoon Foundation (HGF)

Pandit Roopnauth Sharma, President of the Hindu Federation and Founder and Spiritual Leader, Mississauga Ram Mandir (Hindu Temple)

The Rev. Perkin F. Simpson, Executive Director of Urban Alliance (CT) and Former Executive Director, American Baptist Foundation

Dr. Rupinder Singh Brar, Cardiologist and Founding Member of Sikh Community Center, Yuba City, California

Stacy B. Sulman, JD, Chief Legal Officer and Vice President, Personalized Philanthropy, American Committee for the Weizmann Institute of Science

The Rev. David P. Uribe, OMI, Oblate Executive Director/Oblate Chaplain Director for the Missionary Association of Mary Immaculate (MAMI-USA)

DENOMINATIONAL RESOURCES FOR PLANNED GIVING AND FAITH-BASED FOUNDATIONS

This section is clearly not inclusive of the many denominations and faiths which exist today. However, we include these references for your initial use. Please contact your own denomination or others in your faith tradition for more resources.

If you know of another useful resource for other faith traditions and denominations not noted here, please send me a message on my website and I will take the next steps to add that resource to our book's online resources. Thank you.

Contact Jim at *www.murphyjw.com*

CHRISTIAN

Anglican/Episcopal
Episcopal Church Foundation
www.ecf.org/programs/planned-giving-stewardship
www.episcopalgifts.org (for potential donors)

Anglican Church of Canada
www.anglican.ca/gifts/legacy-giving

Baptist
American Baptist Foundation
www.abcofgiving.org

Cooperative Baptist Fellowship Foundation
www.cbf.net/cbf-foundation

Church of the Brethren
www.brethren.givingplan.net/plan-your-gifts-greatest-impact

Community of Christ
www.cofchrist.org

Disciples of Christ
Christian Church Foundation
www.christianchurchfoundation.org

Lutheran

Evangelical Lutheran Church in America

ELCA Foundation

www.ELCA.org/foundation

Lutheran Church—Missouri Synod

Lutheran Church—Missouri Synod Foundation

www.lcmsfoundation.org

Wisconsin Evangelical Lutheran Synod

WELS Foundation

www.wels.net/giving/wels-foundation/

Moravian

Moravian Ministries Foundation in America

www.mmfa.info

Mennonite

Everence Foundation (formerly the Mennonite Foundation)

www.everence.com

Presbyterian Church (USA)

Presbyterian Foundation

www.presbyterianfoundation.org

Presbyterian Church in Canada

www.presbyterian.ca/stewardship/planned-giving

Religious Society of Friends (Quakers)

Friends Fiduciary Corporation

www.friendsfiduciary.org

Roman Catholic

Depending on the legal structure of the Roman Catholic diocese, individual parishes may or may not be able to hold their own invested or endowed funds. Finance councils may check with their local diocesan finance or Development/ Stewardship office regarding ways to manage separate funds as well as for planned giving resources and access to Life Income Gifts.

Independent Roman Catholic organizations, like religious orders or charities, normally oversee their own investments and planned giving efforts but may also have access to diocesan resources.

If you are a Roman Catholic Mission Diocese in the United States and need access to charitable gift annuities, please reach out to:

Catholic Extension
www.catholicextension.org

Unitarian Universalist Association (UUA)
www.uualegacy.org

United Church of Canada
The United Church of Canada Foundation
www.unitedchurchfoundation.ca

United Church of Christ (UCC)
United Church Funds
www.ucfunds.org

United Methodist
For a United Methodist foundation that serves your local regional conference, please check with your local regional leadership or visit the following site.

UMC Foundation Investment Management
www.investumc.org

JEWISH

Jewish Federations of North America
Your local federation or Jewish community foundation may be able to assist your congregation or agency with your planned giving and legacy efforts, or contact Dirk Bird (Dirk.Bird@JewishFederations.org) or Steve Gross (Steve.Gross@JewishFederations.org) in the Planned Giving & Endowments Group directly for assistance.
www.jewishfederations.org/

LIFE & LEGACY®, Harold Grinspoon Foundation
If your Jewish community is interested in becoming part of the LIFE & LEGACY network, contact Arlene D. Schiff, National Director at arlene@hgf.org.
www.jewishlifelegacy.org

Muslim

Islamic Relief USA

There are several commercial resources online for writing a will according to Muslim tradition. You may also view a number of resources on Islamic giving and making a Sharia compliant will on Islamic Relief USA's website.

www.irusa.org/wills

For various other resources beyond planned giving for Islamic communities of faith and charities:

Islamic Society of North America (ISNA)

www.isna.net

ISNA's mission is to foster the development of the Muslim community, interfaith relations, civic engagement, and better understanding of Islam.

Hindu[1]

Hindu Federation (Canada)

www.hindufederation.ca
The Hindu Federation is an amalgamation of temples of varied Hindu denominations and other organizations in Canada.

Hindu American Foundation (USA)

www.hinduamerican.org
HAF focuses on educating the public about Hindus and Hinduism and advocating for policies and practices that ensure the well-being of all people and the planet.

Sikh

Sikh Coalition

www.sikhcoalition.org
Through the community, courtrooms, classrooms, and halls of Congress, the Sikh Coalition works to protect the constitutional right to practice the Sikh faith without fear. We strive to do this with integrity, selflessness, and the belief that our shared work holds a greater purpose.

Sikh Foundation International

www.sikhfoundation.org
Preserving and sharing Sikh heritage through the arts and education since 1967.

---

1. The following organizations listed under the "Hindu" and "Sikh" headings do not have planned giving tools but are excellent resources for your faith tradition.

CPSIA information can be obtained
at www.ICGtesting.com
Printed in the USA
JSHW052007060922
30050JS00004B/5